JOHN CONSTANTINE, HELLBLAZER: RED SEPULCHRE

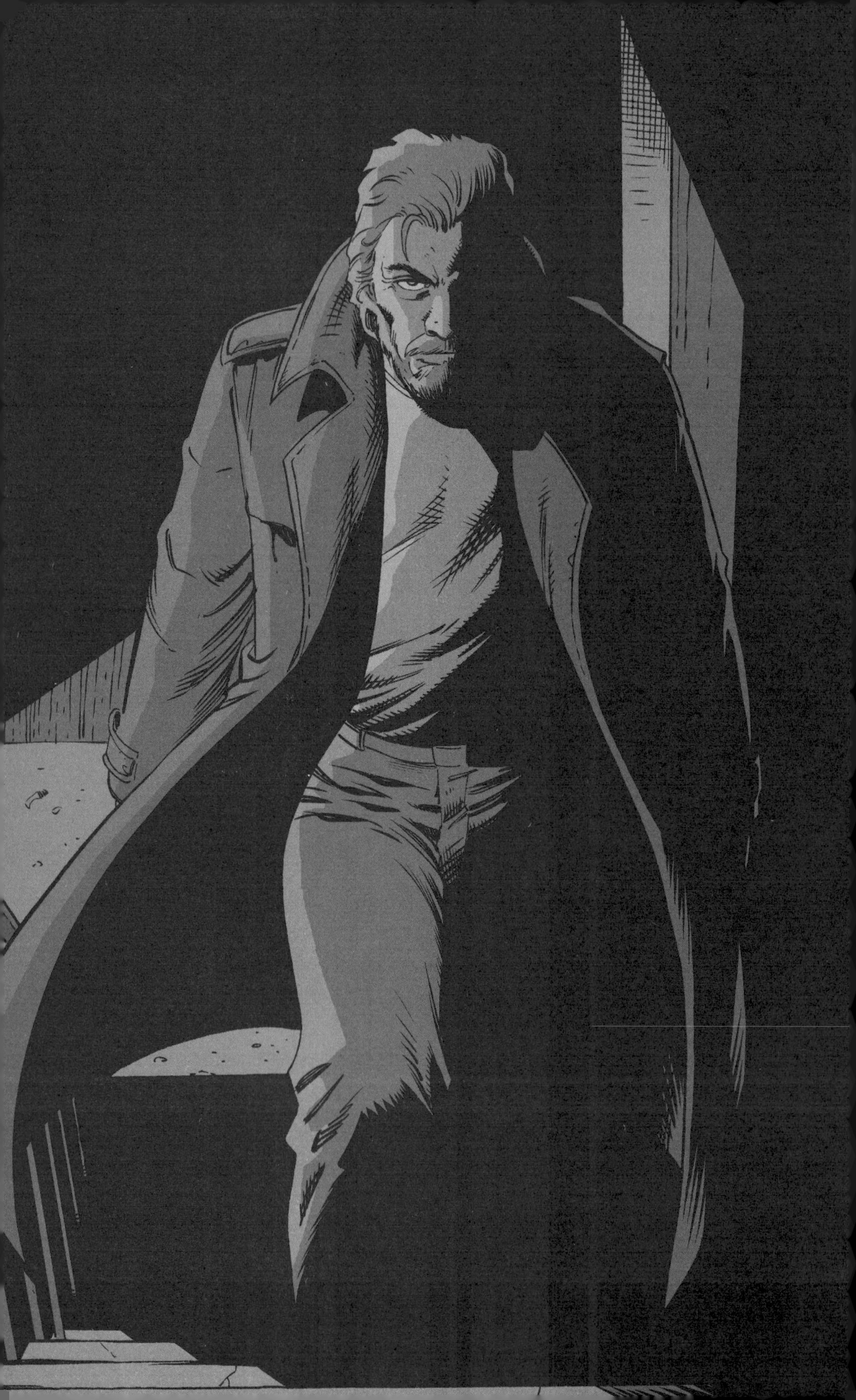

JOHN CONSTANTINE, HELLBLAZER:
RED SEPULCHRE

Mike Carey
Writer

"High on Life"
Steve Dillon
Penciller
Jimmy Palmiotti
Inker

"Red Sepulchre"
Marcelo Frusin
Artist

Lee Loughridge
Colorist

Clem Robins
Letterer

Tim Bradstreet
Original Series Covers

JOHN CONSTANTINE, HELLBLAZER: RED SEPULCHRE

Published by DC Comics. Cover and compilation copyright ©
2005 DC Comics. All Rights Reserved.

Originally published in single magazine form as HELLBLAZER
175-180. Copyright © 2002, 2003 DC Comics. All Rights
Reserved. All characters, their distinctive likenesses and related
elements featured in this publication are trademarks of
DC Comics. The stories, characters and incidents featured in this
publication are entirely fictional. DC Comics does not read or
accept unsolicited submissions of ideas, stories or artwork.

DC Comics, 1700 Broadway, New York, NY 10019
A Warner Bros. Entertainment Company
Printed in Canada. First Printing.

ISBN: 1-4012-0485-6

Cover illustration by Tim Bradstreet.
Logo design by Nessim Higson.

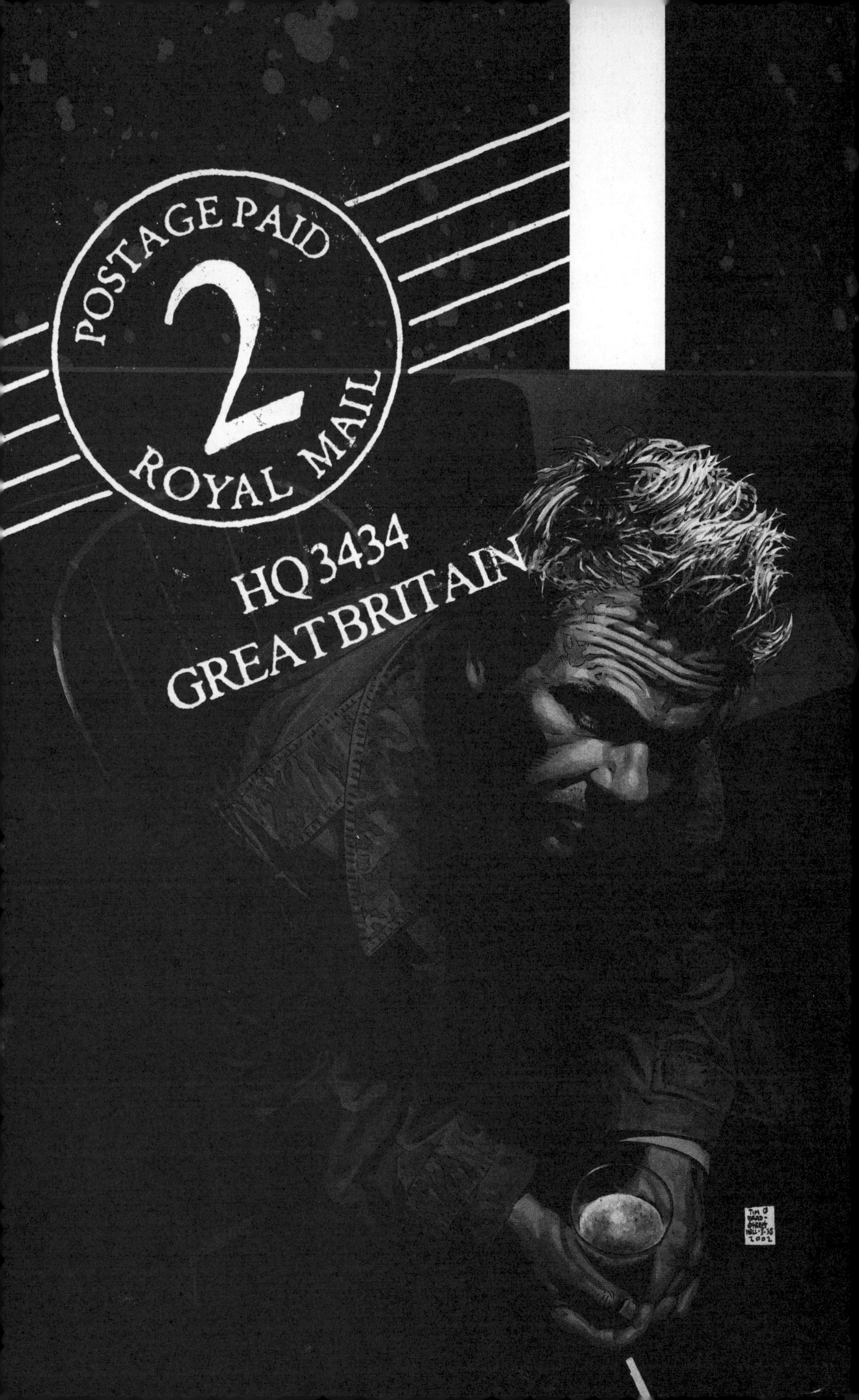
POSTAGE PAID
2
ROYAL MAIL
HQ 3434
GREAT BRITAIN

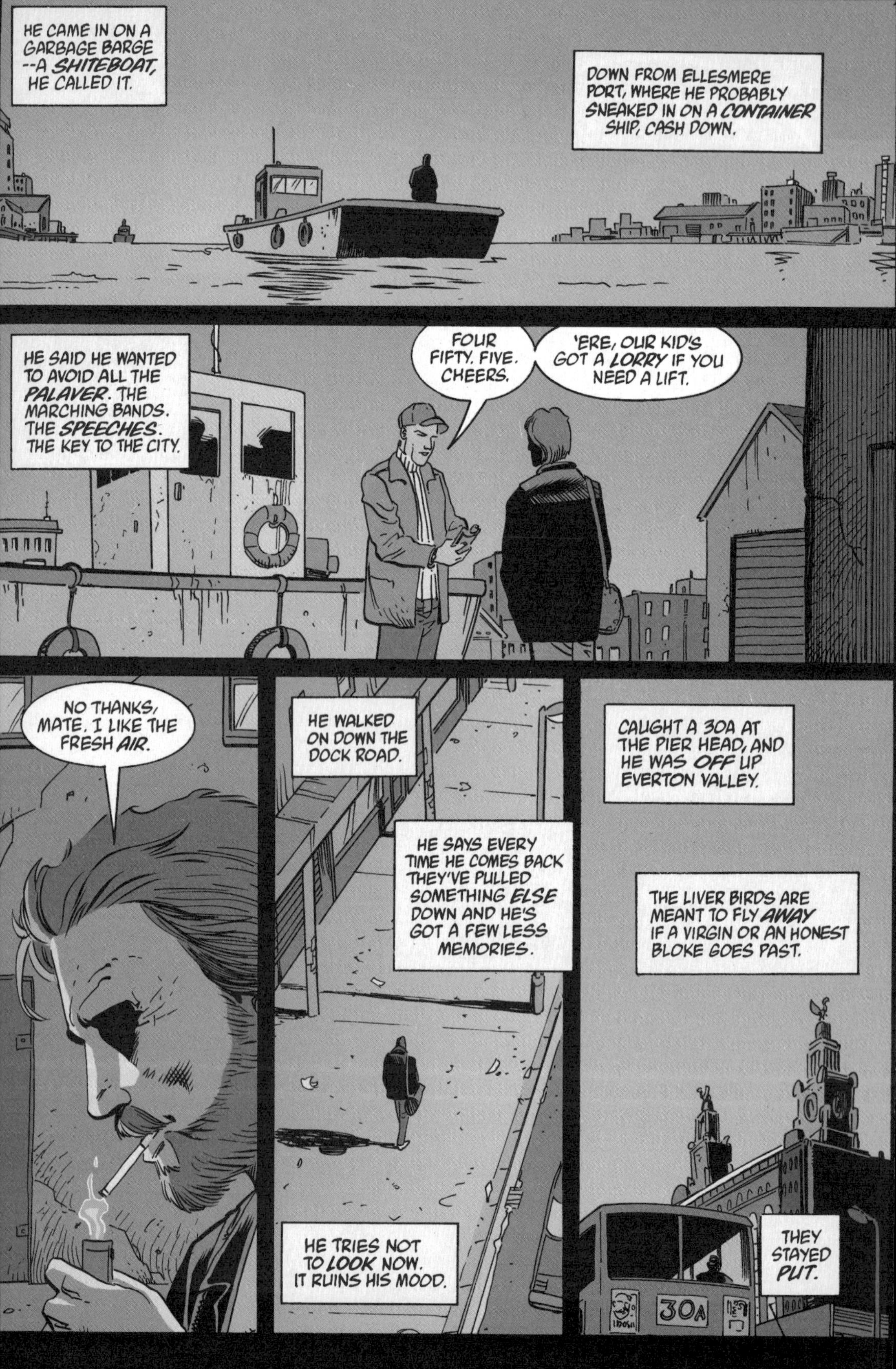
HE CAME IN ON A GARBAGE BARGE --A SHITEBOAT, HE CALLED IT.
DOWN FROM ELLESMERE PORT, WHERE HE PROBABLY SNEAKED IN ON A CONTAINER SHIP, CASH DOWN.
HE SAID HE WANTED TO AVOID ALL THE PALAVER. THE MARCHING BANDS. THE SPEECHES. THE KEY TO THE CITY.
FOUR FIFTY. FIVE. CHEERS.
'ERE, OUR KID'S GOT A LORRY IF YOU NEED A LIFT.
NO THANKS, MATE. I LIKE THE FRESH AIR.
HE WALKED ON DOWN THE DOCK ROAD.
HE SAYS EVERY TIME HE COMES BACK THEY'VE PULLED SOMETHING ELSE DOWN AND HE'S GOT A FEW LESS MEMORIES.
HE TRIES NOT TO LOOK NOW. IT RUINS HIS MOOD.
CAUGHT A 30A AT THE PIER HEAD, AND HE WAS OFF UP EVERTON VALLEY.
THE LIVER BIRDS ARE MEANT TO FLY AWAY IF A VIRGIN OR AN HONEST BLOKE GOES PAST.
THEY STAYED PUT.
30A

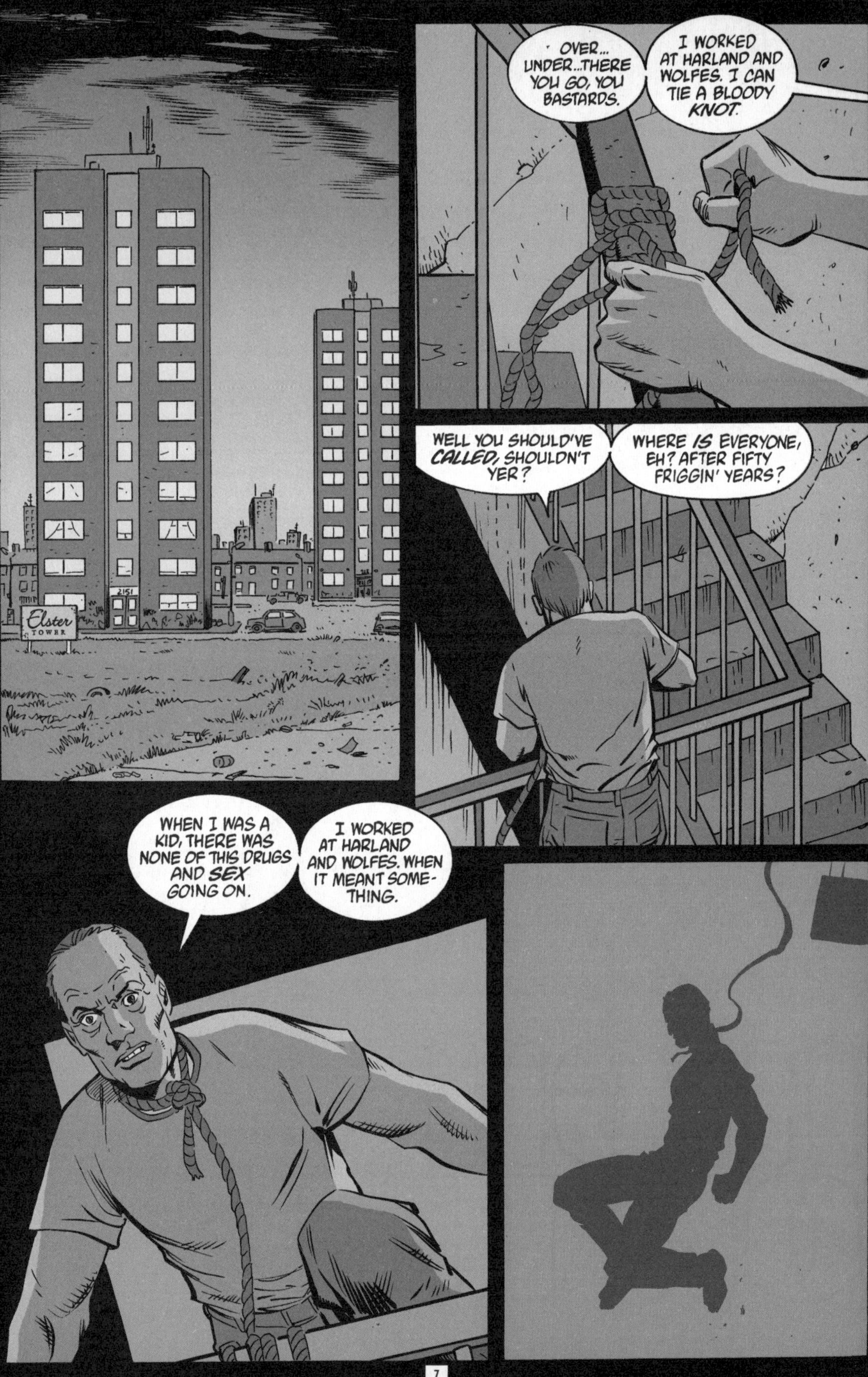
Elster TOWER
2151
OVER... UNDER...THERE YOU GO, YOU BASTARDS.
I WORKED AT HARLAND AND WOLFES. I CAN TIE A BLOODY KNOT.
WELL YOU SHOULD'VE CALLED, SHOULDN'T YER?
WHERE IS EVERYONE, EH? AFTER FIFTY FRIGGIN' YEARS?
WHEN I WAS A KID, THERE WAS NONE OF THIS DRUGS AND SEX GOING ON.
I WORKED AT HARLAND AND WOLFES. WHEN IT MEANT SOME-THING.

SOD IT! A BLOODY REEF KNOT!
ALL RIGHT, COME ON OUT OF IT. WE'RE NOT SELLING TICKETS.
POLICE
HIGH ON LIFE

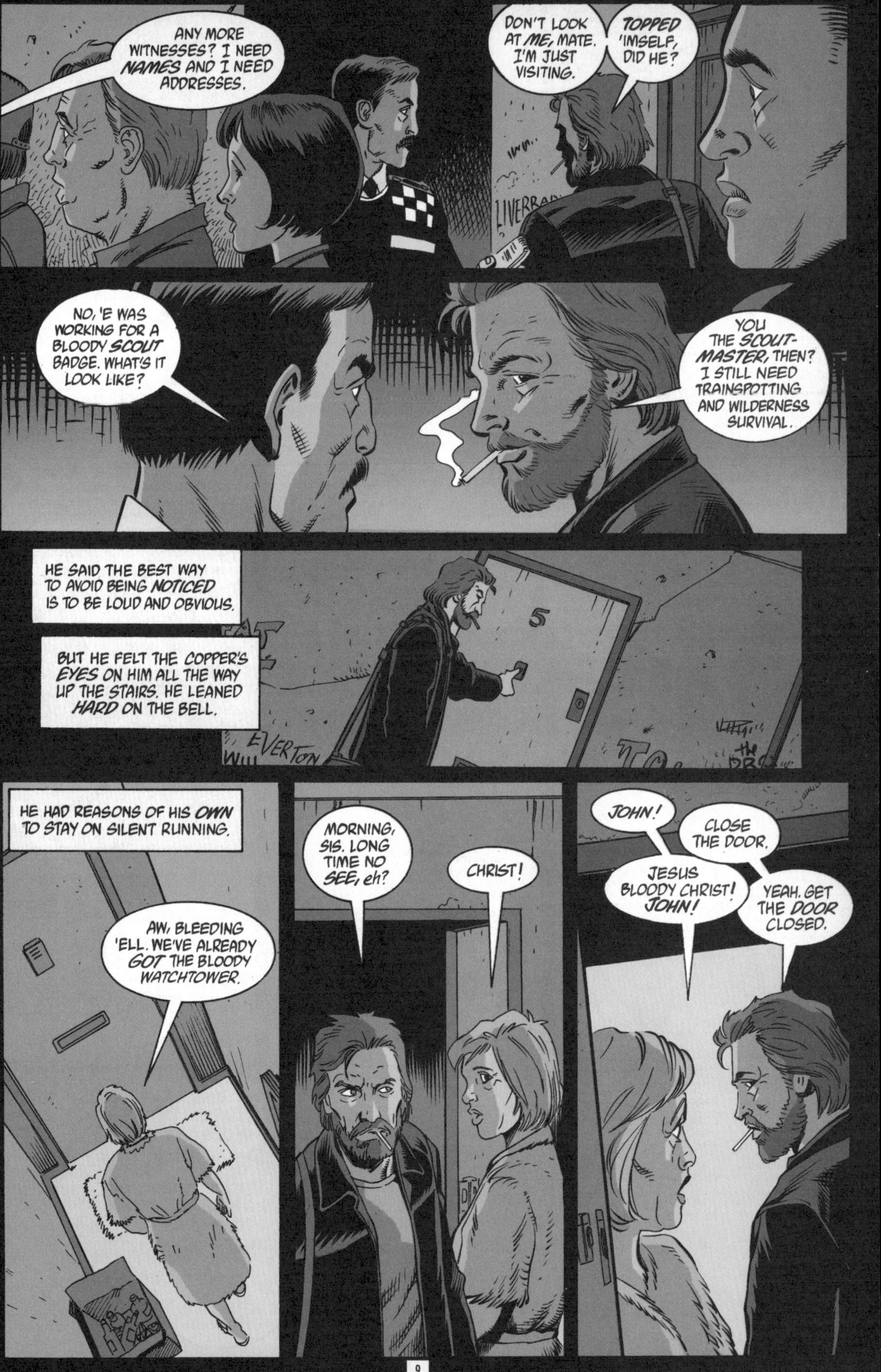
ANY MORE WITNESSES? I NEED NAMES AND I NEED ADDRESSES.
DON'T LOOK AT ME, MATE. I'M JUST VISITING.
TOPPED 'IMSELF, DID HE?
LIVERPA
NO, 'E WAS WORKING FOR A BLOODY SCOUT BADGE. WHAT'S IT LOOK LIKE?
YOU THE SCOUT-MASTER, THEN? I STILL NEED TRAINSPOTTING AND WILDERNESS SURVIVAL.
HE SAID THE BEST WAY TO AVOID BEING NOTICED IS TO BE LOUD AND OBVIOUS.
BUT HE FELT THE COPPER'S EYES ON HIM ALL THE WAY UP THE STAIRS. HE LEANED HARD ON THE BELL.
5
EVERTON
HE HAD REASONS OF HIS OWN TO STAY ON SILENT RUNNING.
AW, BLEEDING 'ELL. WE'VE ALREADY GOT THE BLOODY WATCHTOWER.
MORNING, SIS. LONG TIME NO SEE, eh?
CHRIST!
JOHN!
CLOSE THE DOOR.
JESUS BLOODY CHRIST! JOHN!
YEAH. GET THE DOOR CLOSED.

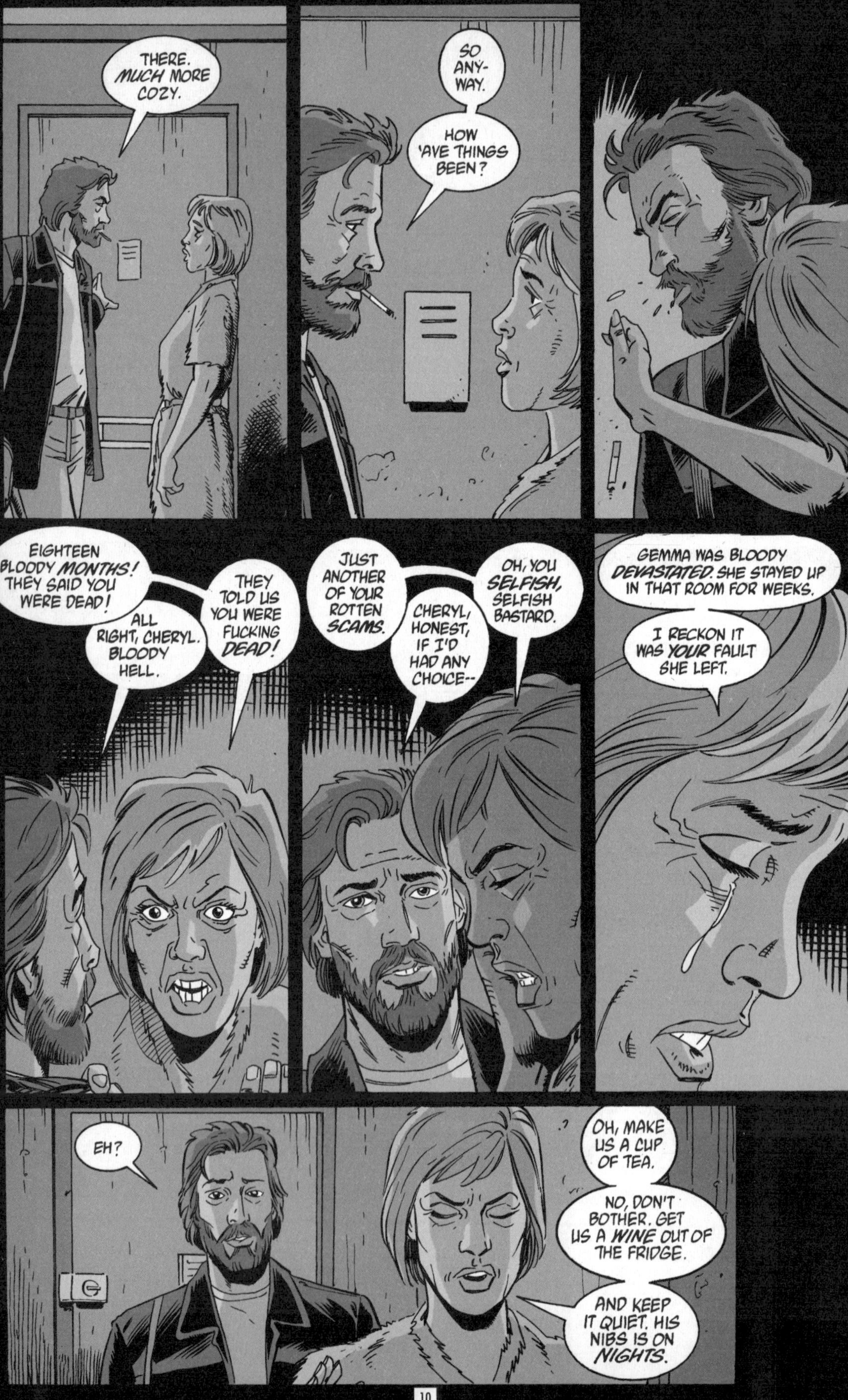
THERE. MUCH MORE COZY.
SO ANY-WAY.
HOW 'AVE THINGS BEEN?
EIGHTEEN BLOODY MONTHS! THEY SAID YOU WERE DEAD!
THEY TOLD US YOU WERE FUCKING DEAD!
ALL RIGHT, CHERYL. BLOODY HELL.
JUST ANOTHER OF YOUR ROTTEN SCAMS.
OH, YOU SELFISH, SELFISH BASTARD.
CHERYL, HONEST, IF I'D HAD ANY CHOICE--
GEMMA WAS BLOODY DEVASTATED. SHE STAYED UP IN THAT ROOM FOR WEEKS.
I RECKON IT WAS YOUR FAULT SHE LEFT.
EH?
OH, MAKE US A CUP OF TEA.
NO, DON'T BOTHER. GET US A WINE OUT OF THE FRIDGE.
AND KEEP IT QUIET. HIS NIBS IS ON NIGHTS.

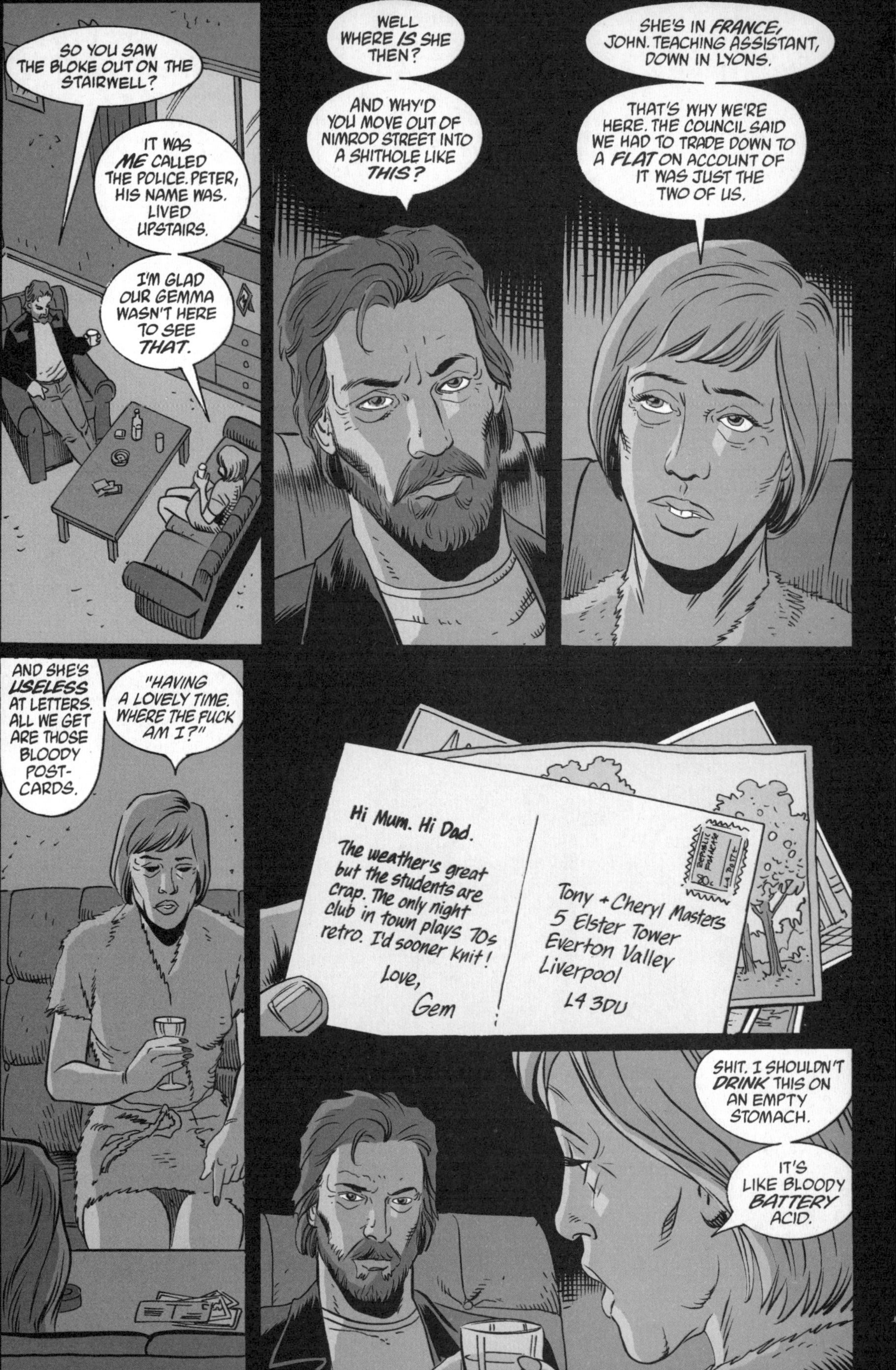
SO YOU SAW THE BLOKE OUT ON THE STAIRWELL?
IT WAS ME CALLED THE POLICE. PETER, HIS NAME WAS. LIVED UPSTAIRS.
I'M GLAD OUR GEMMA WASN'T HERE TO SEE THAT.
WELL WHERE IS SHE THEN?
AND WHY'D YOU MOVE OUT OF NIMROD STREET INTO A SHITHOLE LIKE THIS?
SHE'S IN FRANCE, JOHN. TEACHING ASSISTANT, DOWN IN LYONS.
THAT'S WHY WE'RE HERE. THE COUNCIL SAID WE HAD TO TRADE DOWN TO A FLAT ON ACCOUNT OF IT WAS JUST THE TWO OF US.
AND SHE'S USELESS AT LETTERS. ALL WE GET ARE THOSE BLOODY POST-CARDS.
"HAVING A LOVELY TIME. WHERE THE FUCK AM I?"
Hi Mum. Hi Dad.
The weather's great but the students are crap. The only night club in town plays 70s retro. I'd sooner knit!
Love,
Gem
Tony + Cheryl Masters
5 Elster Tower
Everton Valley
Liverpool
L4 3DU
SHIT. I SHOULDN'T DRINK THIS ON AN EMPTY STOMACH.
IT'S LIKE BLOODY BATTERY ACID.

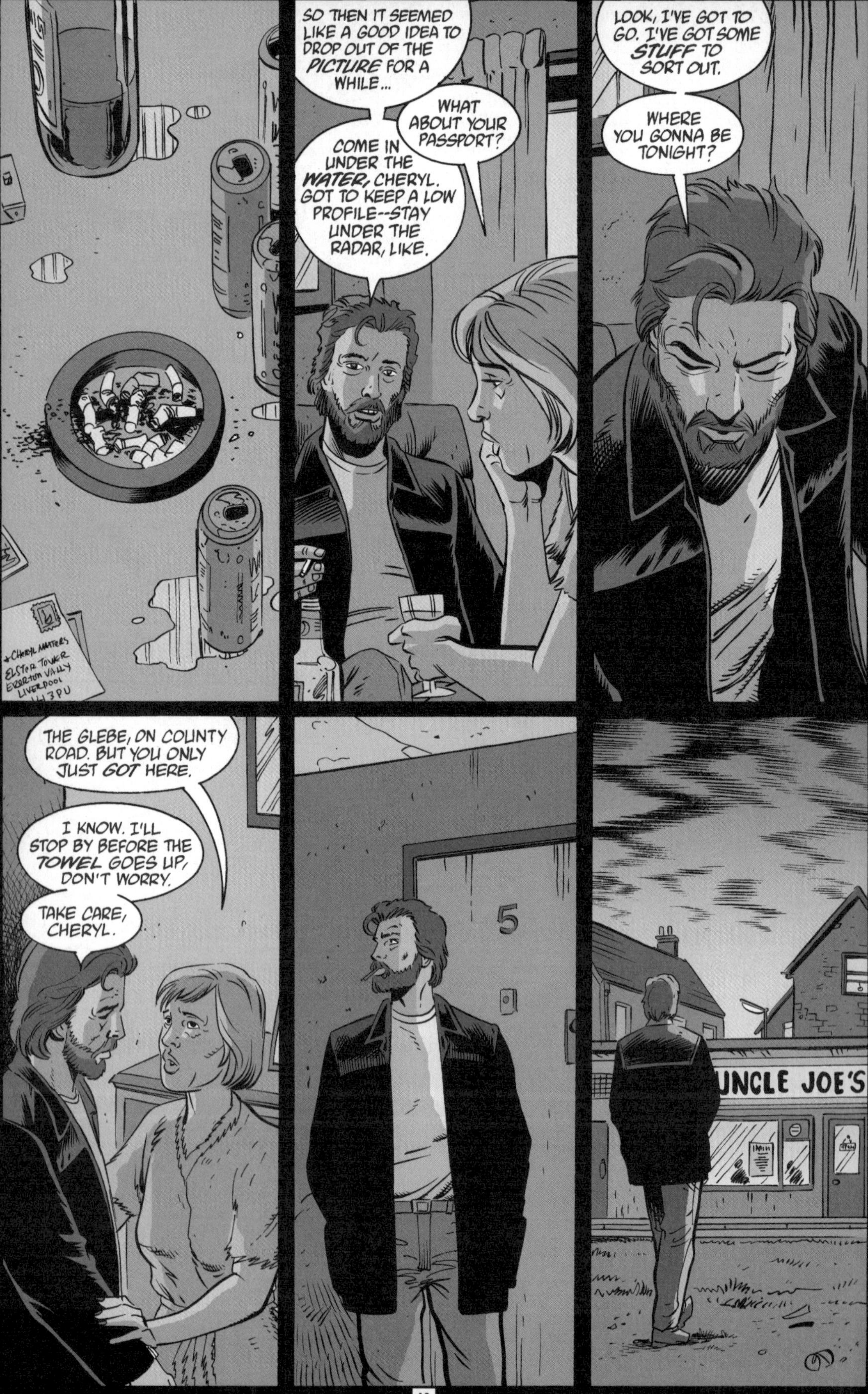
SO THEN IT SEEMED LIKE A GOOD IDEA TO DROP OUT OF THE PICTURE FOR A WHILE...
WHAT ABOUT YOUR PASSPORT?
COME IN UNDER THE WATER, CHERYL. GOT TO KEEP A LOW PROFILE--STAY UNDER THE RADAR, LIKE.
LOOK, I'VE GOT TO GO. I'VE GOT SOME STUFF TO SORT OUT.
WHERE YOU GONNA BE TONIGHT?
THE GLEBE, ON COUNTY ROAD. BUT YOU ONLY JUST GOT HERE.
I KNOW. I'LL STOP BY BEFORE THE TOWEL GOES UP, DON'T WORRY.
TAKE CARE, CHERYL.
5
UNCLE JOE'S

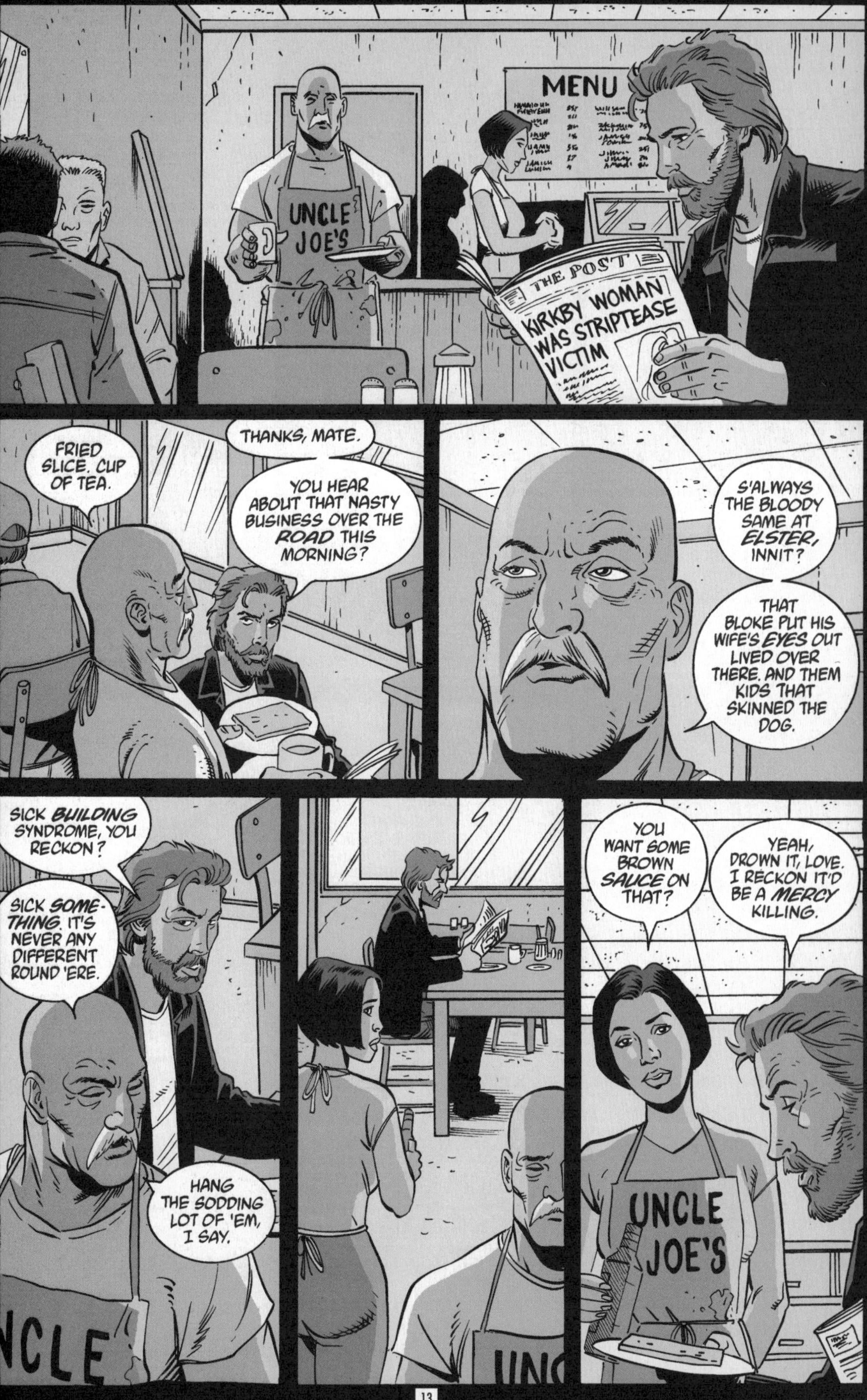
MENU
UNCLE JOE'S
THE POST
KIRKBY WOMAN WAS STRIPTEASE VICTIM
FRIED SLICE. CUP OF TEA.
THANKS, MATE.
YOU HEAR ABOUT THAT NASTY BUSINESS OVER THE ROAD THIS MORNING?
S'ALWAYS THE BLOODY SAME AT ELSTER, INNIT?
THAT BLOKE PUT HIS WIFE'S EYES OUT LIVED OVER THERE. AND THEM KIDS THAT SKINNED THE DOG.
SICK BUILDING SYNDROME, YOU RECKON?
SICK SOME-THING. IT'S NEVER ANY DIFFERENT ROUND 'ERE.
HANG THE SODDING LOT OF 'EM, I SAY.
YOU WANT SOME BROWN SAUCE ON THAT?
YEAH, DROWN IT, LOVE. I RECKON IT'D BE A MERCY KILLING.
UNCLE JOE'S

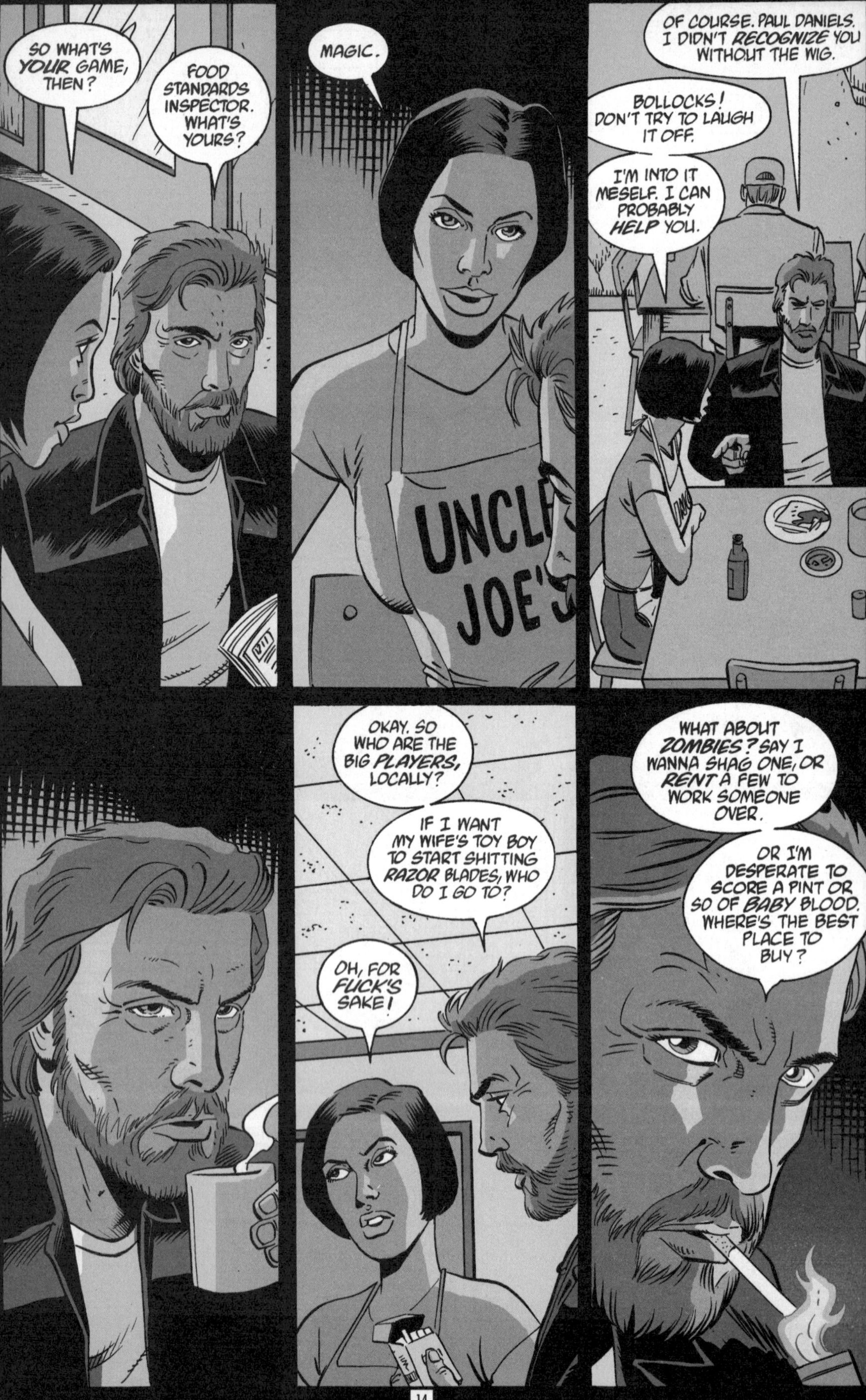
SO WHAT'S YOUR GAME, THEN?
FOOD STANDARDS INSPECTOR. WHAT'S YOURS?
MAGIC.
UNCLE JOE'S
OF COURSE. PAUL DANIELS. I DIDN'T RECOGNIZE YOU WITHOUT THE WIG.
BOLLOCKS! DON'T TRY TO LAUGH IT OFF.
I'M INTO IT MESELF. I CAN PROBABLY HELP YOU.
OKAY. SO WHO ARE THE BIG PLAYERS, LOCALLY?
IF I WANT MY WIFE'S TOY BOY TO START SHITTING RAZOR BLADES, WHO DO I GO TO?
OH, FOR FUCK'S SAKE!
WHAT ABOUT ZOMBIES? SAY I WANNA SHAG ONE, OR RENT A FEW TO WORK SOMEONE OVER.
OR I'M DESPERATE TO SCORE A PINT OR SO OF BABY BLOOD. WHERE'S THE BEST PLACE TO BUY?

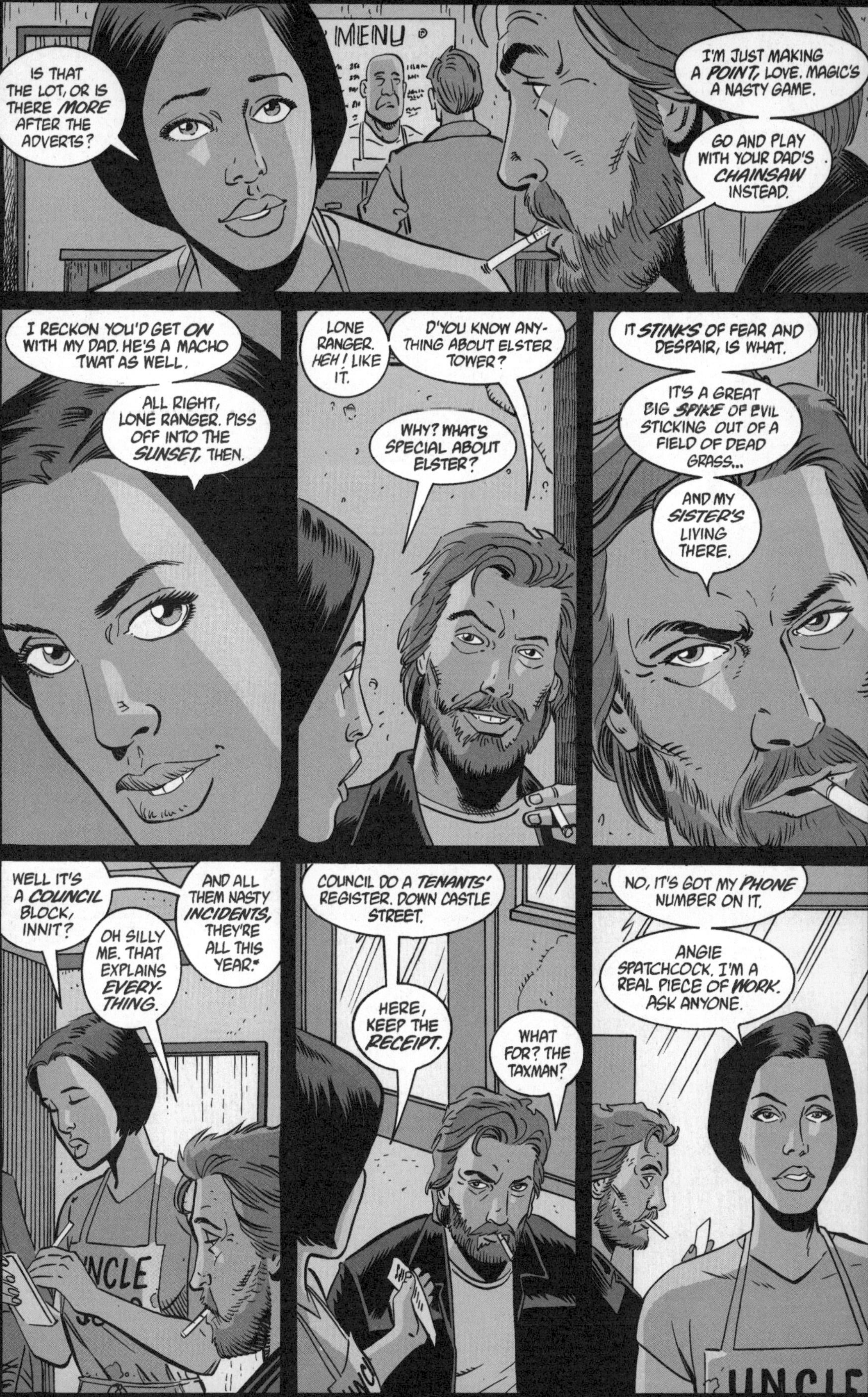

MENU
IS THAT THE LOT, OR IS THERE MORE AFTER THE ADVERTS?
I'M JUST MAKING A POINT, LOVE. MAGIC'S A NASTY GAME.
GO AND PLAY WITH YOUR DAD'S CHAINSAW INSTEAD.
I RECKON YOU'D GET ON WITH MY DAD. HE'S A MACHO TWAT AS WELL.
ALL RIGHT, LONE RANGER. PISS OFF INTO THE SUNSET, THEN.
LONE RANGER. HEH! LIKE IT.
D'YOU KNOW ANYTHING ABOUT ELSTER TOWER?
WHY? WHAT'S SPECIAL ABOUT ELSTER?
IT STINKS OF FEAR AND DESPAIR, IS WHAT.
IT'S A GREAT BIG SPIKE OF EVIL STICKING OUT OF A FIELD OF DEAD GRASS...
AND MY SISTER'S LIVING THERE.
WELL IT'S A COUNCIL BLOCK, INNIT?
OH SILLY ME. THAT EXPLAINS EVERYTHING.
AND ALL THEM NASTY INCIDENTS, THEY'RE ALL THIS YEAR.*
UNCLE
COUNCIL DO A TENANTS' REGISTER. DOWN CASTLE STREET.
HERE, KEEP THE RECEIPT.
WHAT FOR? THE TAXMAN?
NO, IT'S GOT MY PHONE NUMBER ON IT.
ANGIE SPATCHCOCK. I'M A REAL PIECE OF WORK. ASK ANYONE.
UNCLE

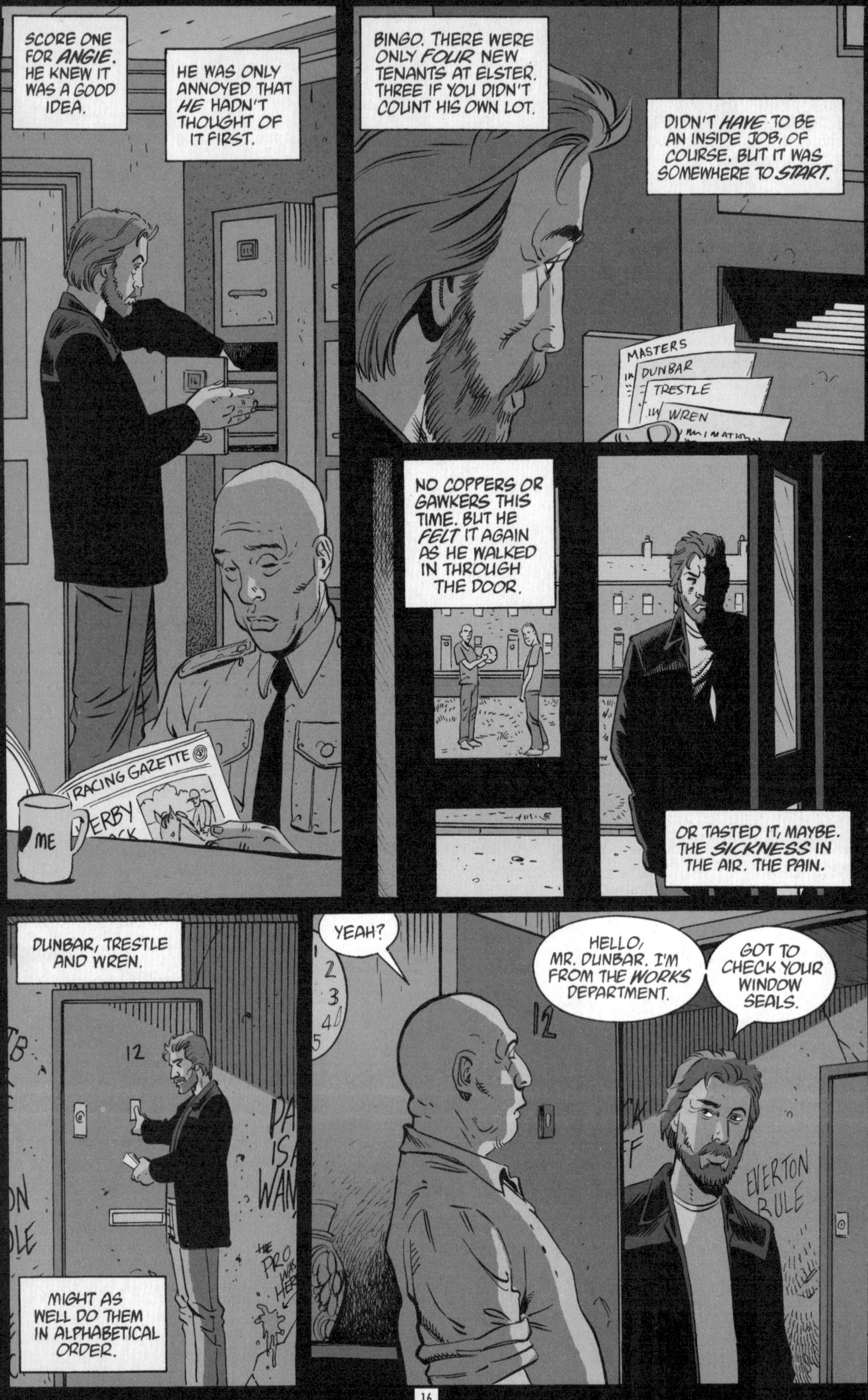
SCORE ONE FOR *ANGIE*. HE KNEW IT WAS A GOOD IDEA.
HE WAS ONLY ANNOYED THAT *HE* HADN'T THOUGHT OF IT FIRST.
RACING GAZETTE
ME
BINGO. THERE WERE ONLY *FOUR* NEW TENANTS AT ELSTER. THREE IF YOU DIDN'T COUNT HIS OWN LOT.
DIDN'T *HAVE* TO BE AN INSIDE JOB, OF COURSE. BUT IT WAS SOMEWHERE TO *START*.
MASTERS
DUNBAR
TRESTLE
WREN
NO COPPERS OR GAWKERS THIS TIME. BUT HE *FELT* IT AGAIN AS HE WALKED IN THROUGH THE DOOR.
OR TASTED IT, MAYBE. THE *SICKNESS* IN THE AIR. THE PAIN.
DUNBAR, TRESTLE AND WREN.
12
MIGHT AS WELL DO THEM IN ALPHABETICAL ORDER.
YEAH?
HELLO, MR. DUNBAR. I'M FROM THE *WORKS* DEPARTMENT.
GOT TO CHECK YOUR WINDOW SEALS.
12
EVERTON RULE

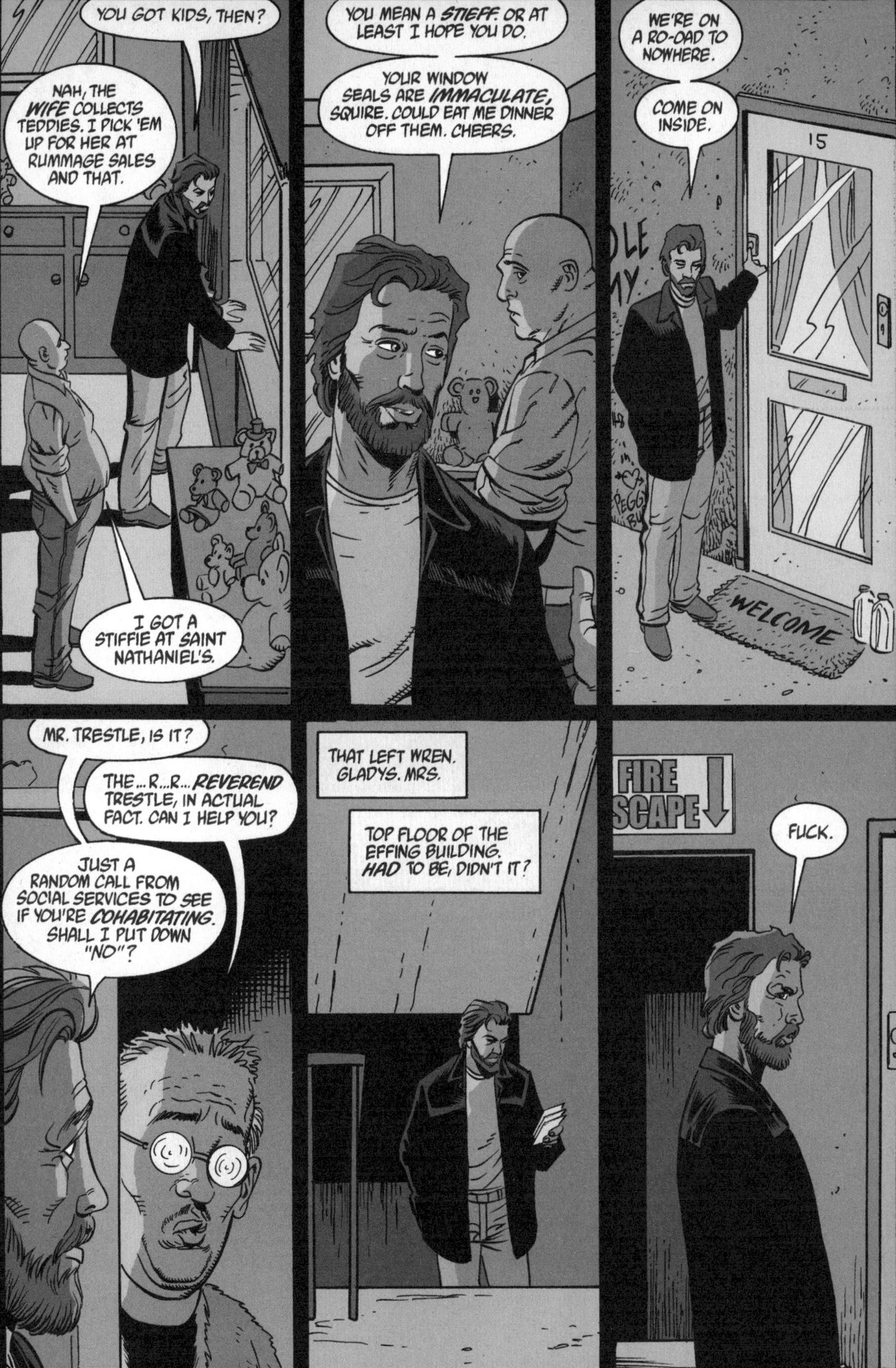
YOU GOT KIDS, THEN?
NAH, THE WIFE COLLECTS TEDDIES. I PICK 'EM UP FOR HER AT RUMMAGE SALES AND THAT.
I GOT A STIFFIE AT SAINT NATHANIEL'S.
YOU MEAN A STIFF. OR AT LEAST I HOPE YOU DO.
YOUR WINDOW SEALS ARE IMMACULATE, SQUIRE. COULD EAT ME DINNER OFF THEM. CHEERS.
WE'RE ON A RO-OAD TO NOWHERE.
COME ON INSIDE.
15
WELCOME
MR. TRESTLE, IS IT?
THE... R...R... REVEREND TRESTLE, IN ACTUAL FACT. CAN I HELP YOU?
JUST A RANDOM CALL FROM SOCIAL SERVICES TO SEE IF YOU'RE COHABITATING. SHALL I PUT DOWN "NO"?
THAT LEFT WREN. GLADYS. MRS.
TOP FLOOR OF THE EFFING BUILDING. HAD TO BE, DIDN'T IT?
FIRE SCAPE
FUCK.

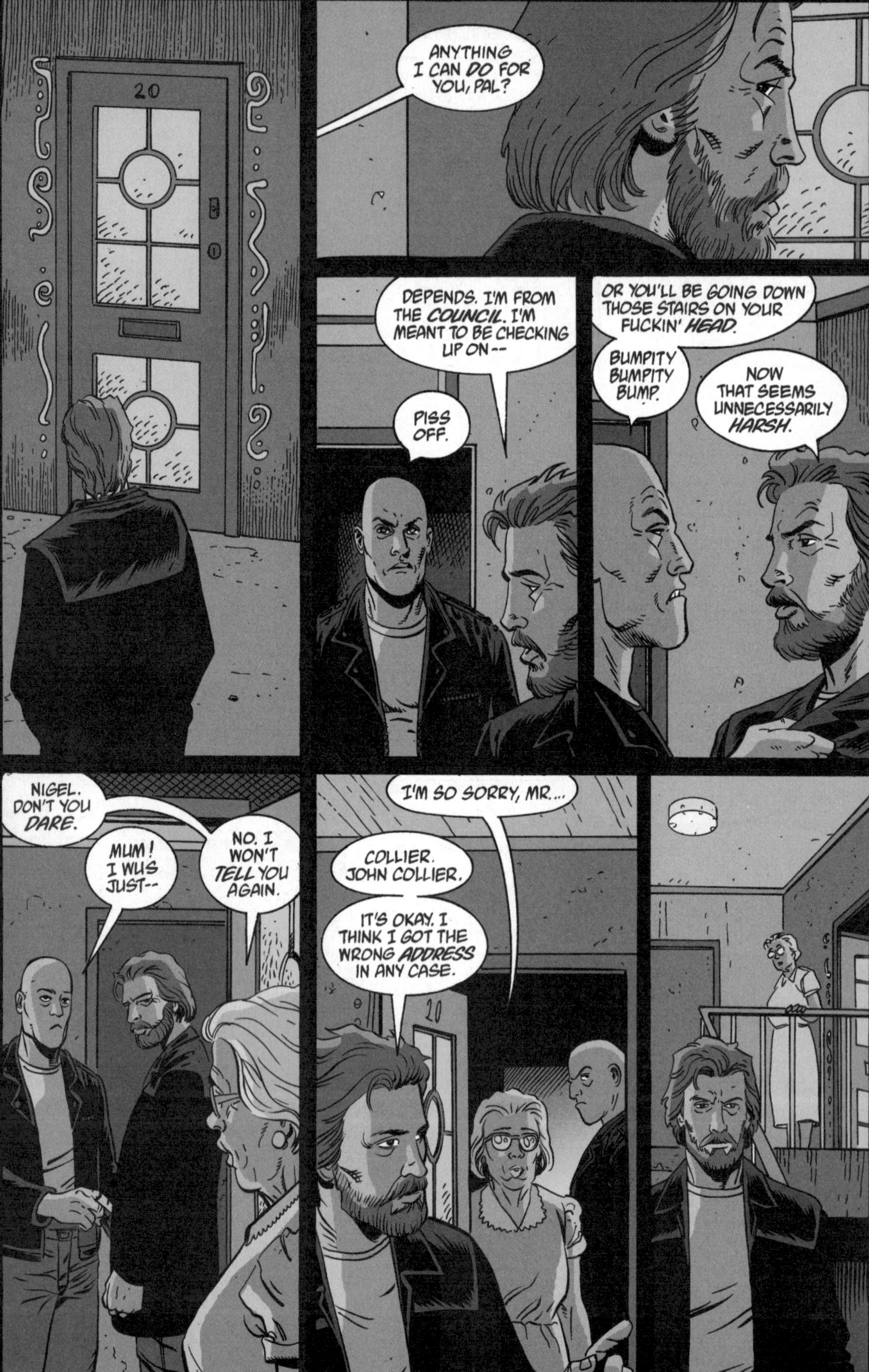

ANYTHING I CAN DO FOR YOU, PAL?
DEPENDS. I'M FROM THE COUNCIL. I'M MEANT TO BE CHECKING UP ON--
PISS OFF.
OR YOU'LL BE GOING DOWN THOSE STAIRS ON YOUR FUCKIN' HEAD.
BUMPITY BUMPITY BUMP.
NOW THAT SEEMS UNNECESSARILY HARSH.
NIGEL. DON'T YOU DARE.
MUM! I WUS JUST--
NO. I WON'T TELL YOU AGAIN.
I'M SO SORRY, MR....
COLLIER. JOHN COLLIER.
IT'S OKAY. I THINK I GOT THE WRONG ADDRESS IN ANY CASE.

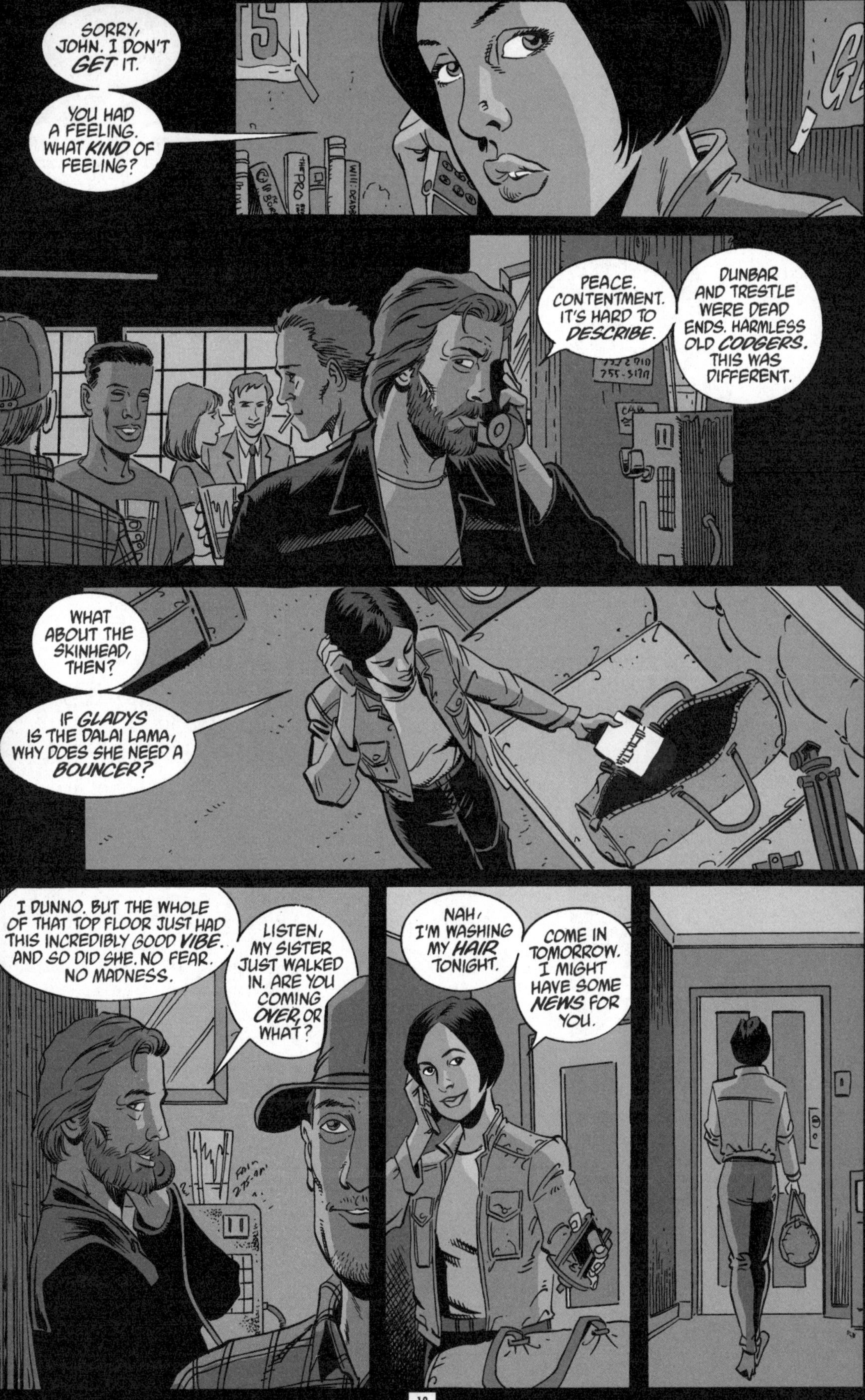
SORRY, JOHN. I DON'T GET IT.
YOU HAD A FEELING. WHAT KIND OF FEELING?
PEACE. CONTENTMENT. IT'S HARD TO DESCRIBE.
DUNBAR AND TRESTLE WERE DEAD ENDS. HARMLESS OLD CODGERS. THIS WAS DIFFERENT.
WHAT ABOUT THE SKINHEAD, THEN?
IF GLADYS IS THE DALAI LAMA, WHY DOES SHE NEED A BOUNCER?
I DUNNO. BUT THE WHOLE OF THAT TOP FLOOR JUST HAD THIS INCREDIBLY GOOD VIBE. AND SO DID SHE. NO FEAR. NO MADNESS.
LISTEN, MY SISTER JUST WALKED IN. ARE YOU COMING OVER, OR WHAT?
NAH, I'M WASHING MY HAIR TONIGHT.
COME IN TOMORROW. I MIGHT HAVE SOME NEWS FOR YOU.

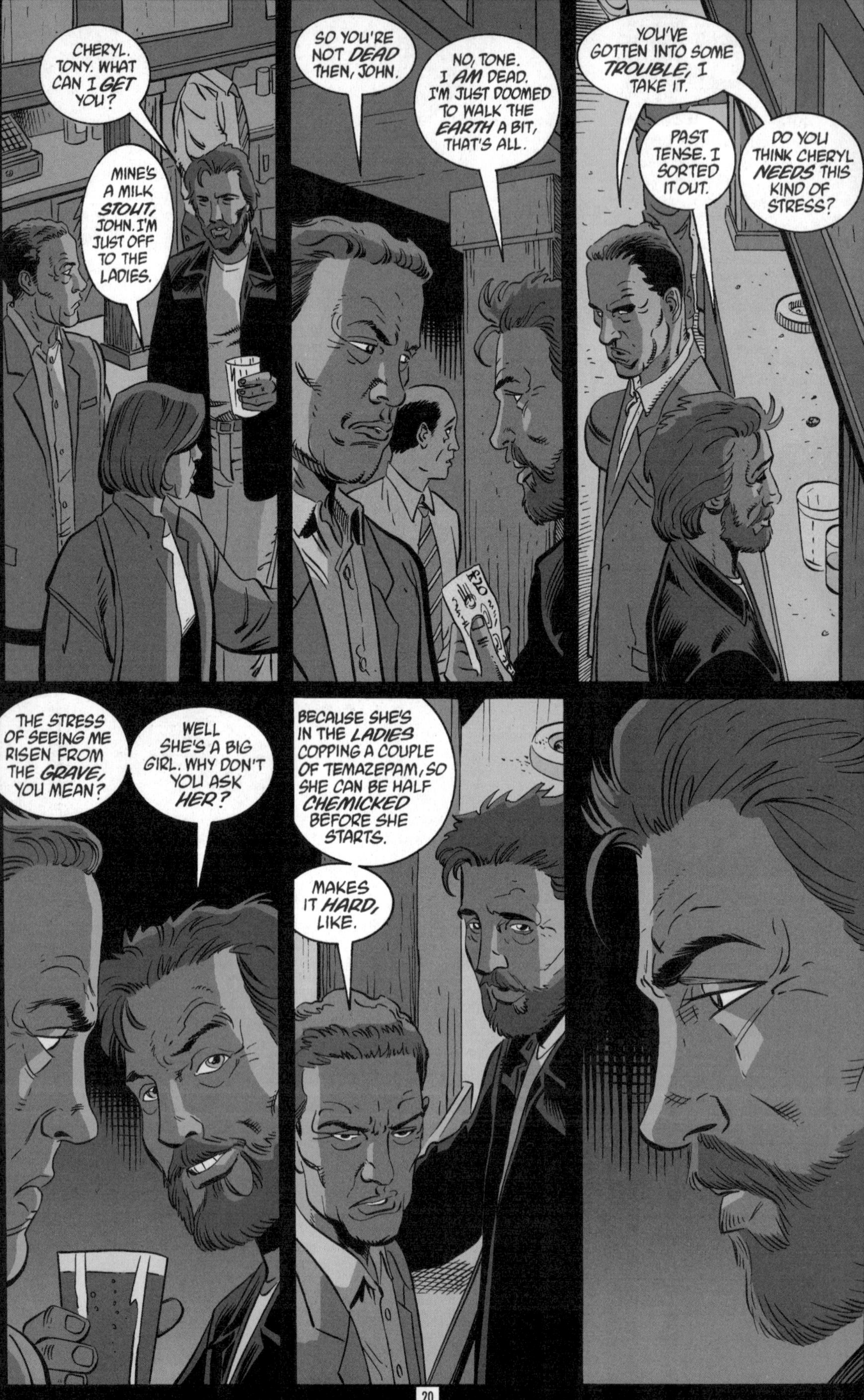

CHERYL. TONY. WHAT CAN I GET YOU?
MINE'S A MILK STOUT, JOHN. I'M JUST OFF TO THE LADIES.
SO YOU'RE NOT DEAD THEN, JOHN.
NO, TONE. I AM DEAD. I'M JUST DOOMED TO WALK THE EARTH A BIT, THAT'S ALL.
YOU'VE GOTTEN INTO SOME TROUBLE, I TAKE IT.
PAST TENSE. I SORTED IT OUT.
DO YOU THINK CHERYL NEEDS THIS KIND OF STRESS?
THE STRESS OF SEEING ME RISEN FROM THE GRAVE, YOU MEAN?
WELL SHE'S A BIG GIRL. WHY DON'T YOU ASK HER?
BECAUSE SHE'S IN THE LADIES COPPING A COUPLE OF TEMAZEPAM, SO SHE CAN BE HALF CHEMICKED BEFORE SHE STARTS.
MAKES IT HARD, LIKE.

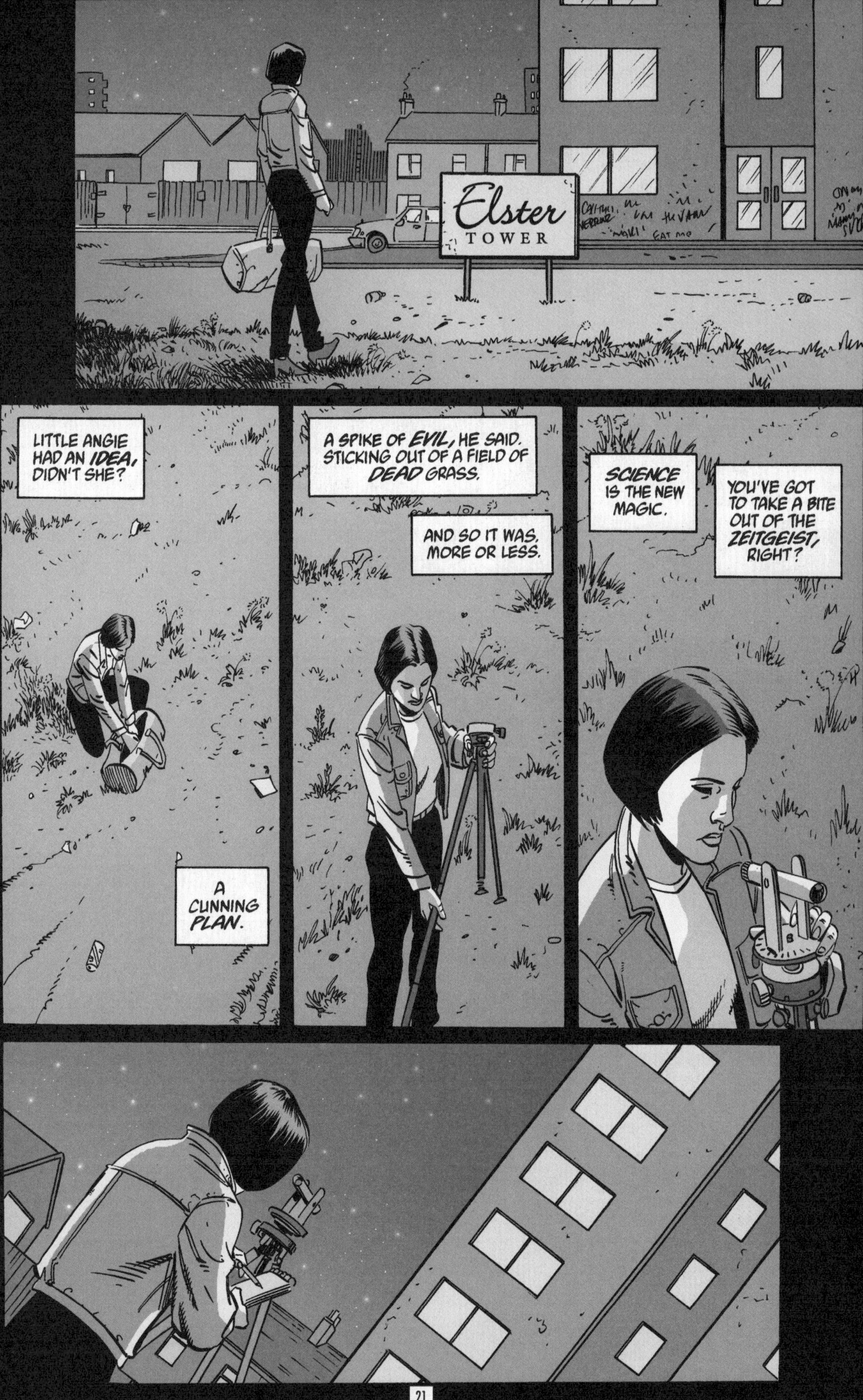
Elster
TOWER
LITTLE ANGIE HAD AN IDEA, DIDN'T SHE?
A CUNNING PLAN.
A SPIKE OF EVIL, HE SAID. STICKING OUT OF A FIELD OF DEAD GRASS.
AND SO IT WAS. MORE OR LESS.
SCIENCE IS THE NEW MAGIC.
YOU'VE GOT TO TAKE A BITE OUT OF THE ZEITGEIST, RIGHT?

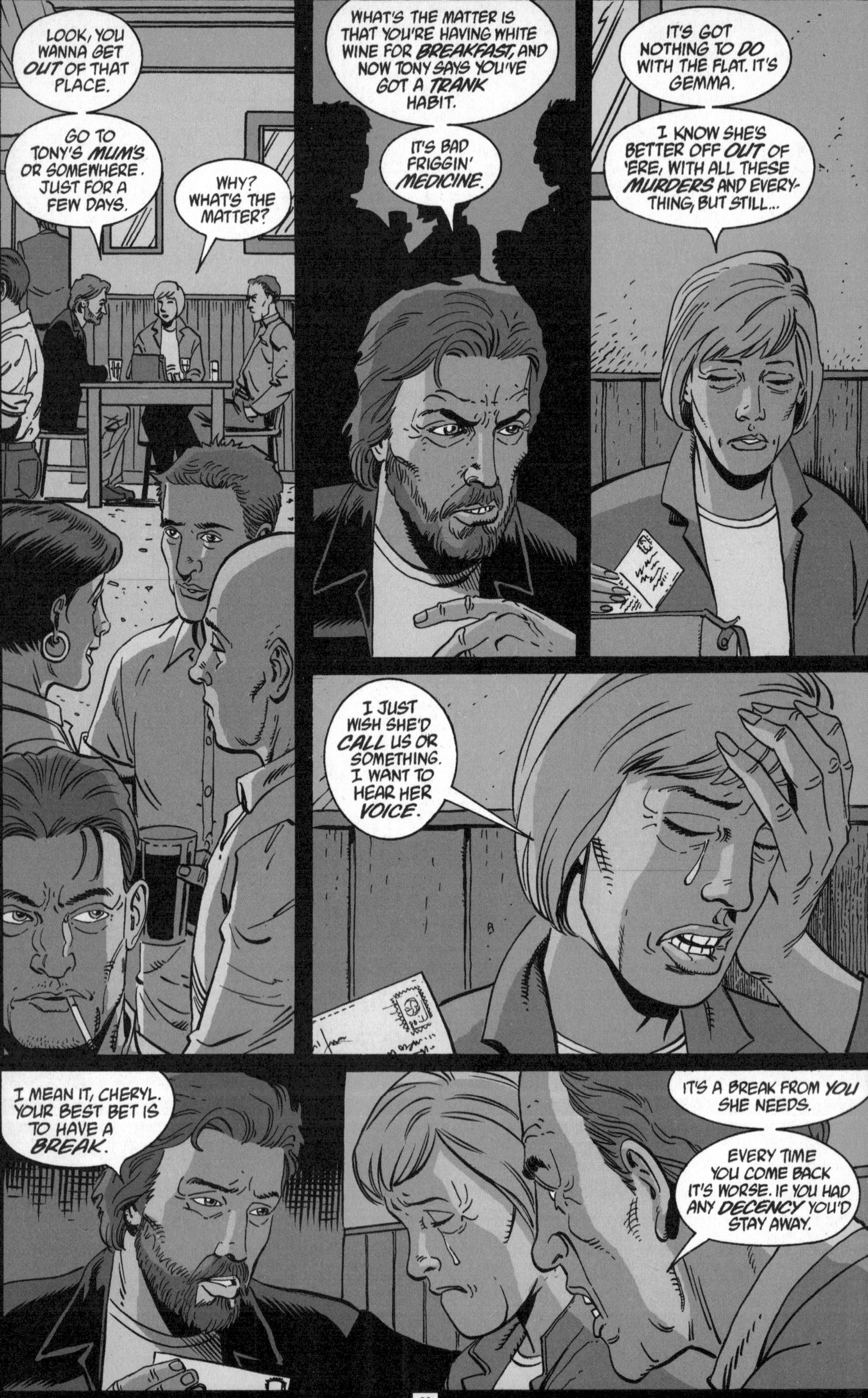
LOOK, YOU WANNA GET OUT OF THAT PLACE.
GO TO TONY'S MUM'S OR SOMEWHERE. JUST FOR A FEW DAYS.
WHY? WHAT'S THE MATTER?
WHAT'S THE MATTER IS THAT YOU'RE HAVING WHITE WINE FOR BREAKFAST, AND NOW TONY SAYS YOU'VE GOT A TRANK HABIT.
IT'S BAD FRIGGIN' MEDICINE.
IT'S GOT NOTHING TO DO WITH THE FLAT. IT'S GEMMA.
I KNOW SHE'S BETTER OFF OUT OF 'ERE, WITH ALL THESE MURDERS AND EVERY-THING, BUT STILL...
I JUST WISH SHE'D CALL US OR SOMETHING. I WANT TO HEAR HER VOICE.
I MEAN IT, CHERYL. YOUR BEST BET IS TO HAVE A BREAK.
IT'S A BREAK FROM YOU SHE NEEDS.
EVERY TIME YOU COME BACK IT'S WORSE. IF YOU HAD ANY DECENCY YOU'D STAY AWAY.

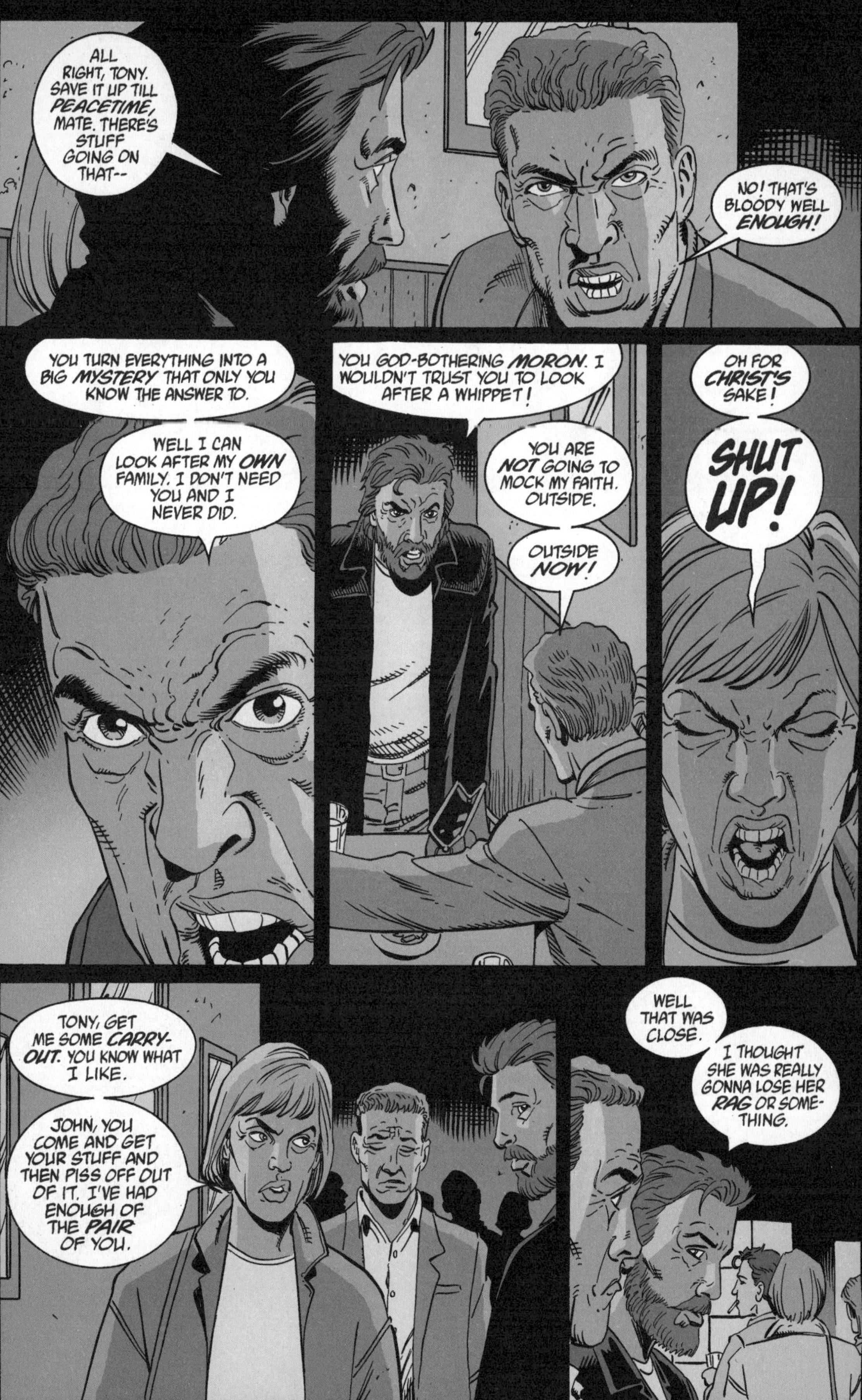
ALL RIGHT, TONY. SAVE IT UP TILL PEACETIME, MATE. THERE'S STUFF GOING ON THAT--
NO! THAT'S BLOODY WELL ENOUGH!
YOU TURN EVERYTHING INTO A BIG MYSTERY THAT ONLY YOU KNOW THE ANSWER TO.
WELL I CAN LOOK AFTER MY OWN FAMILY. I DON'T NEED YOU AND I NEVER DID.
YOU GOD-BOTHERING MORON. I WOULDN'T TRUST YOU TO LOOK AFTER A WHIPPET!
YOU ARE NOT GOING TO MOCK MY FAITH. OUTSIDE.
OUTSIDE NOW!
OH FOR CHRIST'S SAKE!
SHUT UP!
TONY, GET ME SOME CARRY-OUT. YOU KNOW WHAT I LIKE.
JOHN, YOU COME AND GET YOUR STUFF AND THEN PISS OFF OUT OF IT. I'VE HAD ENOUGH OF THE PAIR OF YOU.
WELL THAT WAS CLOSE.
I THOUGHT SHE WAS REALLY GONNA LOSE HER RAG OR SOME-THING.

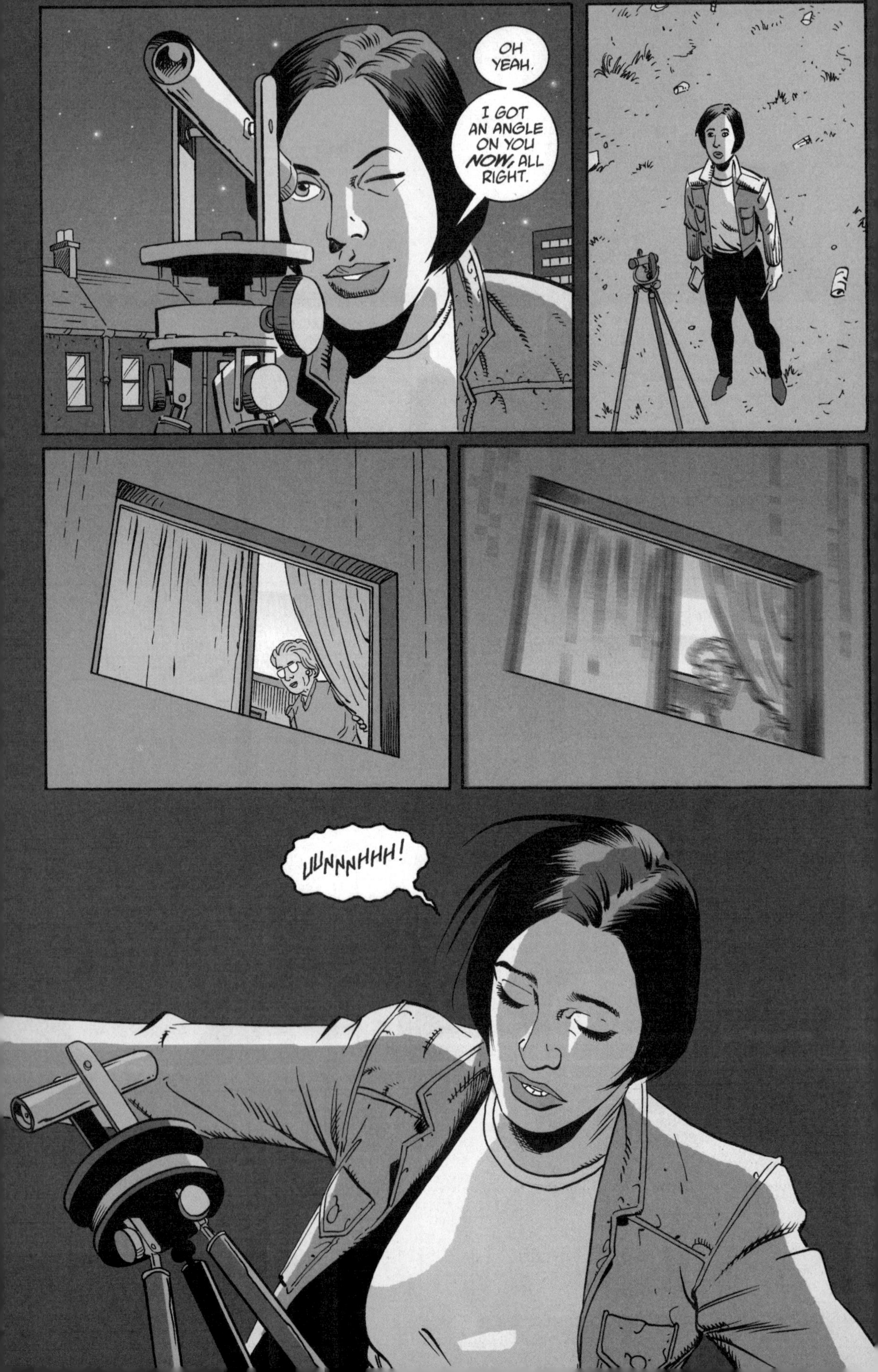
OH YEAH.
I GOT AN ANGLE ON YOU NOW, ALL RIGHT.
UUNNNHHH!

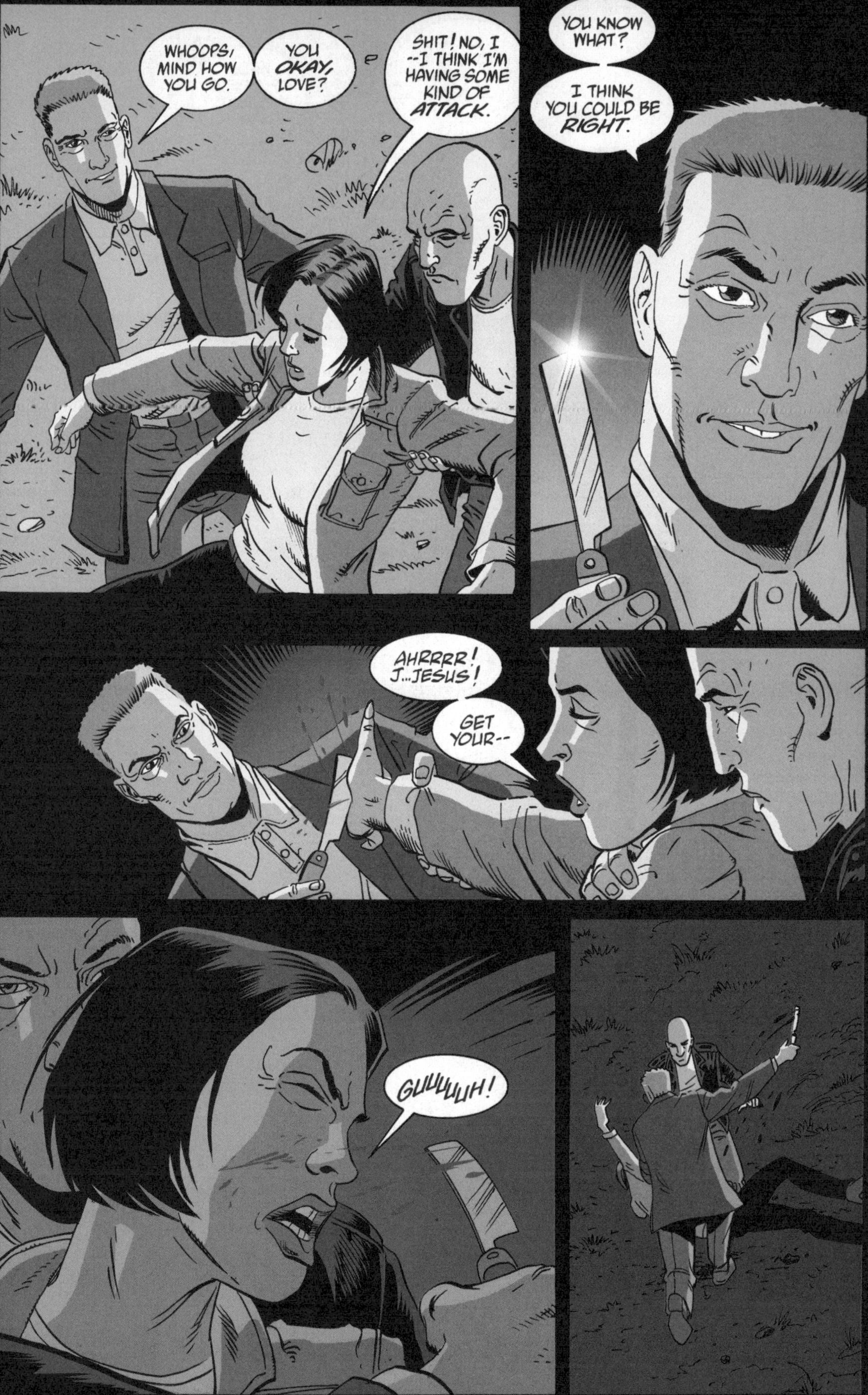
WHOOPS, MIND HOW YOU GO.
YOU *OKAY,* LOVE?
SHIT! NO, I --I THINK I'M HAVING SOME KIND OF *ATTACK.*
YOU KNOW WHAT?
I THINK YOU COULD BE *RIGHT.*
AHRRRR! J...JESUS!
GET YOUR--
GUUUUUH!

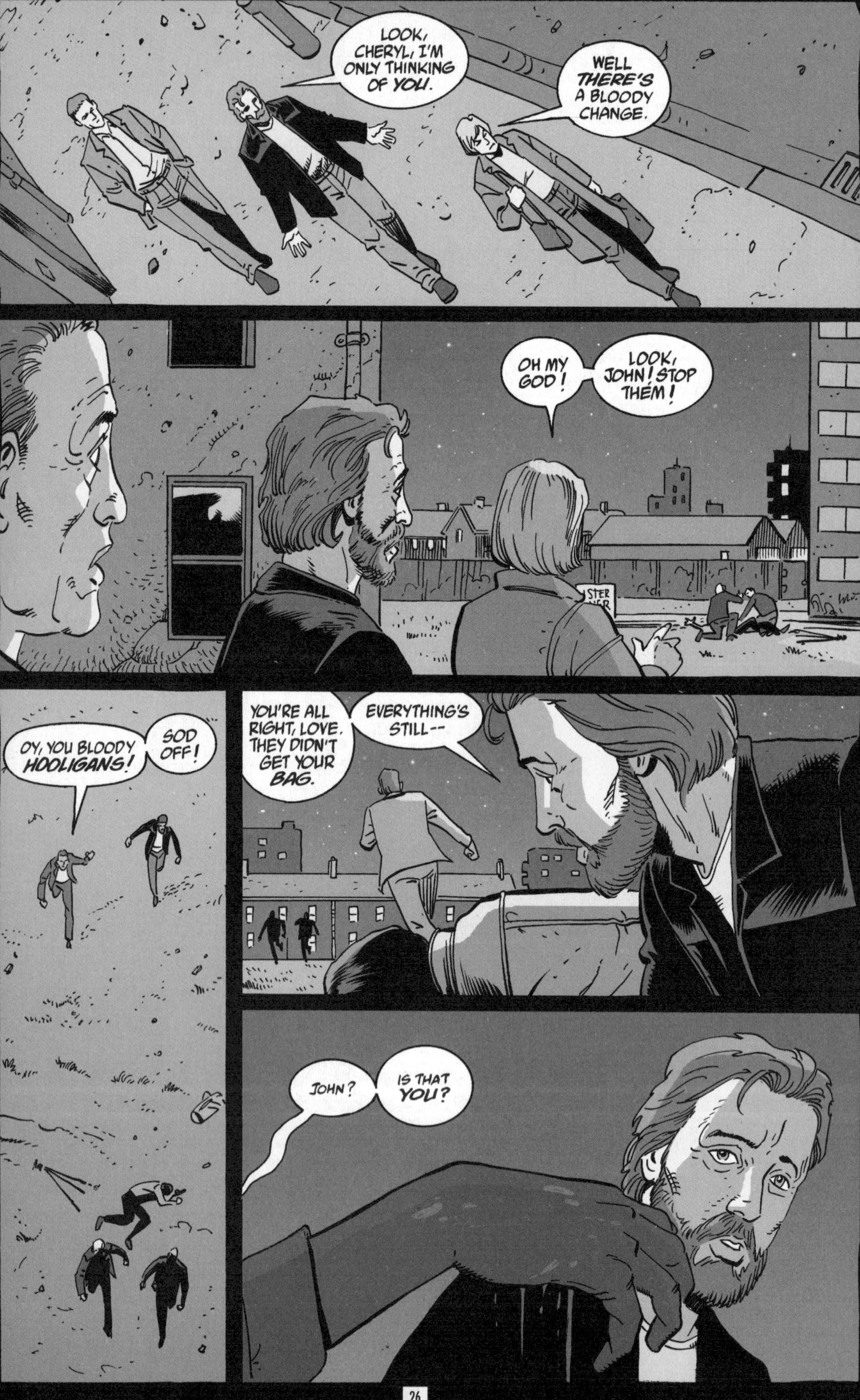
LOOK, CHERYL, I'M ONLY THINKING OF YOU.
WELL THERE'S A BLOODY CHANGE.
OH MY GOD!
LOOK, JOHN! STOP THEM!
OY, YOU BLOODY HOOLIGANS!
SOD OFF!
YOU'RE ALL RIGHT, LOVE. THEY DIDN'T GET YOUR BAG.
EVERYTHING'S STILL--
JOHN?
IS THAT YOU?

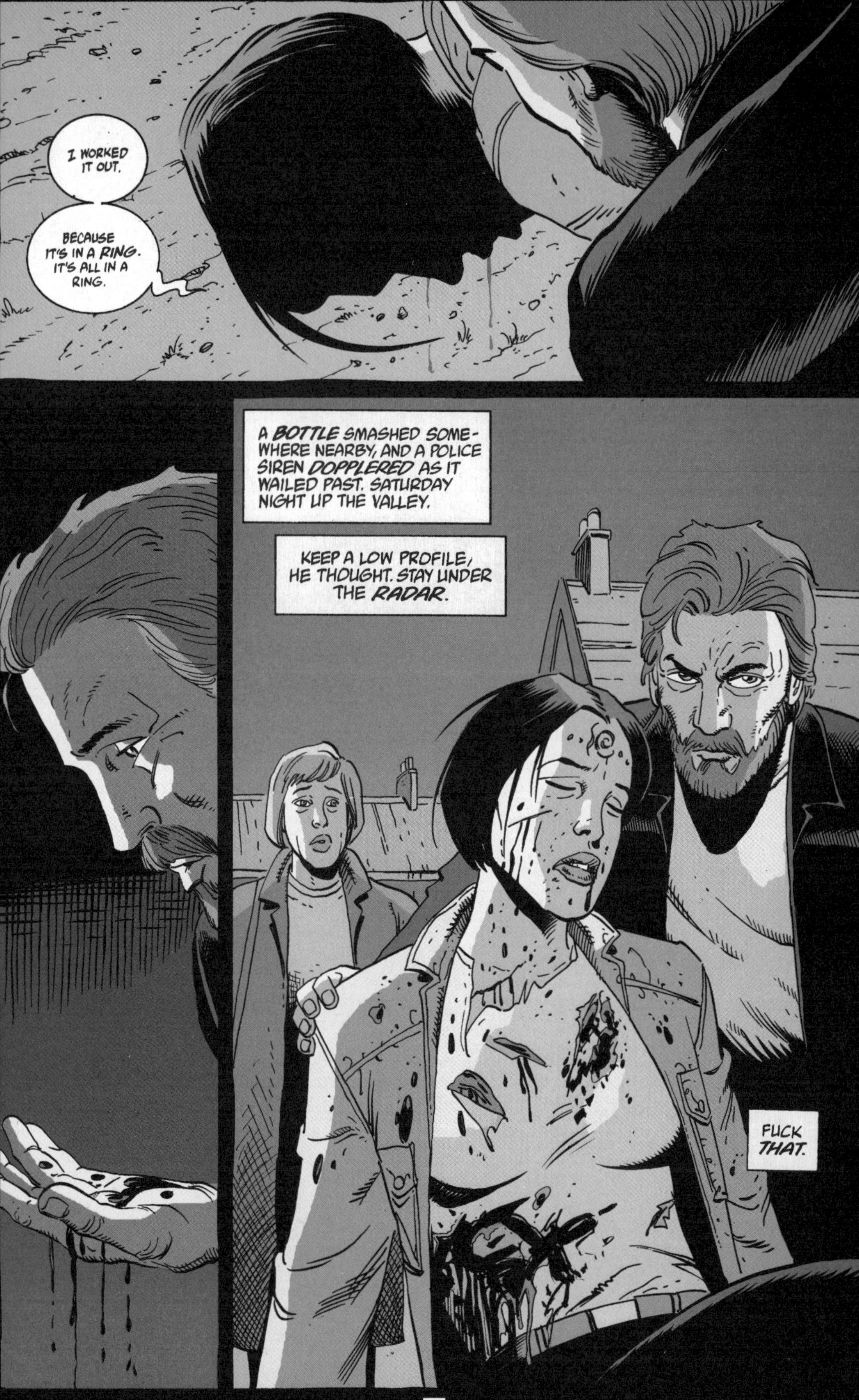
I WORKED IT OUT.
BECAUSE IT'S IN A RING. IT'S ALL IN A RING.
A BOTTLE SMASHED SOMEWHERE NEARBY, AND A POLICE SIREN DOPPLERED AS IT WAILED PAST. SATURDAY NIGHT UP THE VALLEY.
KEEP A LOW PROFILE, HE THOUGHT. STAY UNDER THE RADAR.
FUCK THAT.

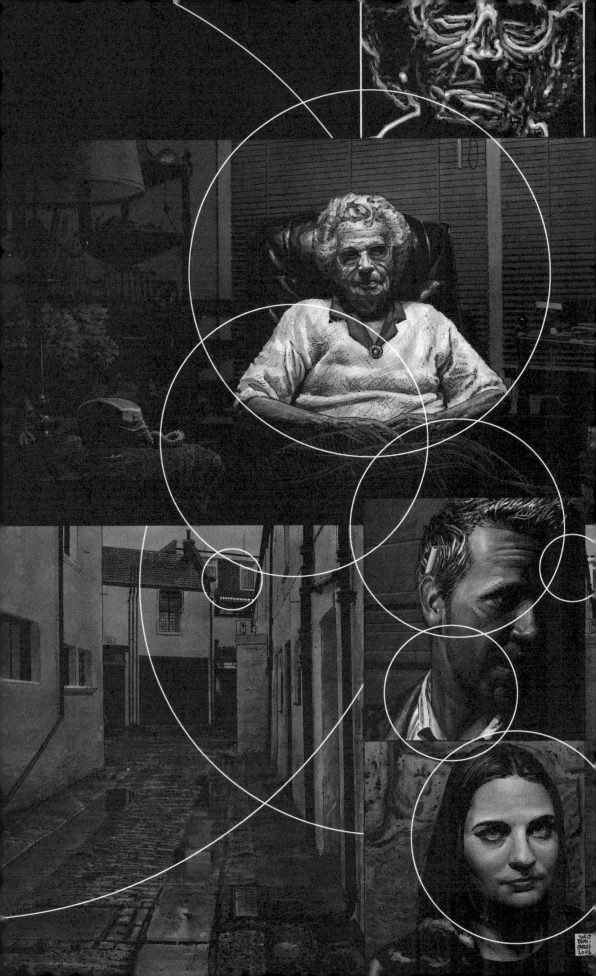

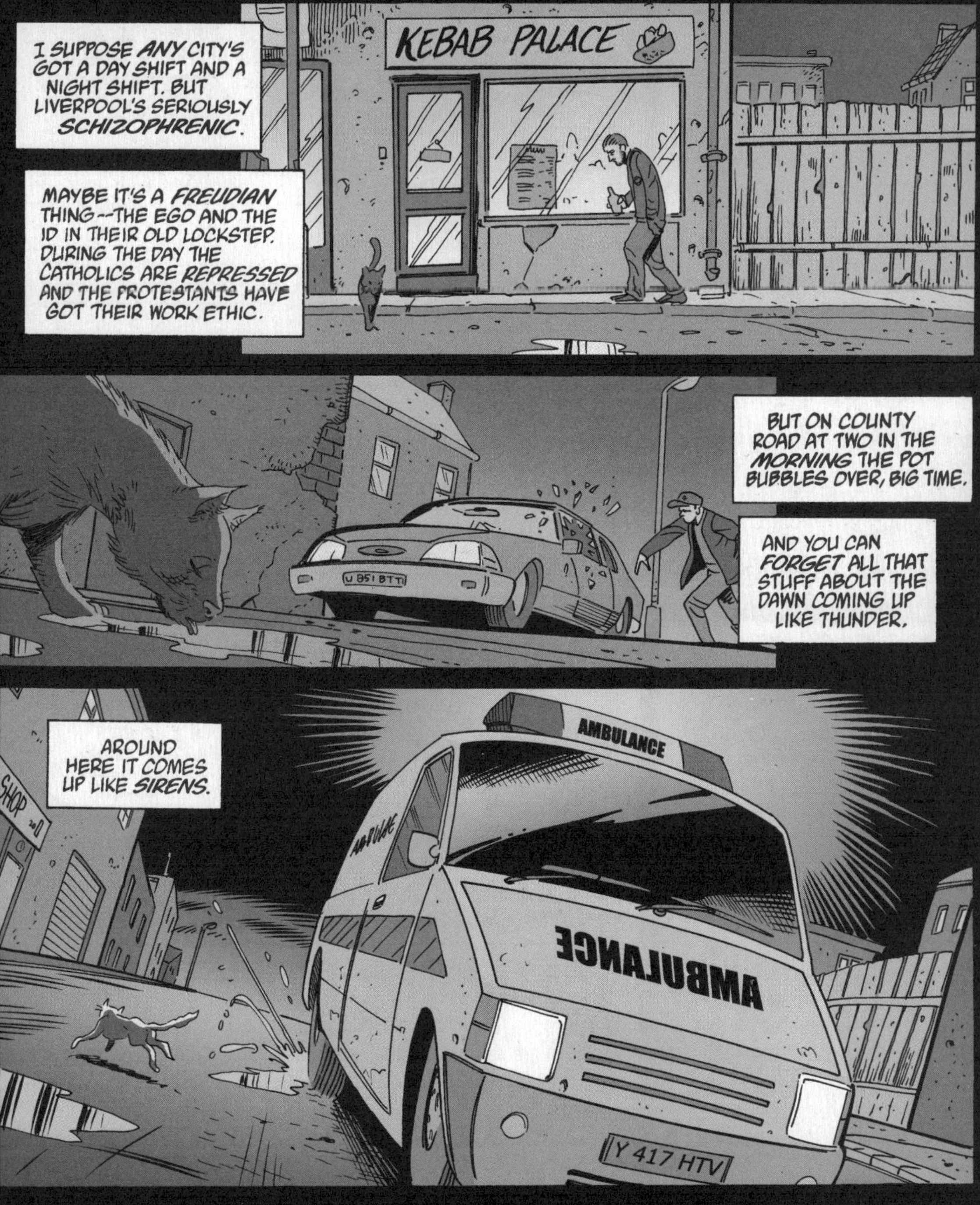
I SUPPOSE ANY CITY'S GOT A DAY SHIFT AND A NIGHT SHIFT. BUT LIVERPOOL'S SERIOUSLY SCHIZOPHRENIC.
MAYBE IT'S A FREUDIAN THING--THE EGO AND THE ID IN THEIR OLD LOCKSTEP. DURING THE DAY THE CATHOLICS ARE REPRESSED AND THE PROTESTANTS HAVE GOT THEIR WORK ETHIC.
KEBAB PALACE
BUT ON COUNTY ROAD AT TWO IN THE MORNING THE POT BUBBLES OVER, BIG TIME.
AND YOU CAN FORGET ALL THAT STUFF ABOUT THE DAWN COMING UP LIKE THUNDER.
U 851 BTT
AROUND HERE IT COMES UP LIKE SIRENS.
AMBULANCE
SHOP
AMBULANCE
Y 417 HTV

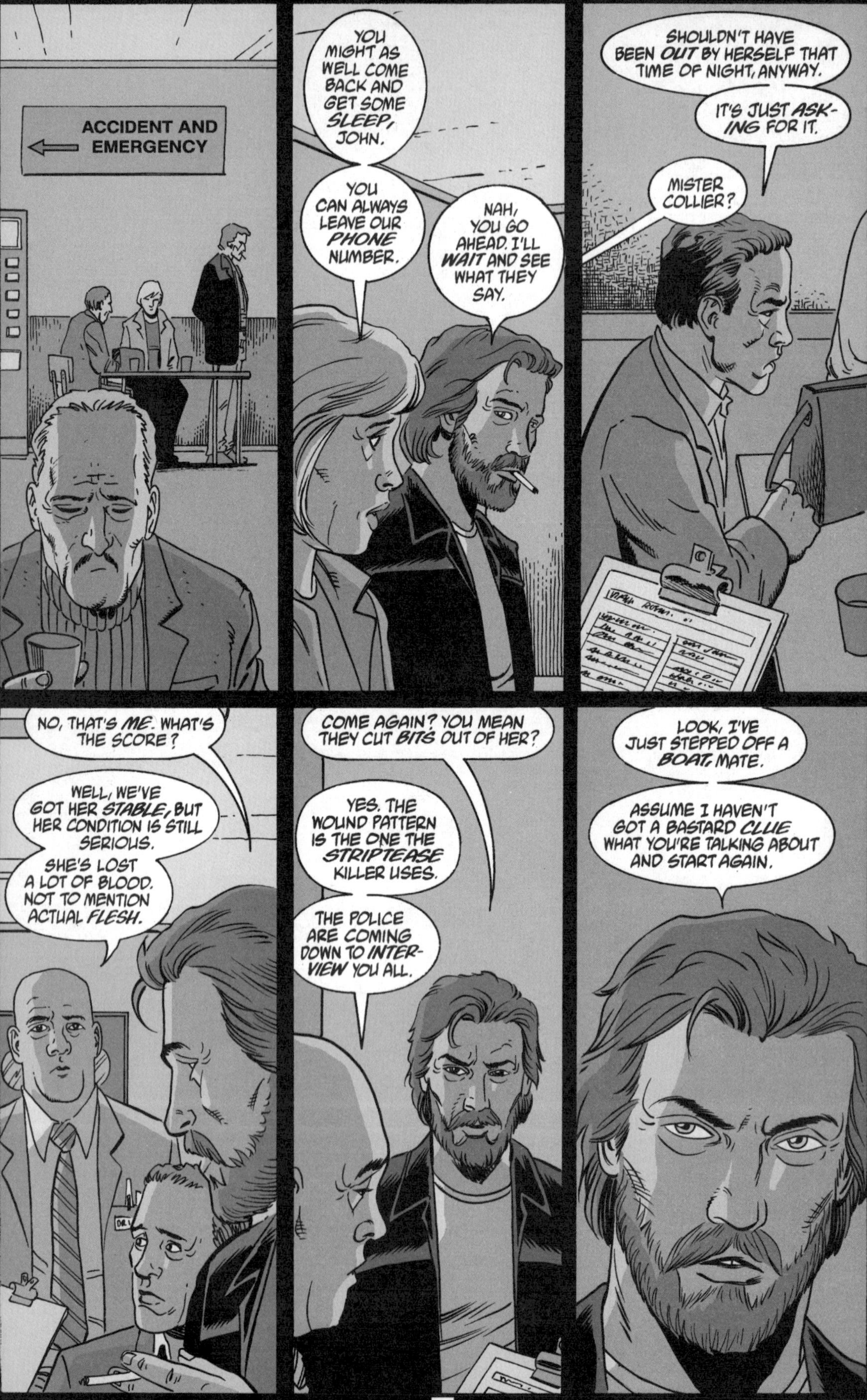
ACCIDENT AND EMERGENCY
YOU MIGHT AS WELL COME BACK AND GET SOME SLEEP, JOHN.
YOU CAN ALWAYS LEAVE OUR PHONE NUMBER.
NAH, YOU GO AHEAD. I'LL WAIT AND SEE WHAT THEY SAY.
SHOULDN'T HAVE BEEN OUT BY HERSELF THAT TIME OF NIGHT, ANYWAY.
IT'S JUST ASKING FOR IT.
MISTER COLLIER?
NO, THAT'S ME. WHAT'S THE SCORE?
WELL, WE'VE GOT HER STABLE, BUT HER CONDITION IS STILL SERIOUS.
SHE'S LOST A LOT OF BLOOD. NOT TO MENTION ACTUAL FLESH.
COME AGAIN? YOU MEAN THEY CUT BITS OUT OF HER?
YES. THE WOUND PATTERN IS THE ONE THE STRIPTEASE KILLER USES.
THE POLICE ARE COMING DOWN TO INTERVIEW YOU ALL.
LOOK, I'VE JUST STEPPED OFF A BOAT, MATE.
ASSUME I HAVEN'T GOT A BASTARD CLUE WHAT YOU'RE TALKING ABOUT AND START AGAIN.

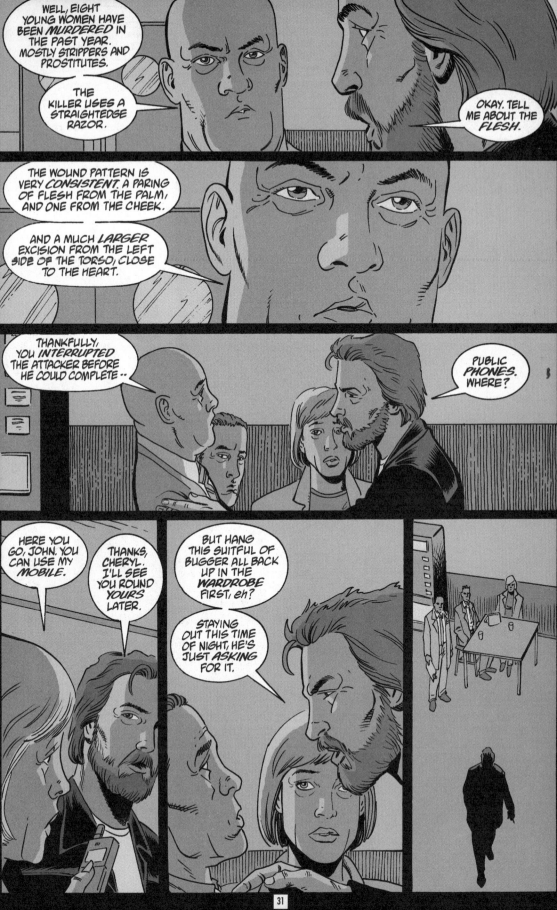

WELL, EIGHT YOUNG WOMEN HAVE BEEN *MURDERED* IN THE PAST YEAR. MOSTLY STRIPPERS AND PROSTITUTES.

THE KILLER USES A *STRAIGHTEDGE* RAZOR.

OKAY. TELL ME ABOUT THE *FLESH.*

THE WOUND PATTERN IS VERY *CONSISTENT.* A PARING OF FLESH FROM THE PALM, AND ONE FROM THE CHEEK.

AND A MUCH *LARGER* EXCISION FROM THE LEFT SIDE OF THE TORSO, CLOSE TO THE HEART.

THANKFULLY, YOU *INTERRUPTED* THE ATTACKER BEFORE HE COULD COMPLETE--

PUBLIC *PHONES.* WHERE?

HERE YOU GO, JOHN. YOU CAN USE MY *MOBILE.*

THANKS, CHERYL. I'LL SEE YOU ROUND YOURS LATER.

BUT HANG THIS SUITFUL OF BUGGER ALL BACK UP IN THE *WARDROBE* FIRST, EH?

STAYING OUT THIS TIME OF NIGHT, HE'S JUST *ASKING* FOR IT.

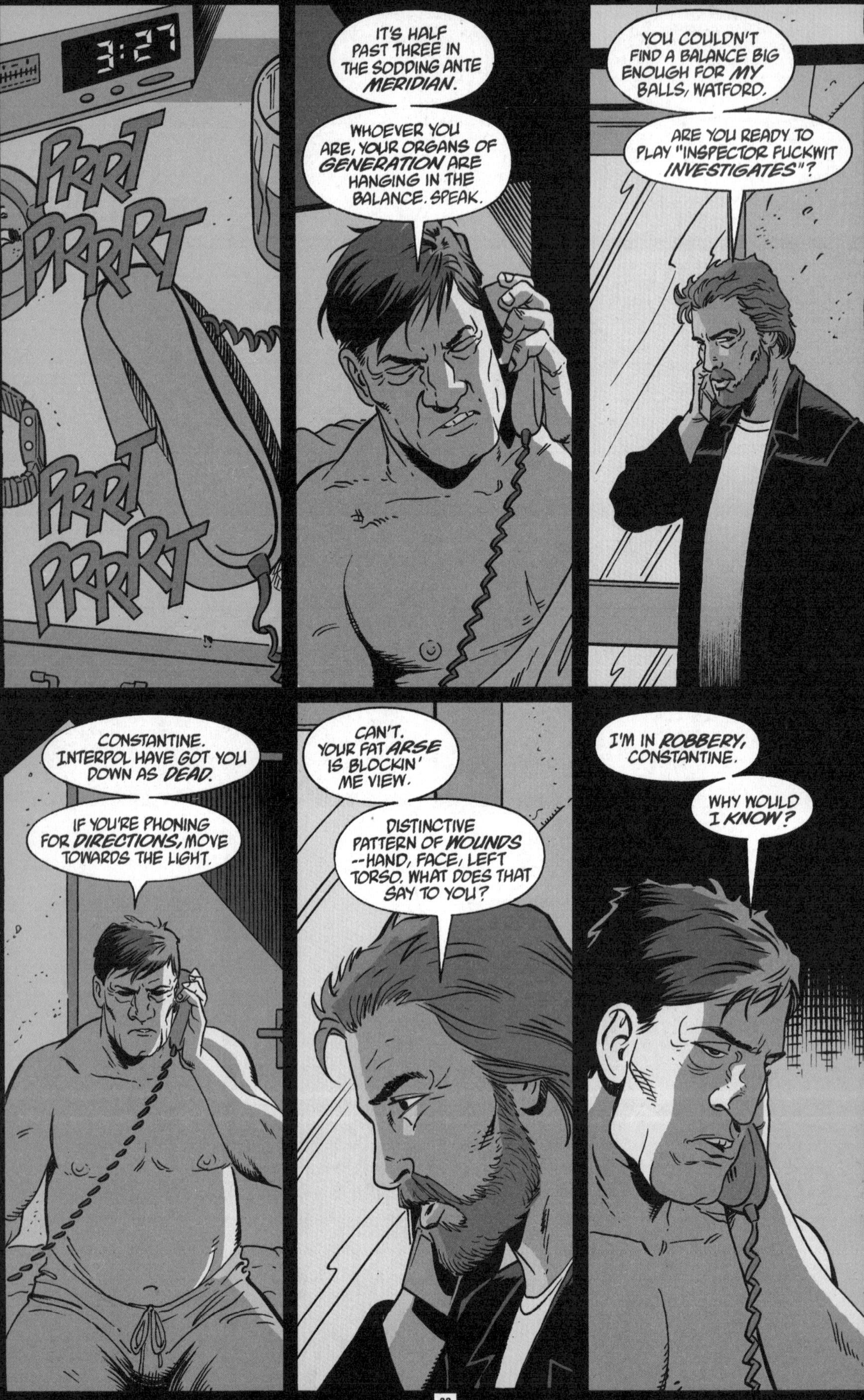
3:27
PRRT PRRRT
PRRT PRRRT
IT'S HALF PAST THREE IN THE SODDING ANTE *MERIDIAN*.
WHOEVER YOU ARE, YOUR ORGANS OF *GENERATION* ARE HANGING IN THE BALANCE. SPEAK.
YOU COULDN'T FIND A BALANCE BIG ENOUGH FOR *MY* BALLS, WATFORD.
ARE YOU READY TO PLAY "INSPECTOR FUCKWIT *INVESTIGATES*"?
CONSTANTINE. INTERPOL HAVE GOT YOU DOWN AS *DEAD*.
IF YOU'RE PHONING FOR *DIRECTIONS*, MOVE TOWARDS THE LIGHT.
CAN'T. YOUR FAT *ARSE* IS BLOCKIN' ME VIEW.
DISTINCTIVE PATTERN OF *WOUNDS* --HAND, FACE, LEFT TORSO. WHAT DOES THAT SAY TO YOU?
I'M IN *ROBBERY*, CONSTANTINE.
WHY WOULD I *KNOW*?

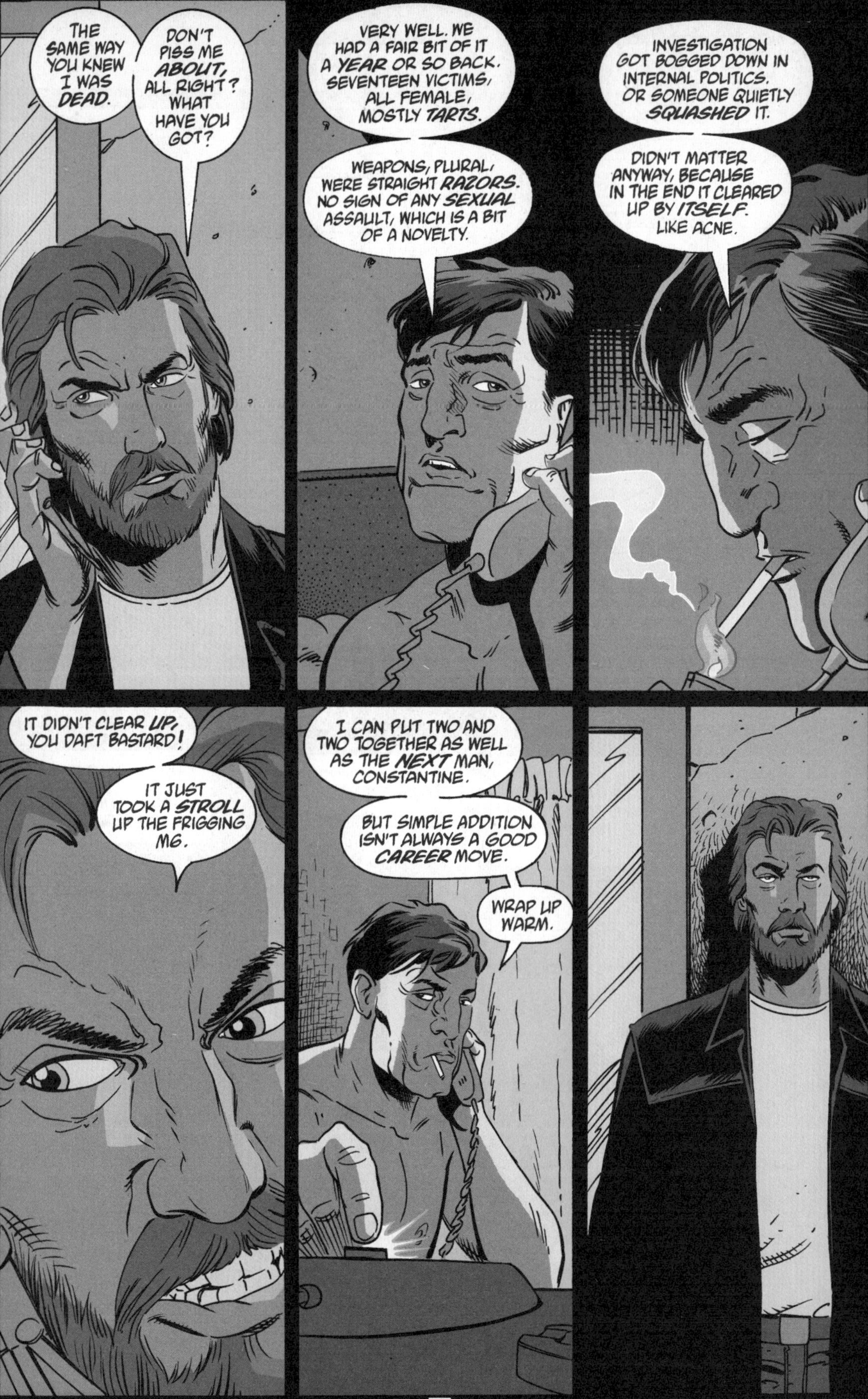
THE SAME WAY YOU KNEW I WAS DEAD.
DON'T PISS ME ABOUT, ALL RIGHT? WHAT HAVE YOU GOT?
VERY WELL. WE HAD A FAIR BIT OF IT A YEAR OR SO BACK. SEVENTEEN VICTIMS, ALL FEMALE, MOSTLY TARTS.
WEAPONS, PLURAL, WERE STRAIGHT RAZORS. NO SIGN OF ANY SEXUAL ASSAULT, WHICH IS A BIT OF A NOVELTY.
INVESTIGATION GOT BOGGED DOWN IN INTERNAL POLITICS. OR SOMEONE QUIETLY SQUASHED IT.
DIDN'T MATTER ANYWAY, BECAUSE IN THE END IT CLEARED UP BY ITSELF. LIKE ACNE.
IT DIDN'T CLEAR UP, YOU DAFT BASTARD!
IT JUST TOOK A STROLL UP THE FRIGGING M6.
I CAN PUT TWO AND TWO TOGETHER AS WELL AS THE NEXT MAN, CONSTANTINE.
BUT SIMPLE ADDITION ISN'T ALWAYS A GOOD CAREER MOVE.
WRAP UP WARM.

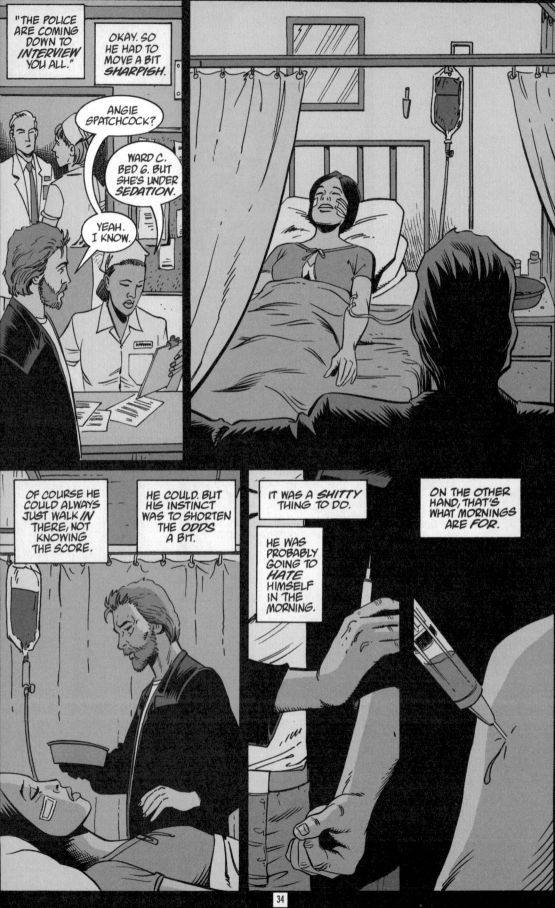

"THE POLICE ARE COMING DOWN TO *INTERVIEW* YOU ALL."

OKAY. SO HE HAD TO MOVE A BIT *SHARPISH.*

ANGIE SPATCHCOCK?

WARD C. BED 6. BUT SHE'S UNDER *SEDATION.*

YEAH. I KNOW.

OF COURSE HE COULD ALWAYS JUST WALK *IN* THERE, NOT KNOWING THE SCORE.

HE COULD. BUT HIS INSTINCT WAS TO SHORTEN THE *ODDS* A BIT.

IT WAS A *SHITTY* THING TO DO.

HE WAS PROBABLY GOING TO *HATE* HIMSELF IN THE MORNING.

ON THE OTHER HAND, THAT'S WHAT MORNINGS ARE *FOR.*

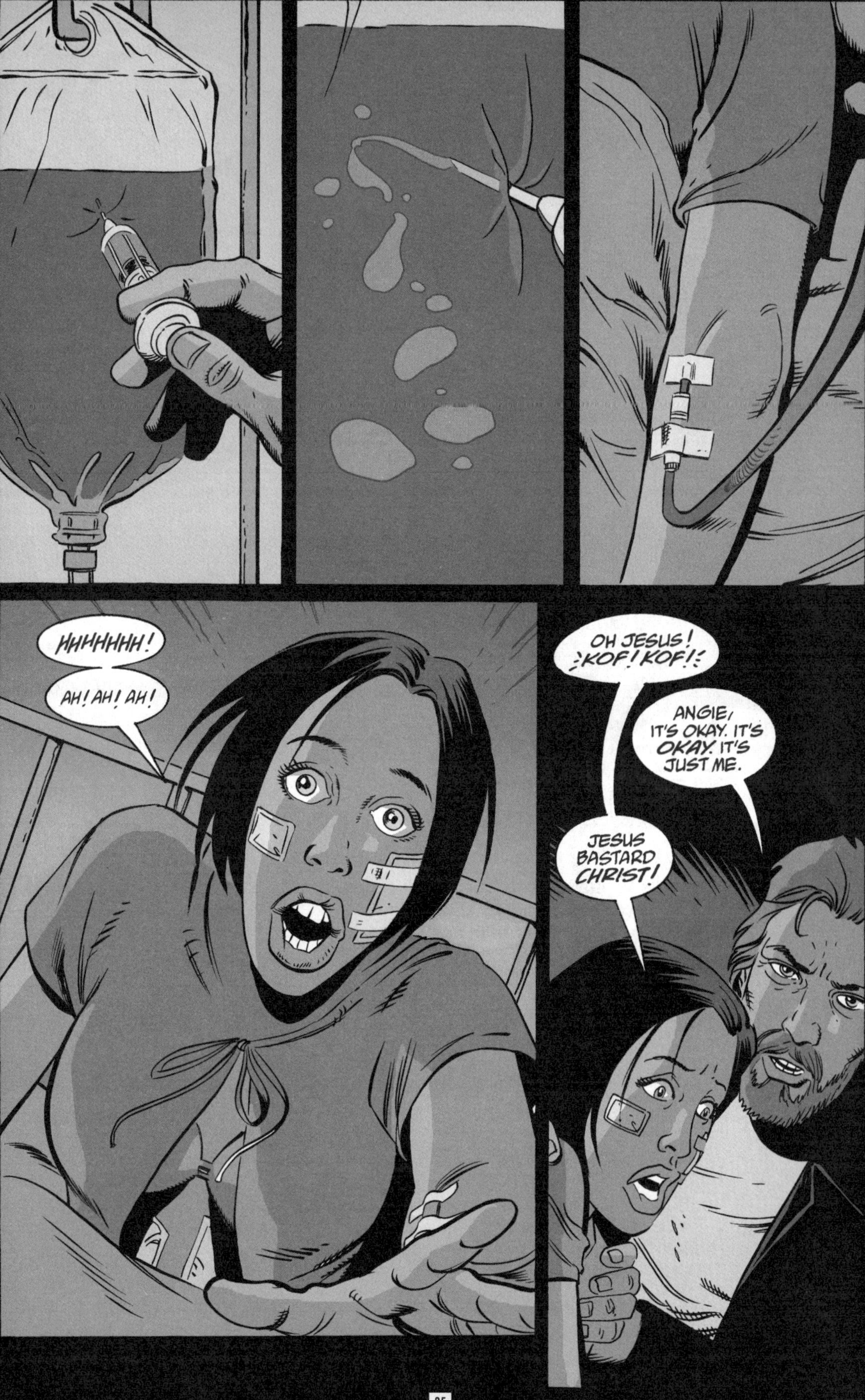
HHHHHHH!
AH! AH! AH!
OH JESUS! KOF! KOF!
ANGIE, IT'S OKAY. IT'S OKAY. IT'S JUST ME.
JESUS BASTARD CHRIST!

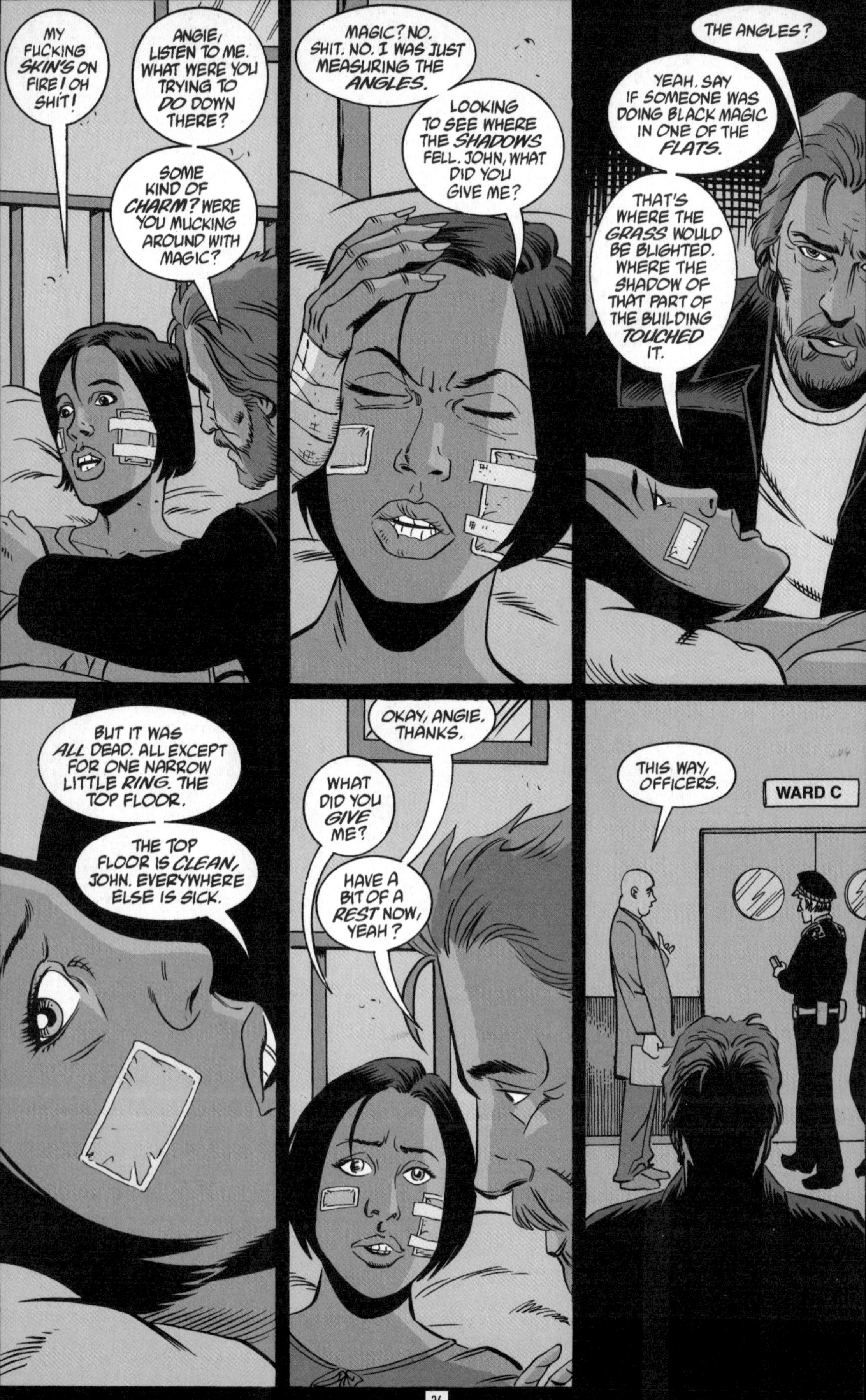

MY FUCKING SKIN'S ON FIRE! OH SHIT!
ANGIE, LISTEN TO ME. WHAT WERE YOU TRYING TO DO DOWN THERE?
SOME KIND OF CHARM? WERE YOU MUCKING AROUND WITH MAGIC?
MAGIC? NO. SHIT. NO. I WAS JUST MEASURING THE ANGLES.
LOOKING TO SEE WHERE THE SHADOWS FELL. JOHN, WHAT DID YOU GIVE ME?
THE ANGLES?
YEAH. SAY IF SOMEONE WAS DOING BLACK MAGIC IN ONE OF THE FLATS.
THAT'S WHERE THE GRASS WOULD BE BLIGHTED. WHERE THE SHADOW OF THAT PART OF THE BUILDING TOUCHED IT.
BUT IT WAS ALL DEAD. ALL EXCEPT FOR ONE NARROW LITTLE RING. THE TOP FLOOR.
THE TOP FLOOR IS CLEAN, JOHN. EVERYWHERE ELSE IS SICK.
OKAY, ANGIE. THANKS.
WHAT DID YOU GIVE ME?
HAVE A BIT OF A REST NOW, YEAH?
THIS WAY, OFFICERS.
WARD C

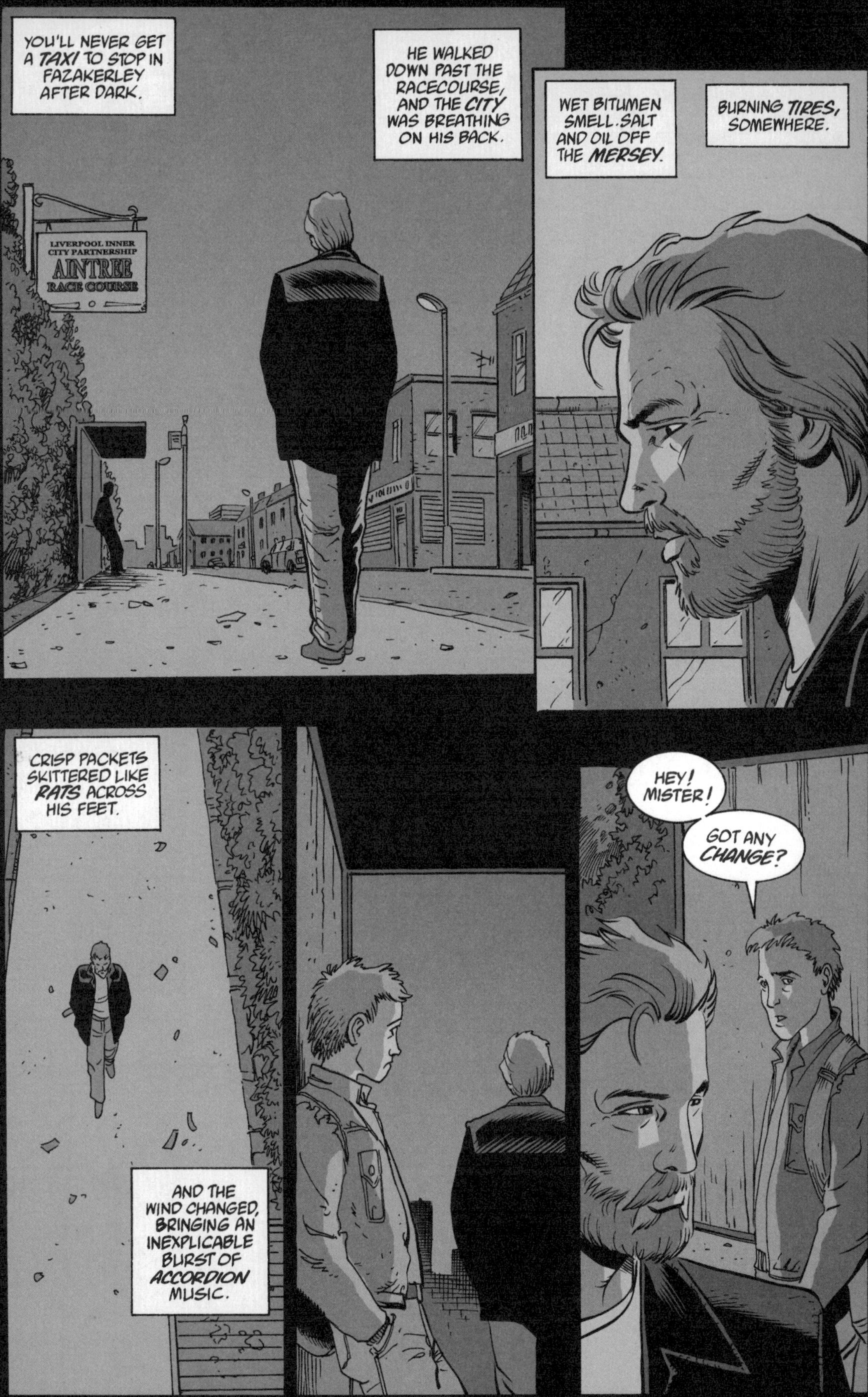
YOU'LL NEVER GET A TAXI TO STOP IN FAZAKERLEY AFTER DARK.
HE WALKED DOWN PAST THE RACECOURSE, AND THE CITY WAS BREATHING ON HIS BACK.
LIVERPOOL INNER CITY PARTNERSHIP
AINTREE
RACE COURSE
WET BITUMEN SMELL. SALT AND OIL OFF THE MERSEY.
BURNING TIRES, SOMEWHERE.
CRISP PACKETS SKITTERED LIKE RATS ACROSS HIS FEET.
AND THE WIND CHANGED, BRINGING AN INEXPLICABLE BURST OF ACCORDION MUSIC.
HEY! MISTER!
GOT ANY CHANGE?

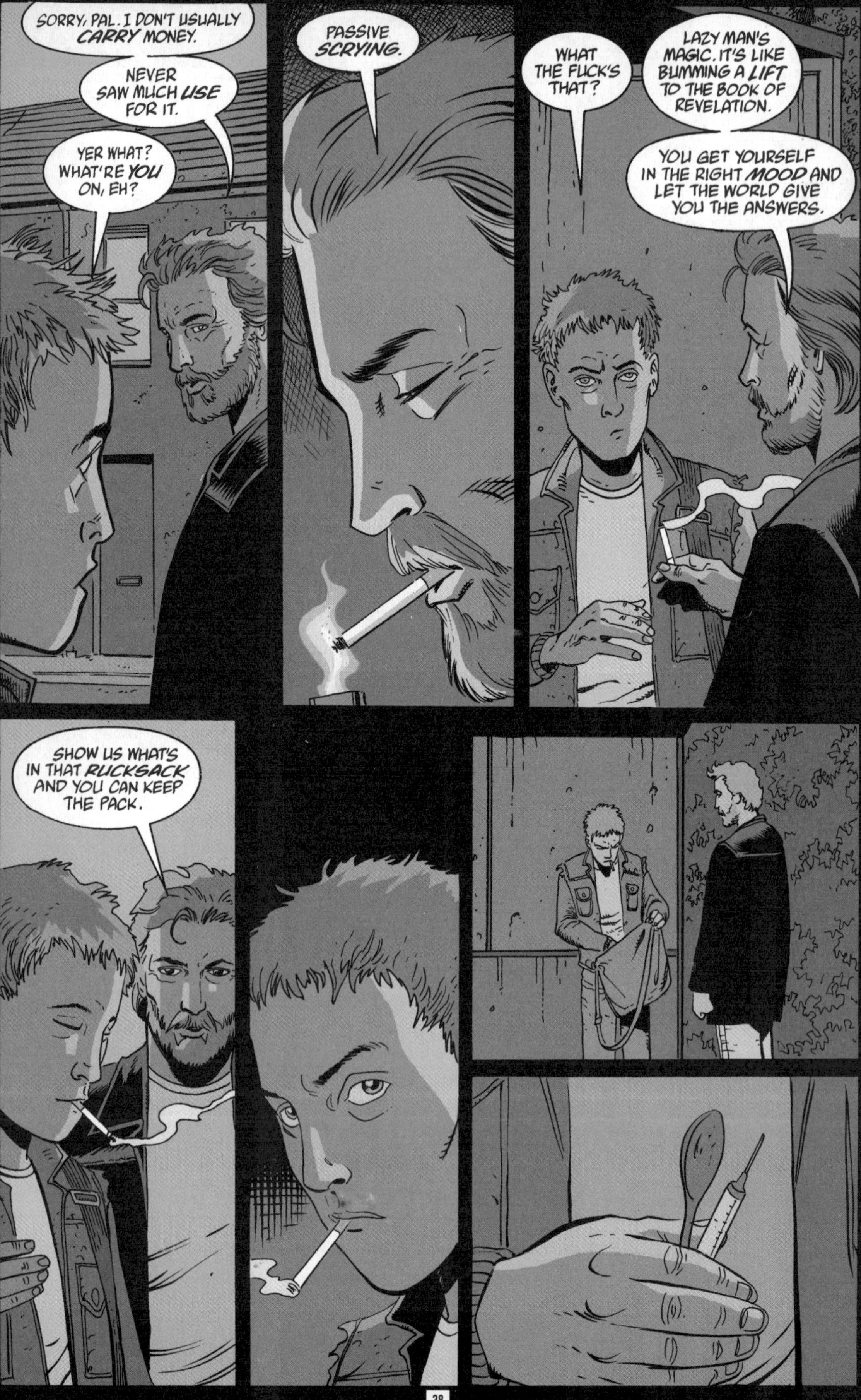
SORRY, PAL. I DON'T USUALLY CARRY MONEY.
NEVER SAW MUCH USE FOR IT.
YER WHAT? WHAT'RE YOU ON, EH?
PASSIVE SCRYING.
WHAT THE FUCK'S THAT?
LAZY MAN'S MAGIC. IT'S LIKE BUMMING A LIFT TO THE BOOK OF REVELATION.
YOU GET YOURSELF IN THE RIGHT MOOD AND LET THE WORLD GIVE YOU THE ANSWERS.
SHOW US WHAT'S IN THAT RUCKSACK AND YOU CAN KEEP THE PACK.

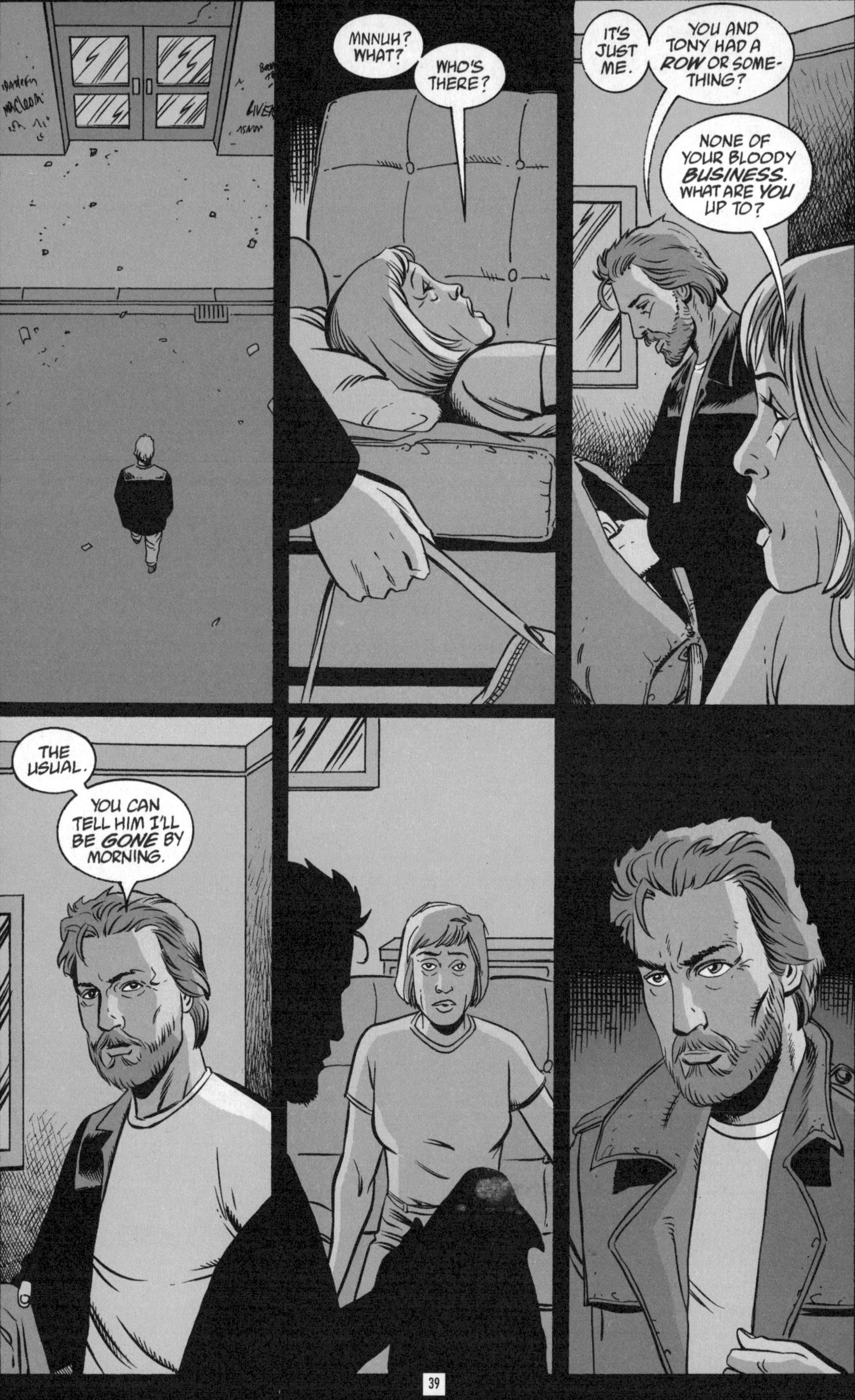
MNNUH? WHAT?
WHO'S THERE?
IT'S JUST ME.
YOU AND TONY HAD A ROW OR SOME-THING?
NONE OF YOUR BLOODY BUSINESS. WHAT ARE YOU UP TO?
THE USUAL.
YOU CAN TELL HIM I'LL BE GONE BY MORNING.

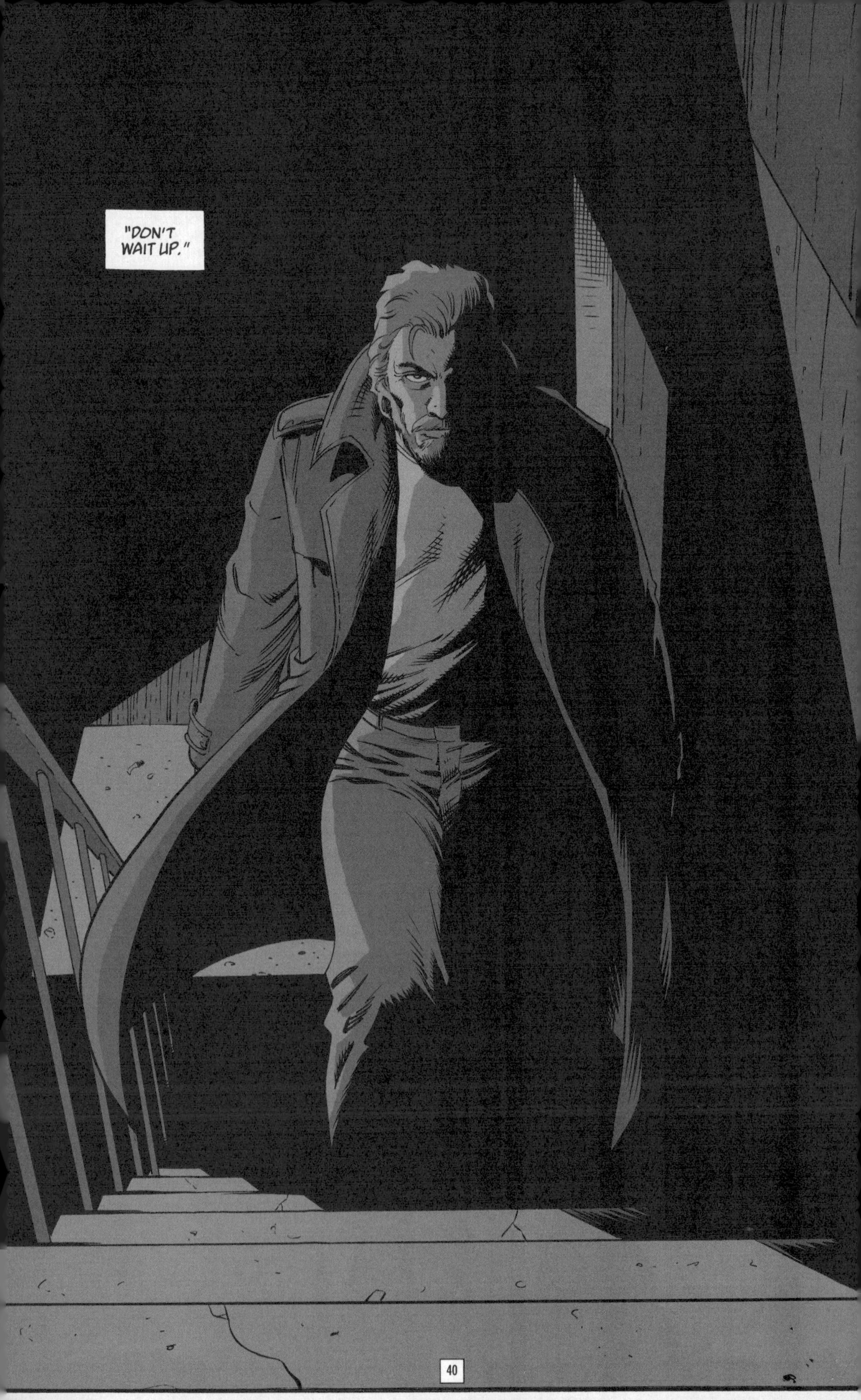
"DON'T WAIT UP."

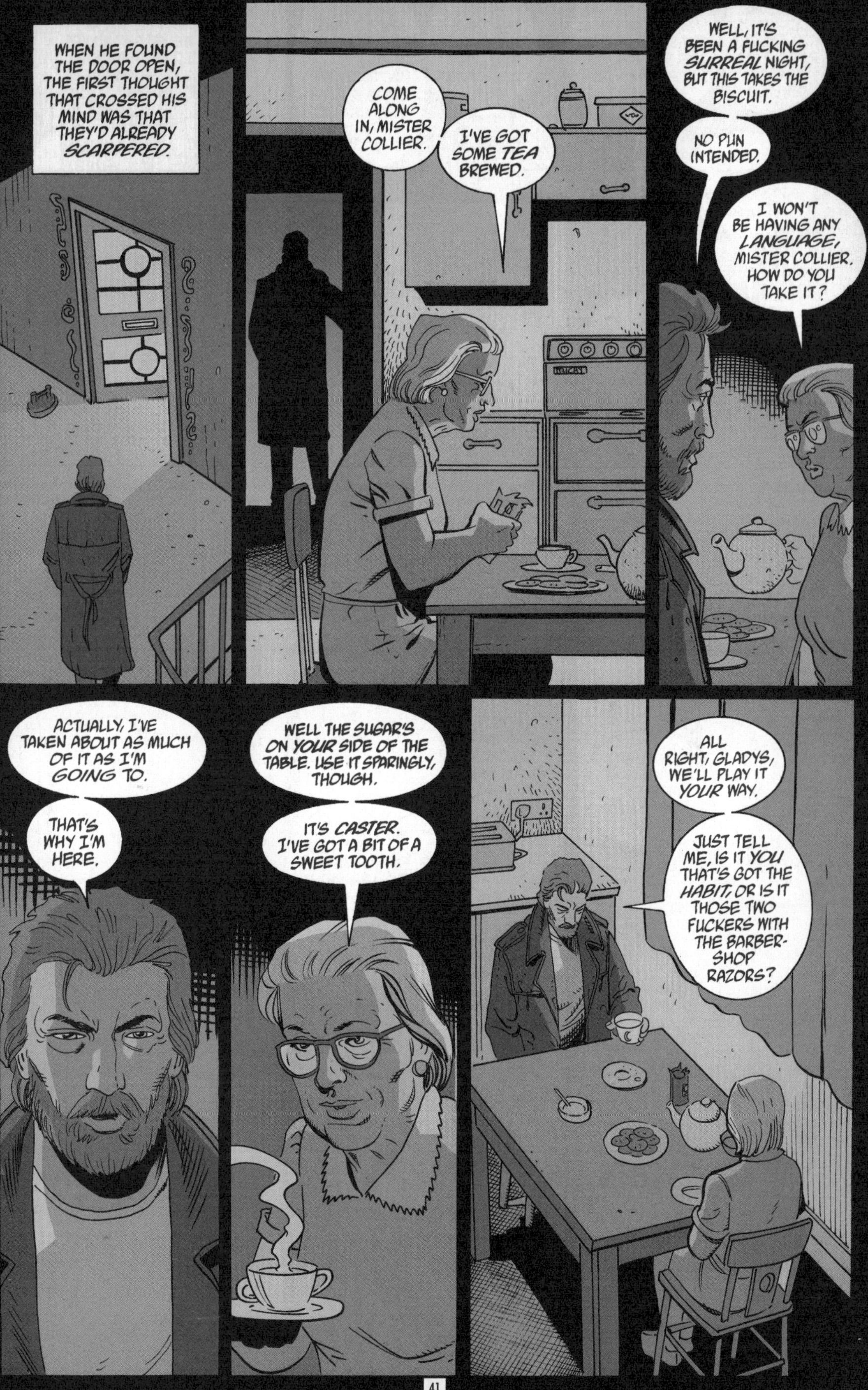
WHEN HE FOUND THE DOOR OPEN, THE FIRST THOUGHT THAT CROSSED HIS MIND WAS THAT THEY'D ALREADY SCARPERED.
COME ALONG IN, MISTER COLLIER.
I'VE GOT SOME TEA BREWED.
WELL, IT'S BEEN A FUCKING SURREAL NIGHT, BUT THIS TAKES THE BISCUIT.
NO PUN INTENDED.
I WON'T BE HAVING ANY LANGUAGE, MISTER COLLIER. HOW DO YOU TAKE IT?
ACTUALLY, I'VE TAKEN ABOUT AS MUCH OF IT AS I'M GOING TO.
THAT'S WHY I'M HERE.
WELL THE SUGAR'S ON YOUR SIDE OF THE TABLE. USE IT SPARINGLY, THOUGH.
IT'S CASTER. I'VE GOT A BIT OF A SWEET TOOTH.
ALL RIGHT, GLADYS, WE'LL PLAY IT YOUR WAY.
JUST TELL ME, IS IT YOU THAT'S GOT THE HABIT, OR IS IT THOSE TWO FUCKERS WITH THE BARBER-SHOP RAZORS?

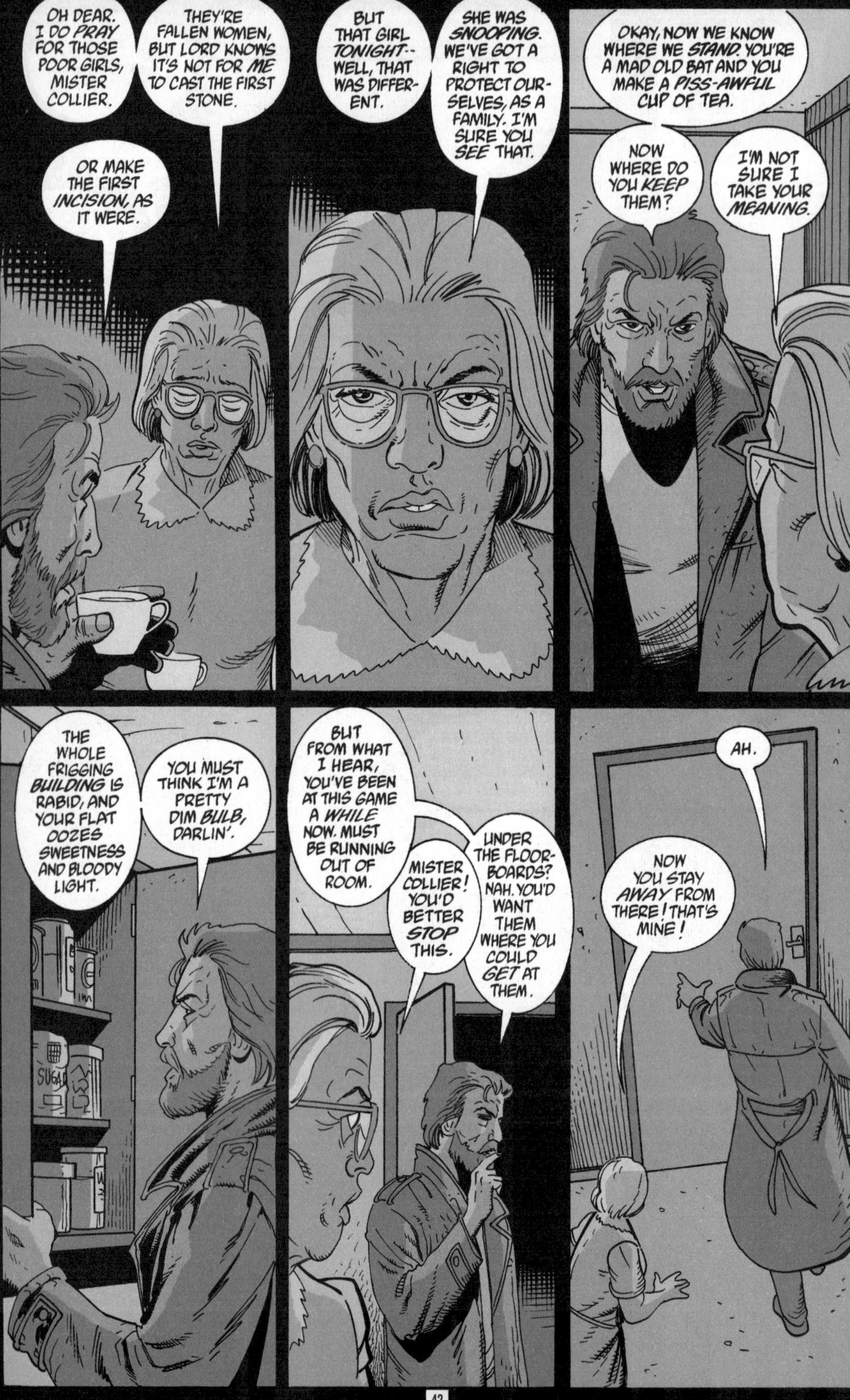

OH DEAR. I DO PRAY FOR THOSE POOR GIRLS, MISTER COLLIER.
THEY'RE FALLEN WOMEN, BUT LORD KNOWS IT'S NOT FOR ME TO CAST THE FIRST STONE.
OR MAKE THE FIRST INCISION, AS IT WERE.
BUT THAT GIRL TONIGHT-- WELL, THAT WAS DIFFER- ENT.
SHE WAS SNOOPING. WE'VE GOT A RIGHT TO PROTECT OUR- SELVES, AS A FAMILY. I'M SURE YOU SEE THAT.
OKAY, NOW WE KNOW WHERE WE STAND. YOU'RE A MAD OLD BAT AND YOU MAKE A PISS-AWFUL CUP OF TEA.
NOW WHERE DO YOU KEEP THEM?
I'M NOT SURE I TAKE YOUR MEANING.
THE WHOLE FRIGGING BUILDING IS RABID, AND YOUR FLAT OOZES SWEETNESS AND BLOODY LIGHT.
YOU MUST THINK I'M A PRETTY DIM BULB, DARLIN'.
SUGA
BUT FROM WHAT I HEAR, YOU'VE BEEN AT THIS GAME A WHILE NOW. MUST BE RUNNING OUT OF ROOM.
UNDER THE FLOOR- BOARDS? NAH. YOU'D WANT THEM WHERE YOU COULD GET AT THEM.
MISTER COLLIER! YOU'D BETTER STOP THIS.
AH.
NOW YOU STAY AWAY FROM THERE! THAT'S MINE!

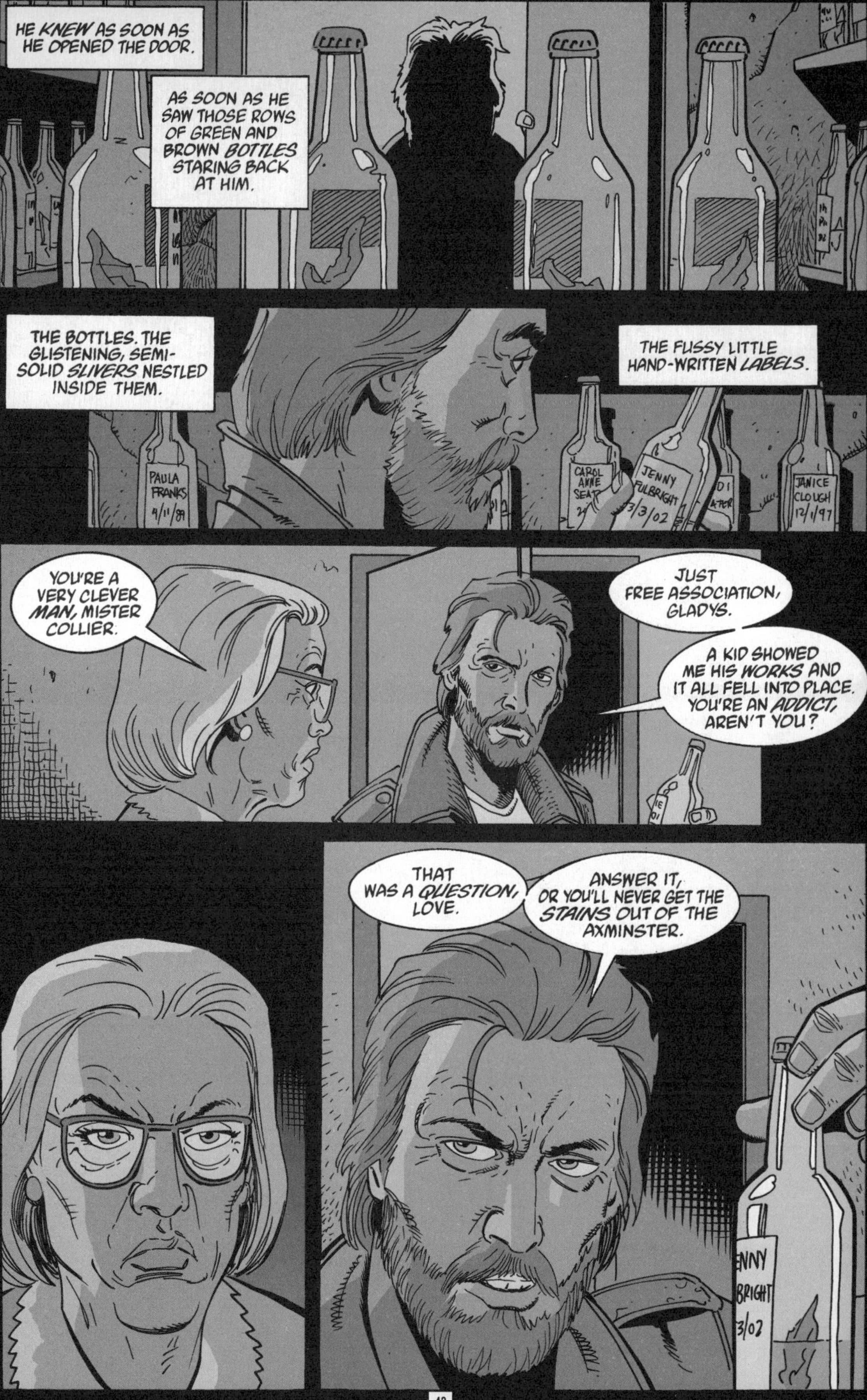
HE KNEW AS SOON AS HE OPENED THE DOOR.
AS SOON AS HE SAW THOSE ROWS OF GREEN AND BROWN BOTTLES STARING BACK AT HIM.
THE BOTTLES. THE GLISTENING, SEMI-SOLID SLIVERS NESTLED INSIDE THEM.
THE FUSSY LITTLE HAND-WRITTEN LABELS.
PAULA FRANKS 4/11/89
CAROL ANNE SEAT
JENNY FULBRIGHT 3/3/02
JANICE CLOUGH 12/1/97
YOU'RE A VERY CLEVER MAN, MISTER COLLIER.
JUST FREE ASSOCIATION, GLADYS.
A KID SHOWED ME HIS WORKS AND IT ALL FELL INTO PLACE. YOU'RE AN ADDICT, AREN'T YOU?
THAT WAS A QUESTION, LOVE.
ANSWER IT, OR YOU'LL NEVER GET THE STAINS OUT OF THE AXMINSTER.

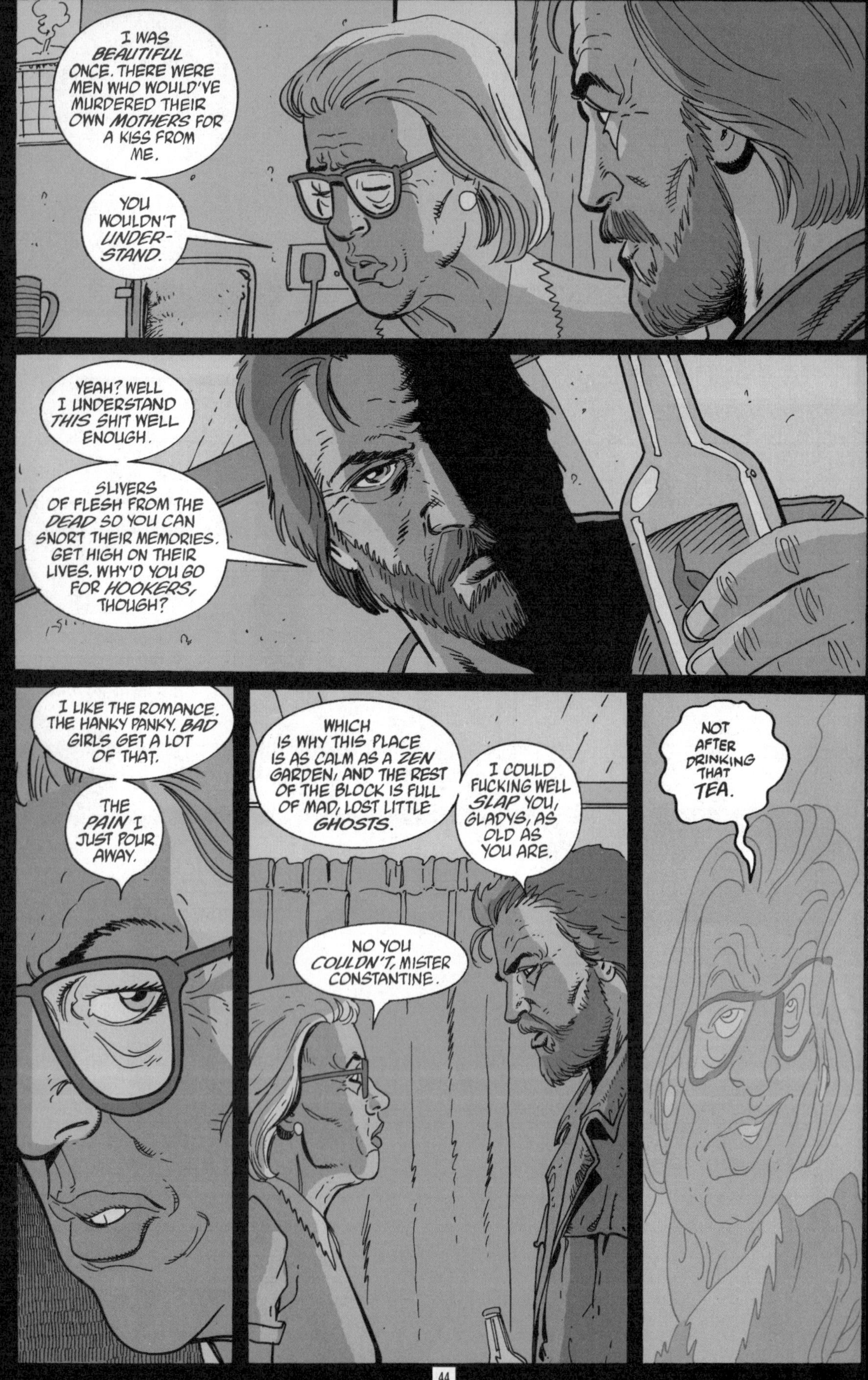
I WAS BEAUTIFUL ONCE. THERE WERE MEN WHO WOULD'VE MURDERED THEIR OWN MOTHERS FOR A KISS FROM ME.
YOU WOULDN'T UNDER-STAND.
YEAH? WELL I UNDERSTAND THIS SHIT WELL ENOUGH.
SLIVERS OF FLESH FROM THE DEAD SO YOU CAN SNORT THEIR MEMORIES. GET HIGH ON THEIR LIVES. WHY'D YOU GO FOR HOOKERS, THOUGH?
I LIKE THE ROMANCE. THE HANKY PANKY. BAD GIRLS GET A LOT OF THAT.
THE PAIN I JUST POUR AWAY.
WHICH IS WHY THIS PLACE IS AS CALM AS A ZEN GARDEN, AND THE REST OF THE BLOCK IS FULL OF MAD, LOST LITTLE GHOSTS.
I COULD FUCKING WELL SLAP YOU, GLADYS, AS OLD AS YOU ARE.
NO YOU COULDN'T, MISTER CONSTANTINE.
NOT AFTER DRINKING THAT TEA.

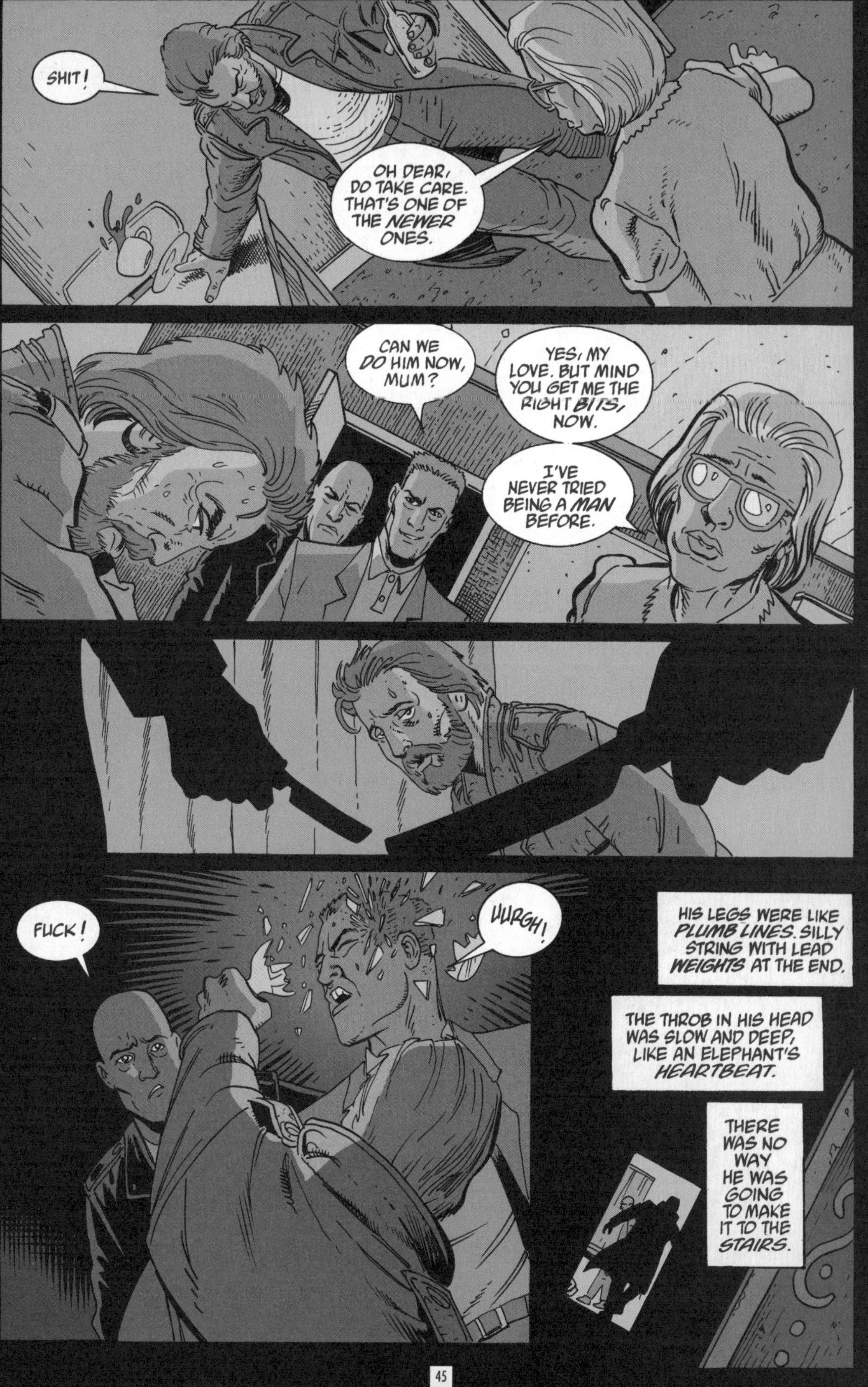
SHIT!
OH DEAR, DO TAKE CARE. THAT'S ONE OF THE NEWER ONES.
CAN WE DO HIM NOW, MUM?
YES, MY LOVE. BUT MIND YOU GET ME THE RIGHT BITS, NOW.
I'VE NEVER TRIED BEING A MAN BEFORE.
FUCK!
UURGH!
HIS LEGS WERE LIKE PLUMB LINES. SILLY STRING WITH LEAD WEIGHTS AT THE END.
THE THROB IN HIS HEAD WAS SLOW AND DEEP, LIKE AN ELEPHANT'S HEARTBEAT.
THERE WAS NO WAY HE WAS GOING TO MAKE IT TO THE STAIRS.

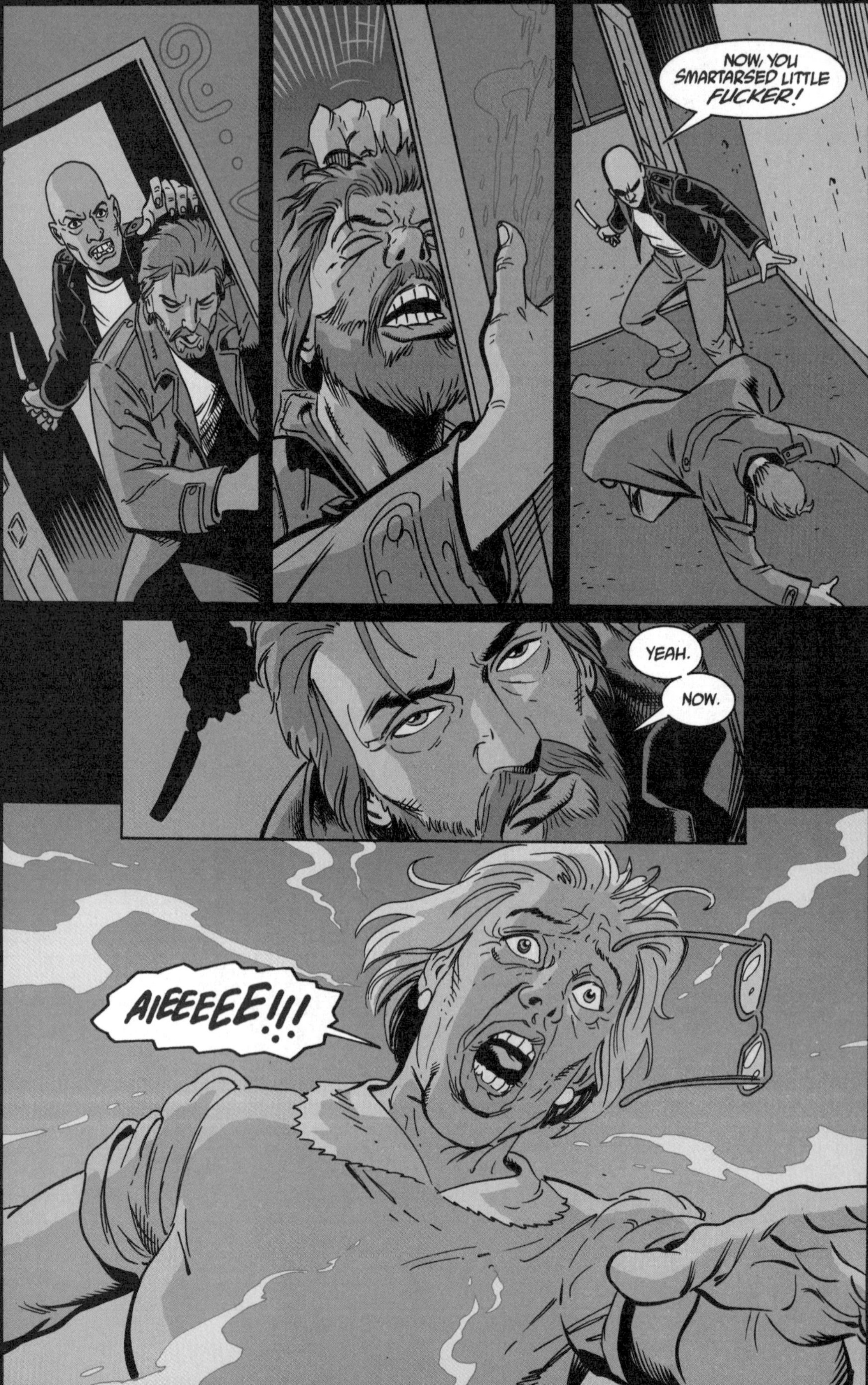
NOW, YOU SMARTARSED LITTLE FUCKER!
YEAH.
NOW.
AIEEEEEE!!!

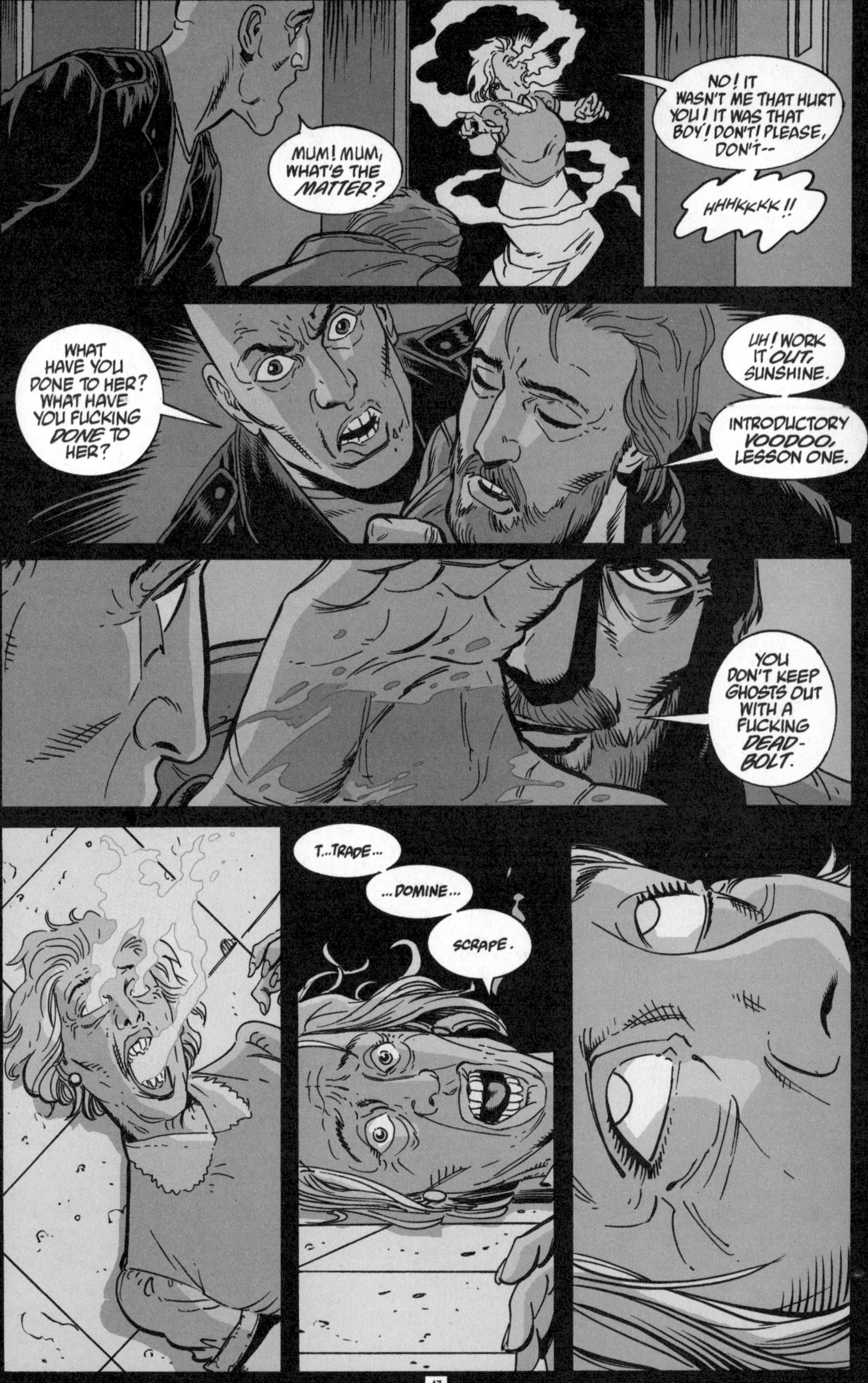
MUM! MUM, WHAT'S THE MATTER?
NO! IT WASN'T ME THAT HURT YOU! IT WAS THAT BOY! DON'T! PLEASE, DON'T--
HHHKKKK!!
WHAT HAVE YOU DONE TO HER? WHAT HAVE YOU FUCKING DONE TO HER?
UH! WORK IT OUT, SUNSHINE.
INTRODUCTORY VOODOO, LESSON ONE.
YOU DON'T KEEP GHOSTS OUT WITH A FUCKING DEAD-BOLT.
T...TRADE...
...DOMINE...
SCRAPE.

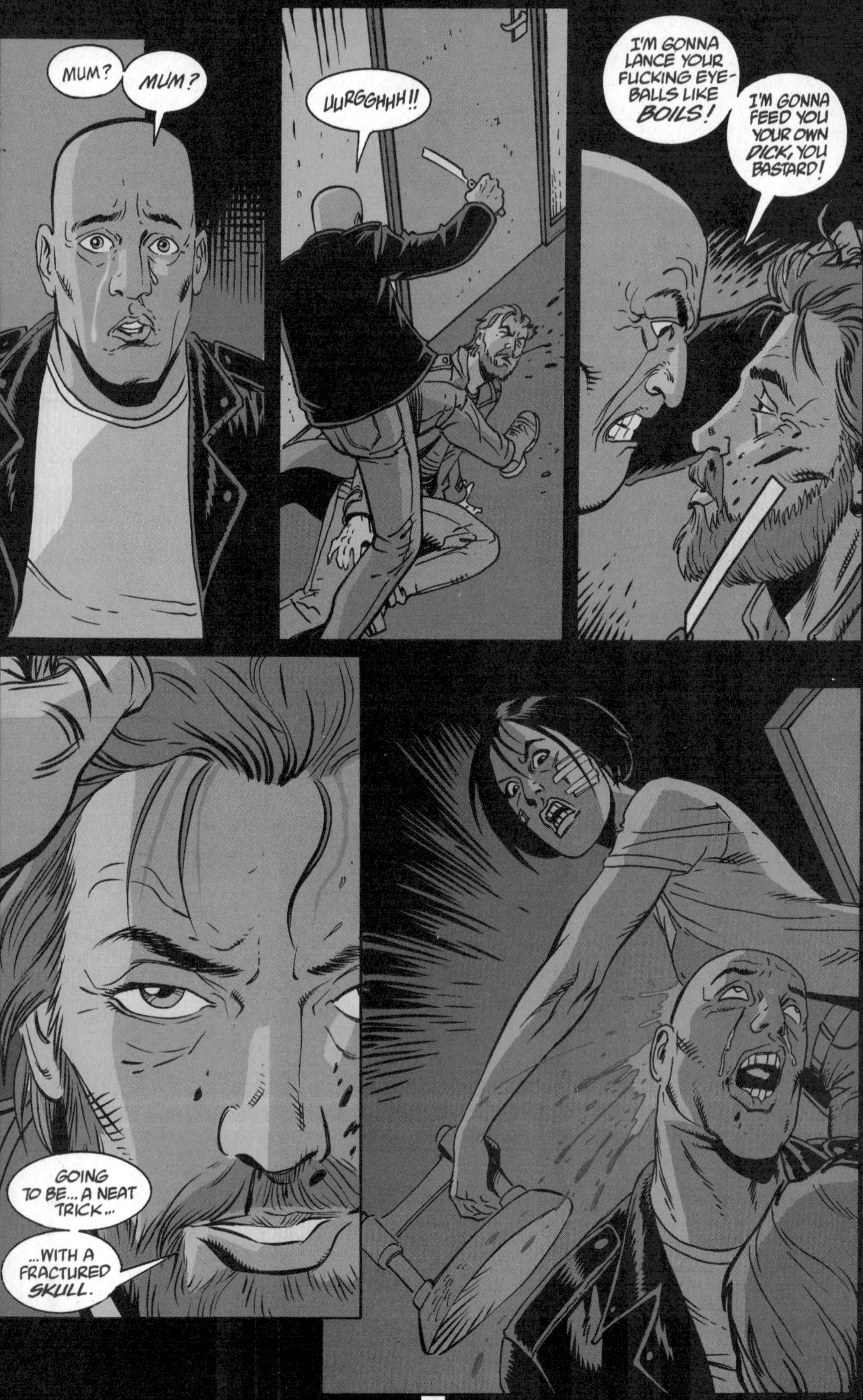
MUM?
MUM?
UURGGHHH!!
I'M GONNA LANCE YOUR FUCKING EYE-BALLS LIKE BOILS!
I'M GONNA FEED YOU YOUR OWN DICK, YOU BASTARD!
GOING TO BE... A NEAT TRICK...
...WITH A FRACTURED SKULL.

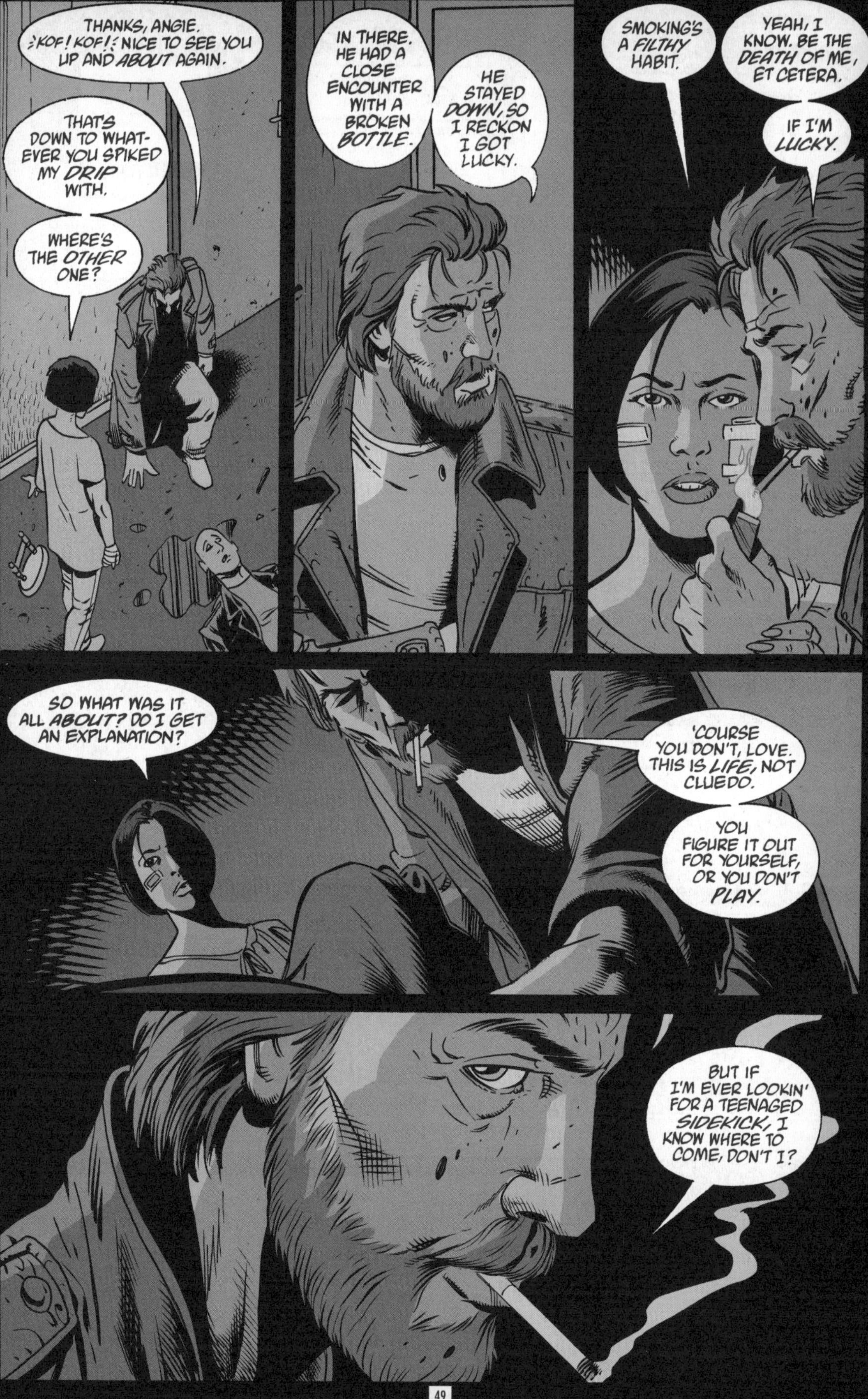

THANKS, ANGIE. ;KOF! KOF!; NICE TO SEE YOU UP AND ABOUT AGAIN.
THAT'S DOWN TO WHAT-EVER YOU SPIKED MY DRIP WITH.
WHERE'S THE OTHER ONE?
IN THERE. HE HAD A CLOSE ENCOUNTER WITH A BROKEN BOTTLE.
HE STAYED DOWN, SO I RECKON I GOT LUCKY.
SMOKING'S A FILTHY HABIT.
YEAH, I KNOW. BE THE DEATH OF ME, ET CETERA.
IF I'M LUCKY.
SO WHAT WAS IT ALL ABOUT? DO I GET AN EXPLANATION?
'COURSE YOU DON'T, LOVE. THIS IS LIFE, NOT CLUEDO.
YOU FIGURE IT OUT FOR YOURSELF, OR YOU DON'T PLAY.
BUT IF I'M EVER LOOKIN' FOR A TEENAGED SIDEKICK, I KNOW WHERE TO COME, DON'T I?

EPILOGUE

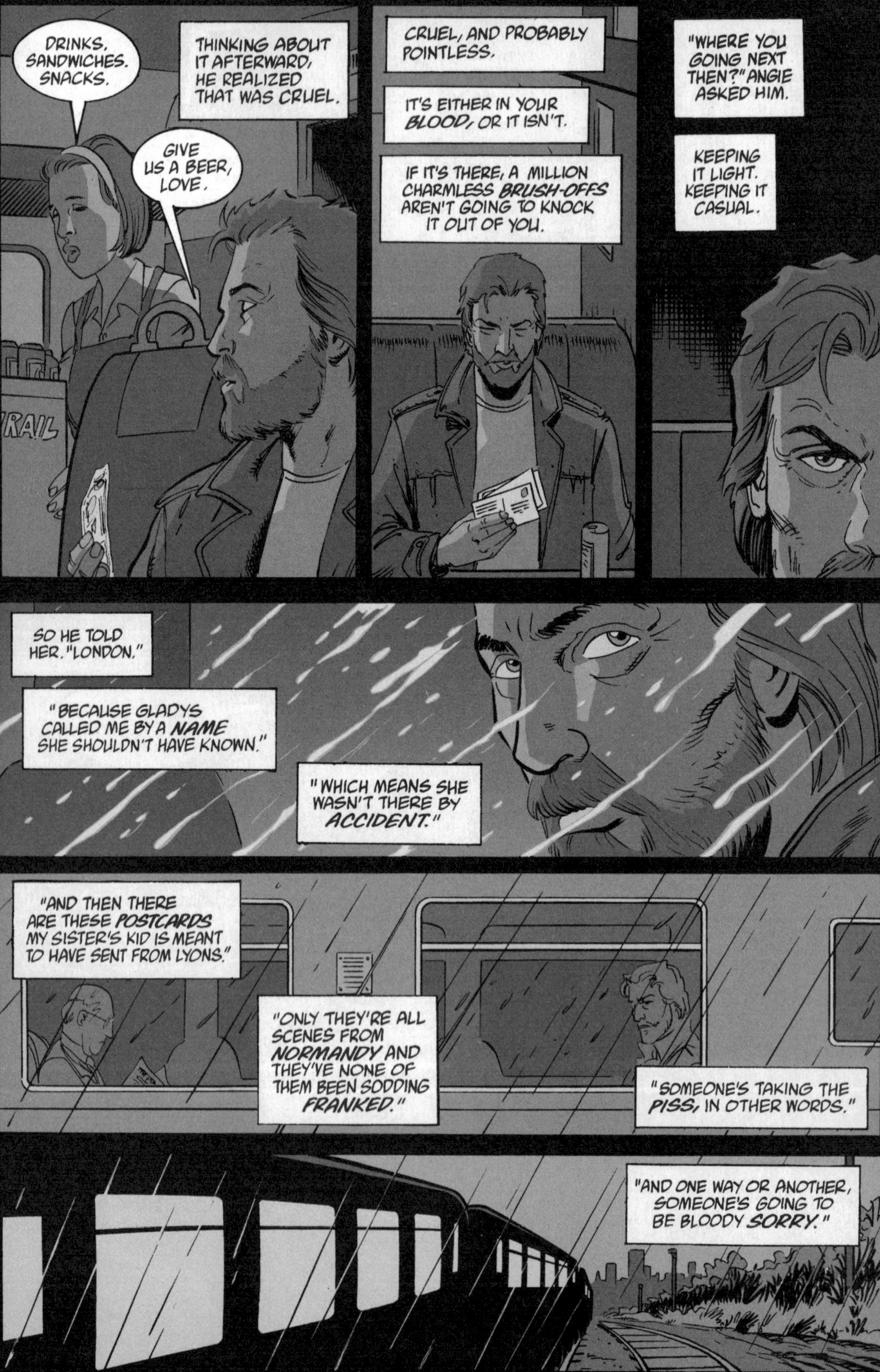
DRINKS, SANDWICHES. SNACKS.
THINKING ABOUT IT AFTERWARD, HE REALIZED THAT WAS CRUEL.
GIVE US A BEER, LOVE.
RAIL
CRUEL, AND PROBABLY POINTLESS.
IT'S EITHER IN YOUR BLOOD, OR IT ISN'T.
IF IT'S THERE, A MILLION CHARMLESS BRUSH-OFFS AREN'T GOING TO KNOCK IT OUT OF YOU.
"WHERE YOU GOING NEXT THEN?" ANGIE ASKED HIM.
KEEPING IT LIGHT. KEEPING IT CASUAL.
SO HE TOLD HER. "LONDON."
"BECAUSE GLADYS CALLED ME BY A NAME SHE SHOULDN'T HAVE KNOWN."
"WHICH MEANS SHE WASN'T THERE BY ACCIDENT."
"AND THEN THERE ARE THESE POSTCARDS MY SISTER'S KID IS MEANT TO HAVE SENT FROM LYONS."
"ONLY THEY'RE ALL SCENES FROM NORMANDY AND THEY'VE NONE OF THEM BEEN SODDING FRANKED."
"SOMEONE'S TAKING THE PISS, IN OTHER WORDS."
"AND ONE WAY OR ANOTHER, SOMEONE'S GOING TO BE BLOODY SORRY."

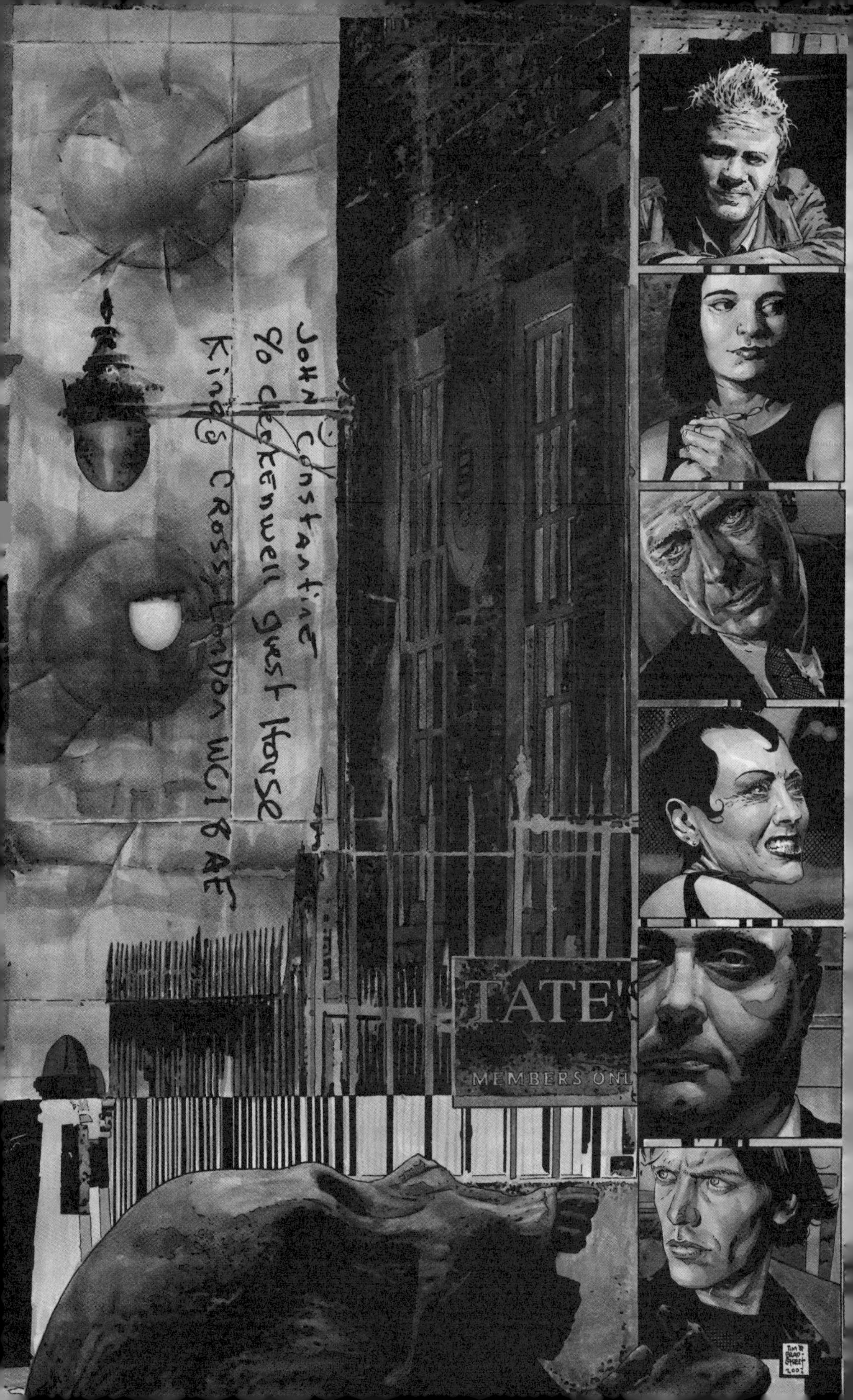
JOHN CONSTANTINE
c/o Clerkenwell Guest House
King's Cross London WC1 8AE
TATE
MEMBERS ONL

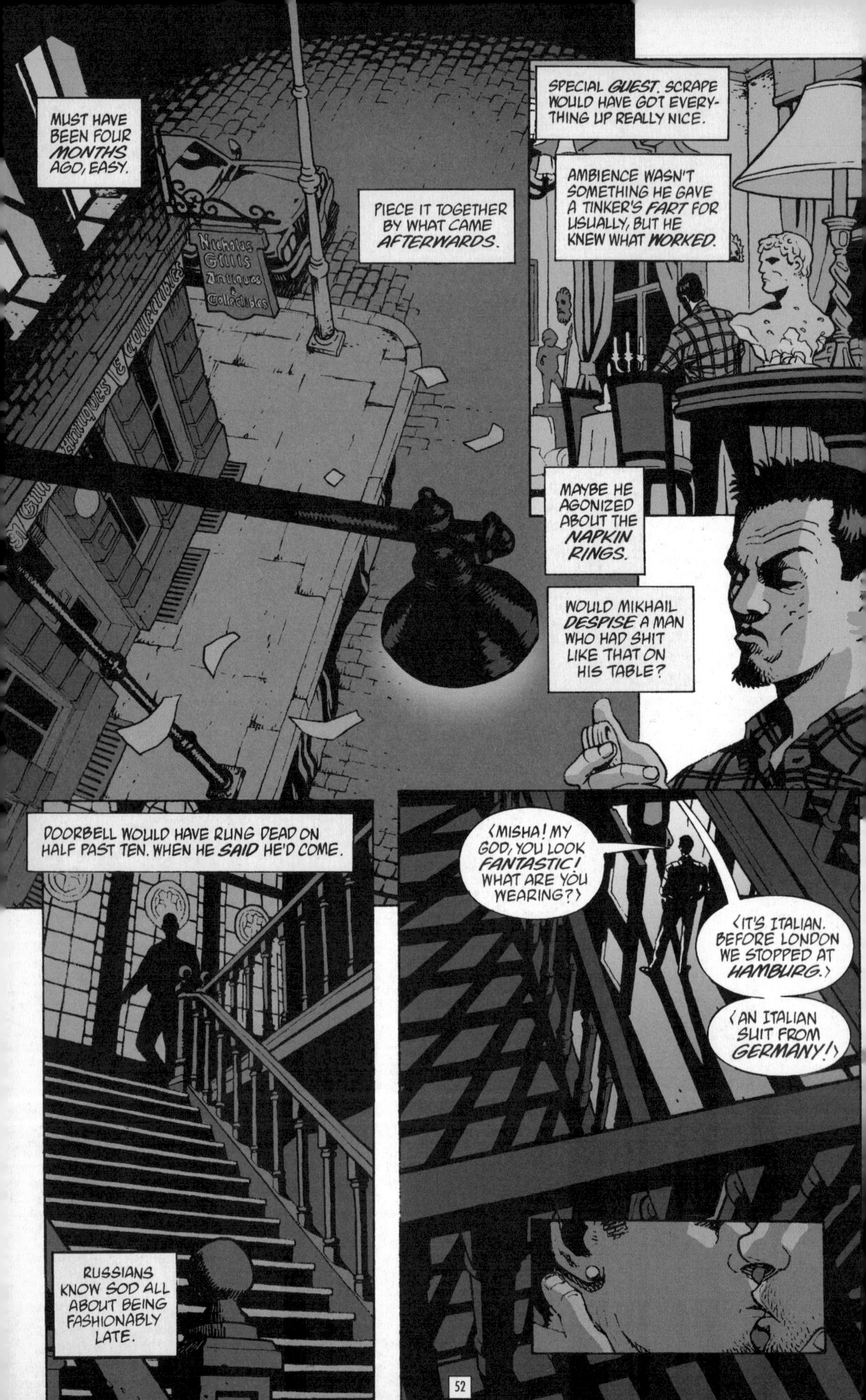
MUST HAVE BEEN FOUR MONTHS AGO, EASY.
PIECE IT TOGETHER BY WHAT CAME AFTERWARDS.
Nicholas Gillis Antiques & Collectibles
SPECIAL GUEST. SCRAPE WOULD HAVE GOT EVERY-THING UP REALLY NICE.
AMBIENCE WASN'T SOMETHING HE GAVE A TINKER'S FART FOR USUALLY, BUT HE KNEW WHAT WORKED.
MAYBE HE AGONIZED ABOUT THE NAPKIN RINGS.
WOULD MIKHAIL DESPISE A MAN WHO HAD SHIT LIKE THAT ON HIS TABLE?
DOORBELL WOULD HAVE RUNG DEAD ON HALF PAST TEN. WHEN HE SAID HE'D COME.
RUSSIANS KNOW SOD ALL ABOUT BEING FASHIONABLY LATE.
‹MISHA! MY GOD, YOU LOOK FANTASTIC! WHAT ARE YOU WEARING?›
‹IT'S ITALIAN. BEFORE LONDON WE STOPPED AT HAMBURG.›
‹AN ITALIAN SUIT FROM GERMANY!›

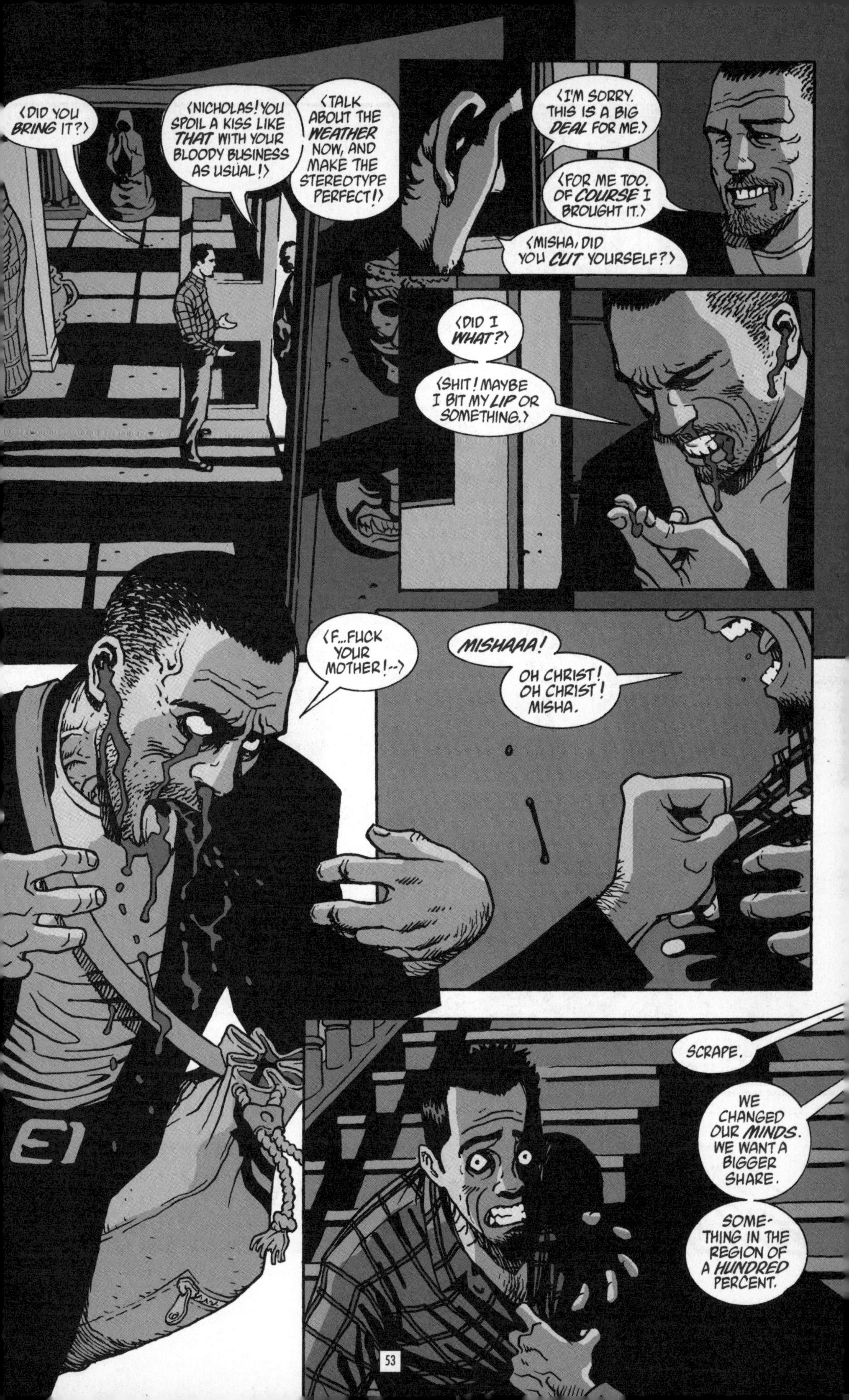

⟨DID YOU BRING IT?⟩
⟨NICHOLAS! YOU SPOIL A KISS LIKE THAT WITH YOUR BLOODY BUSINESS AS USUAL!⟩
⟨TALK ABOUT THE WEATHER NOW, AND MAKE THE STEREOTYPE PERFECT!⟩
⟨I'M SORRY. THIS IS A BIG DEAL FOR ME.⟩
⟨FOR ME TOO. OF COURSE I BROUGHT IT.⟩
⟨MISHA, DID YOU CUT YOURSELF?⟩
⟨DID I WHAT?⟩
⟨SHIT! MAYBE I BIT MY LIP OR SOMETHING.⟩
⟨F...FUCK YOUR MOTHER!--⟩
MISHAAA!
OH CHRIST! OH CHRIST! MISHA.
SCRAPE.
WE CHANGED OUR MINDS. WE WANT A BIGGER SHARE.
SOME-THING IN THE REGION OF A HUNDRED PERCENT.

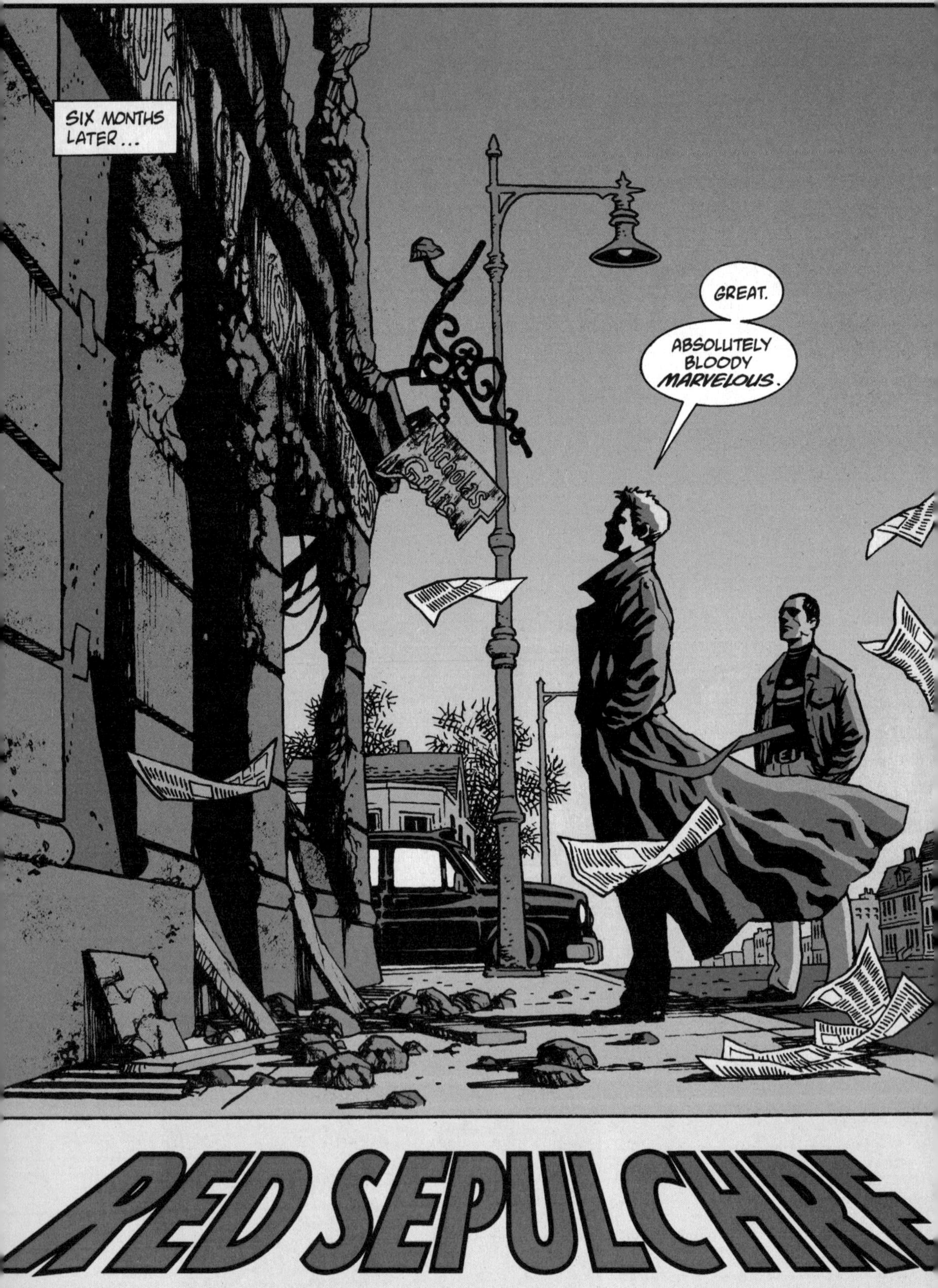
SIX MONTHS LATER...
GREAT.
ABSOLUTELY BLOODY *MARVELOUS*.

RED SEPULCHRE

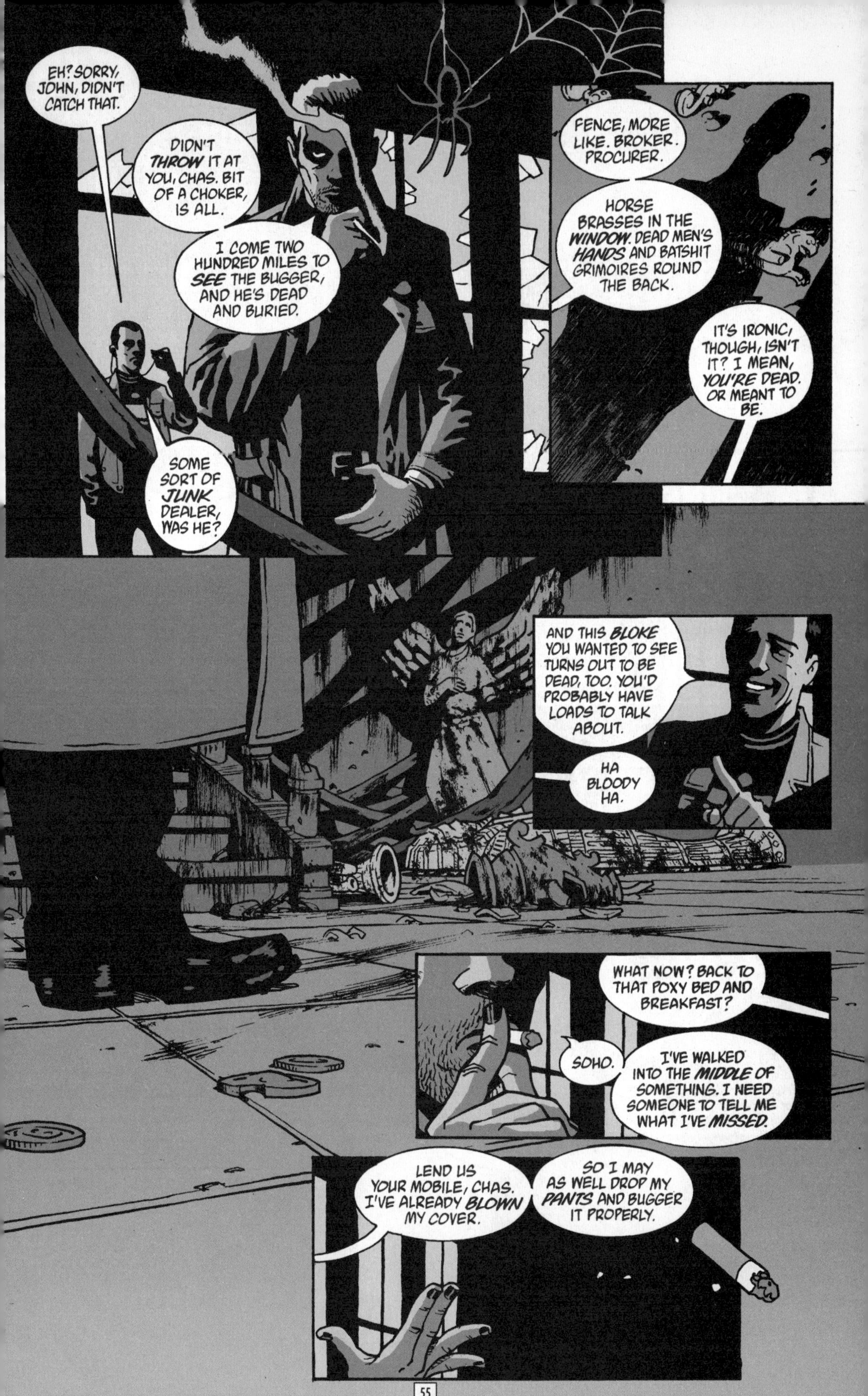
EH? SORRY, JOHN, DIDN'T CATCH THAT.
DIDN'T THROW IT AT YOU, CHAS. BIT OF A CHOKER, IS ALL.
I COME TWO HUNDRED MILES TO SEE THE BUGGER, AND HE'S DEAD AND BURIED.
SOME SORT OF JUNK DEALER, WAS HE?
FENCE, MORE LIKE. BROKER. PROCURER.
HORSE BRASSES IN THE WINDOW. DEAD MEN'S HANDS AND BATSHIT GRIMOIRES ROUND THE BACK.
IT'S IRONIC, THOUGH, ISN'T IT? I MEAN, YOU'RE DEAD. OR MEANT TO BE.
AND THIS BLOKE YOU WANTED TO SEE TURNS OUT TO BE DEAD, TOO. YOU'D PROBABLY HAVE LOADS TO TALK ABOUT.
HA BLOODY HA.
WHAT NOW? BACK TO THAT POXY BED AND BREAKFAST?
SOHO.
I'VE WALKED INTO THE MIDDLE OF SOMETHING. I NEED SOMEONE TO TELL ME WHAT I'VE MISSED.
LEND US YOUR MOBILE, CHAS. I'VE ALREADY BLOWN MY COVER.
SO I MAY AS WELL DROP MY PANTS AND BUGGER IT PROPERLY.

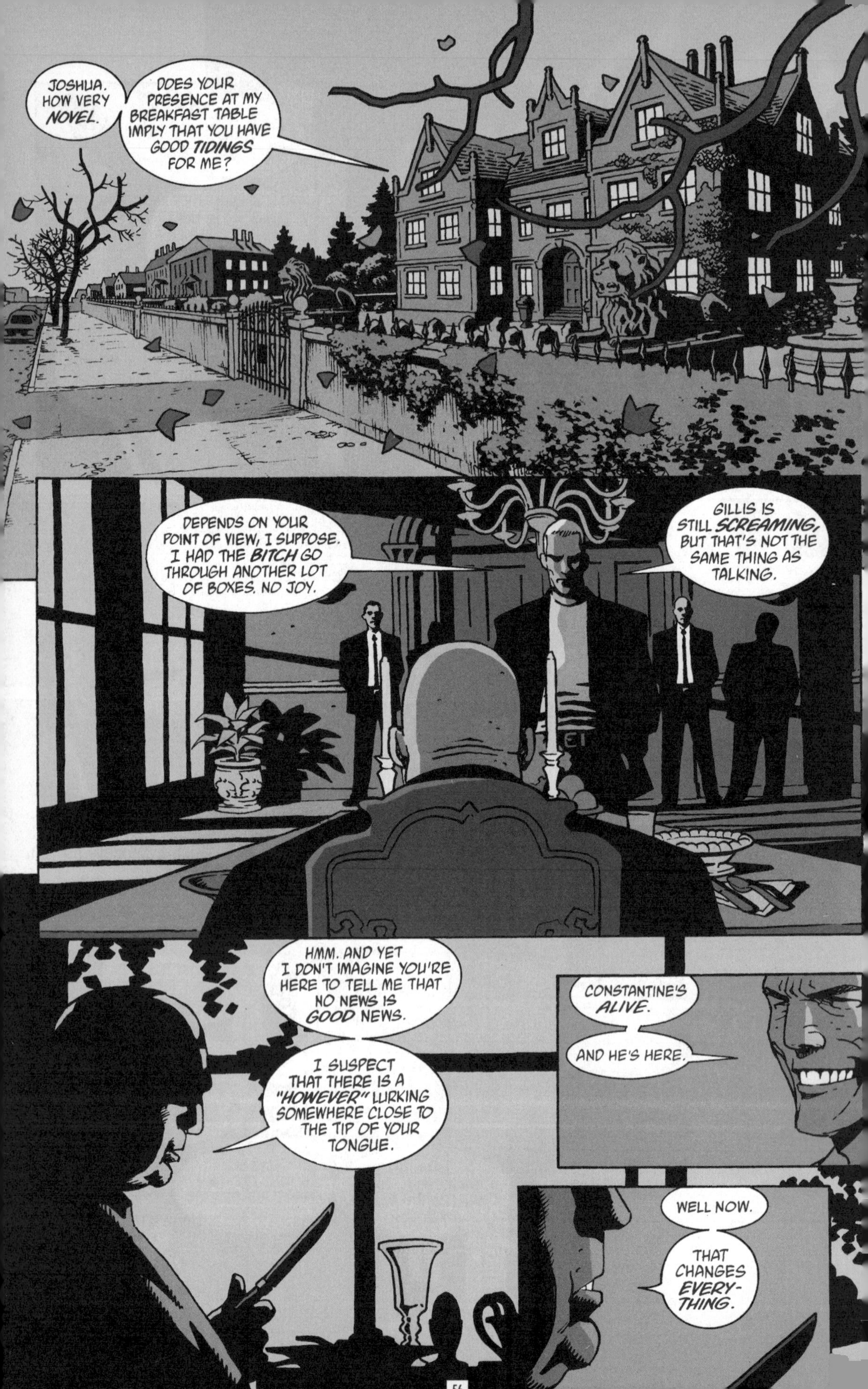
JOSHUA. HOW VERY NOVEL.
DOES YOUR PRESENCE AT MY BREAKFAST TABLE IMPLY THAT YOU HAVE GOOD TIDINGS FOR ME?
DEPENDS ON YOUR POINT OF VIEW, I SUPPOSE. I HAD THE BITCH GO THROUGH ANOTHER LOT OF BOXES. NO JOY.
GILLIS IS STILL SCREAMING, BUT THAT'S NOT THE SAME THING AS TALKING.
HMM. AND YET I DON'T IMAGINE YOU'RE HERE TO TELL ME THAT NO NEWS IS GOOD NEWS.
I SUSPECT THAT THERE IS A "HOWEVER" LURKING SOMEWHERE CLOSE TO THE TIP OF YOUR TONGUE.
CONSTANTINE'S ALIVE.
AND HE'S HERE.
WELL NOW.
THAT CHANGES EVERYTHING.

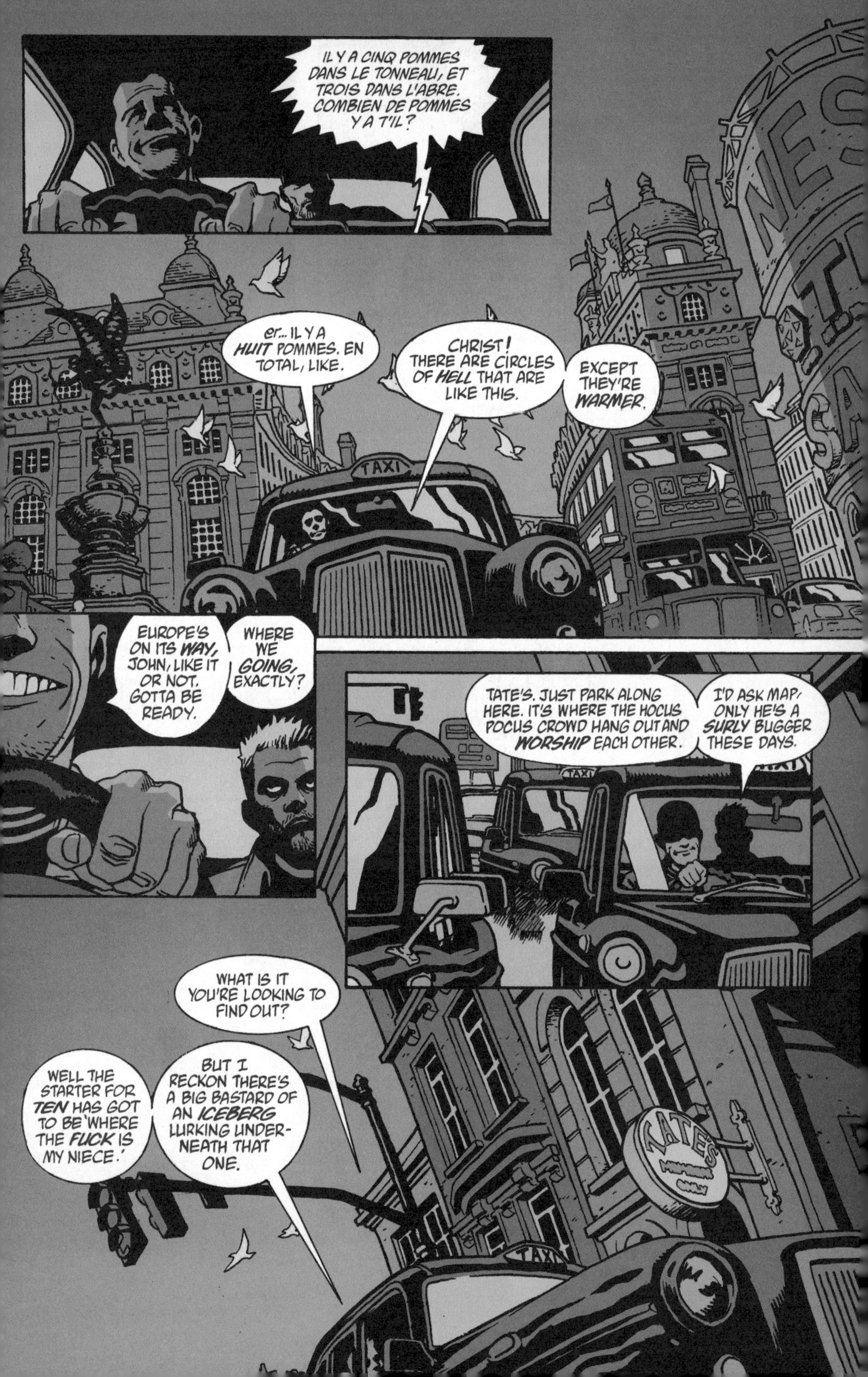
IL Y A CINQ POMMES DANS LE TONNEAU, ET TROIS DANS L'ABRE. COMBIEN DE POMMES Y A T'IL?
er... IL Y A HUIT POMMES. EN TOTAL, LIKE.
CHRIST! THERE ARE CIRCLES OF HELL THAT ARE LIKE THIS.
EXCEPT THEY'RE WARMER.
TAXI
EUROPE'S ON ITS WAY, JOHN, LIKE IT OR NOT. GOTTA BE READY.
WHERE WE GOING, EXACTLY?
TATE'S. JUST PARK ALONG HERE. IT'S WHERE THE HOCUS POCUS CROWD HANG OUT AND WORSHIP EACH OTHER.
I'D ASK MAP, ONLY HE'S A SURLY BUGGER THESE DAYS.
WHAT IS IT YOU'RE LOOKING TO FIND OUT?
WELL THE STARTER FOR TEN HAS GOT TO BE 'WHERE THE FUCK IS MY NIECE.'
BUT I RECKON THERE'S A BIG BASTARD OF AN ICEBERG LURKING UNDER-NEATH THAT ONE.
TATE'S
TAXI

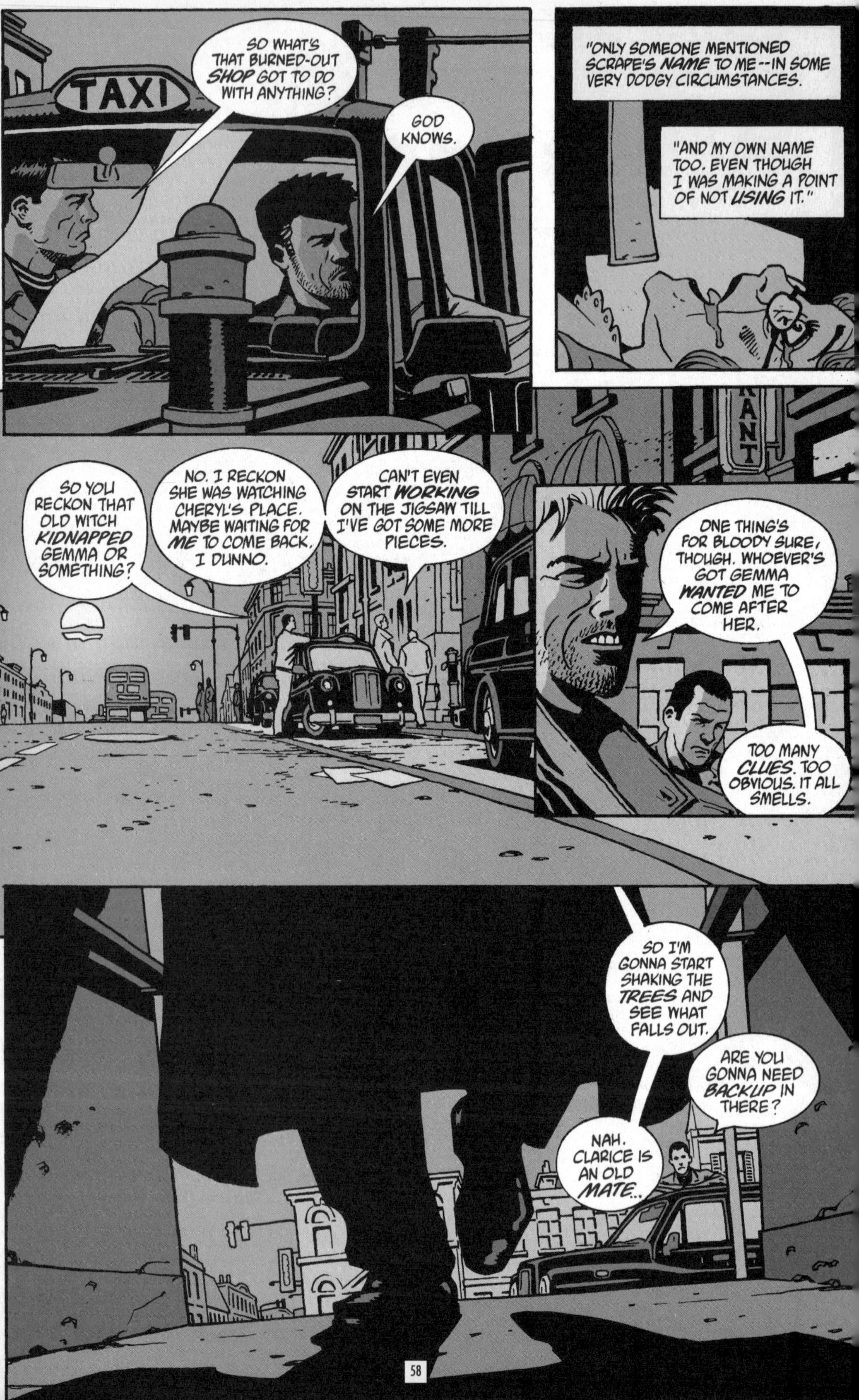

TAXI
SO WHAT'S THAT BURNED-OUT SHOP GOT TO DO WITH ANYTHING?
GOD KNOWS.
"ONLY SOMEONE MENTIONED SCRAPE'S NAME TO ME--IN SOME VERY DODGY CIRCUMSTANCES.
"AND MY OWN NAME TOO. EVEN THOUGH I WAS MAKING A POINT OF NOT USING IT."
SO YOU RECKON THAT OLD WITCH KIDNAPPED GEMMA OR SOMETHING?
NO. I RECKON SHE WAS WATCHING CHERYL'S PLACE. MAYBE WAITING FOR ME TO COME BACK, I DUNNO.
CAN'T EVEN START WORKING ON THE JIGSAW TILL I'VE GOT SOME MORE PIECES.
ONE THING'S FOR BLOODY SURE, THOUGH. WHOEVER'S GOT GEMMA WANTED ME TO COME AFTER HER.
TOO MANY CLUES. TOO OBVIOUS. IT ALL SMELLS.
SO I'M GONNA START SHAKING THE TREES AND SEE WHAT FALLS OUT.
ARE YOU GONNA NEED BACKUP IN THERE?
NAH. CLARICE IS AN OLD MATE..

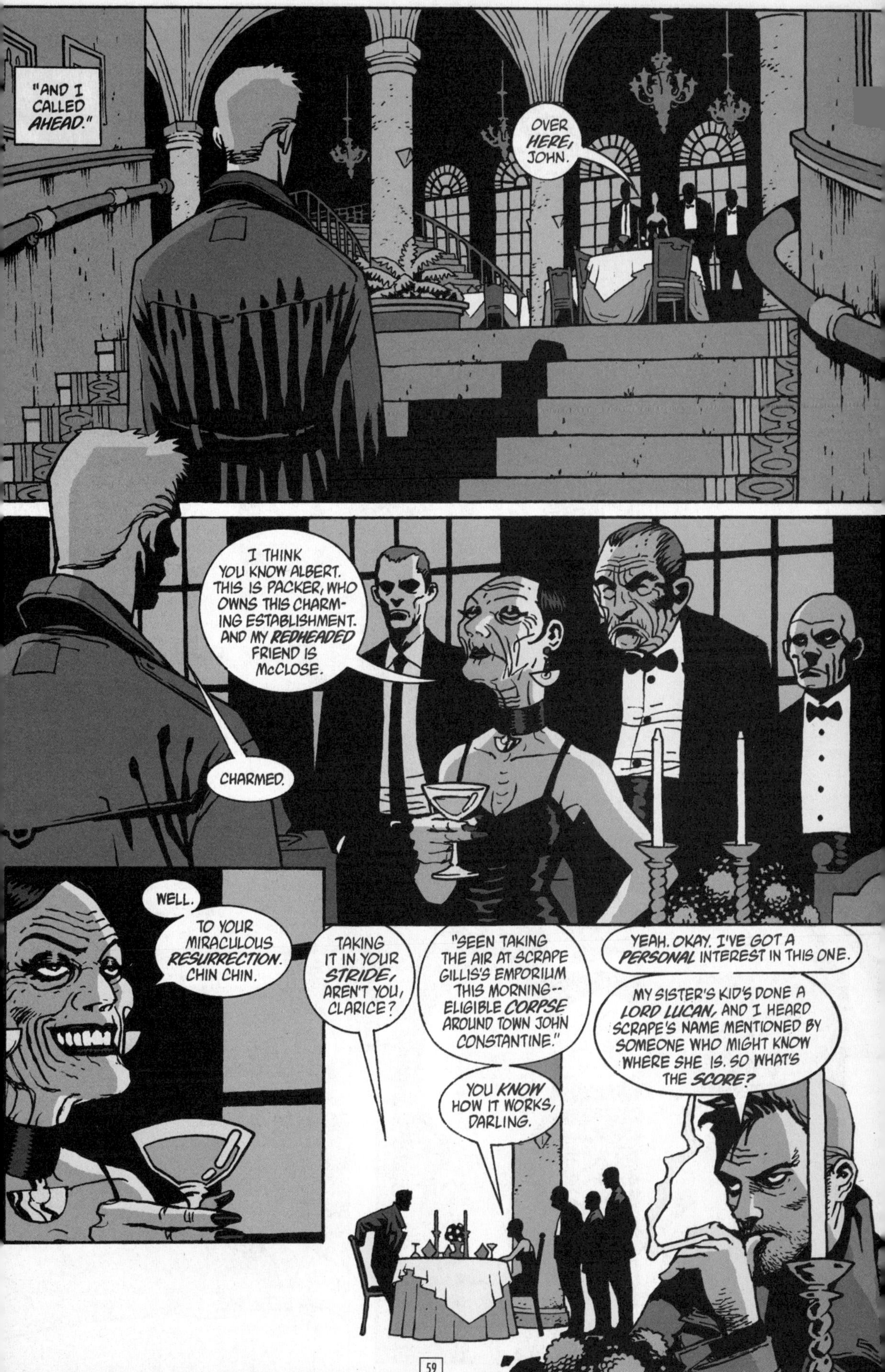
"AND I CALLED AHEAD."
OVER HERE, JOHN.
I THINK YOU KNOW ALBERT. THIS IS PACKER, WHO OWNS THIS CHARMING ESTABLISHMENT. AND MY REDHEADED FRIEND IS McCLOSE.
CHARMED.
WELL.
TO YOUR MIRACULOUS RESURRECTION. CHIN CHIN.
TAKING IT IN YOUR STRIDE, AREN'T YOU, CLARICE?
"SEEN TAKING THE AIR AT SCRAPE GILLIS'S EMPORIUM THIS MORNING-- ELIGIBLE CORPSE AROUND TOWN JOHN CONSTANTINE."
YOU KNOW HOW IT WORKS, DARLING.
YEAH. OKAY. I'VE GOT A PERSONAL INTEREST IN THIS ONE.
MY SISTER'S KID'S DONE A LORD LUCAN, AND I HEARD SCRAPE'S NAME MENTIONED BY SOMEONE WHO MIGHT KNOW WHERE SHE IS. SO WHAT'S THE SCORE?

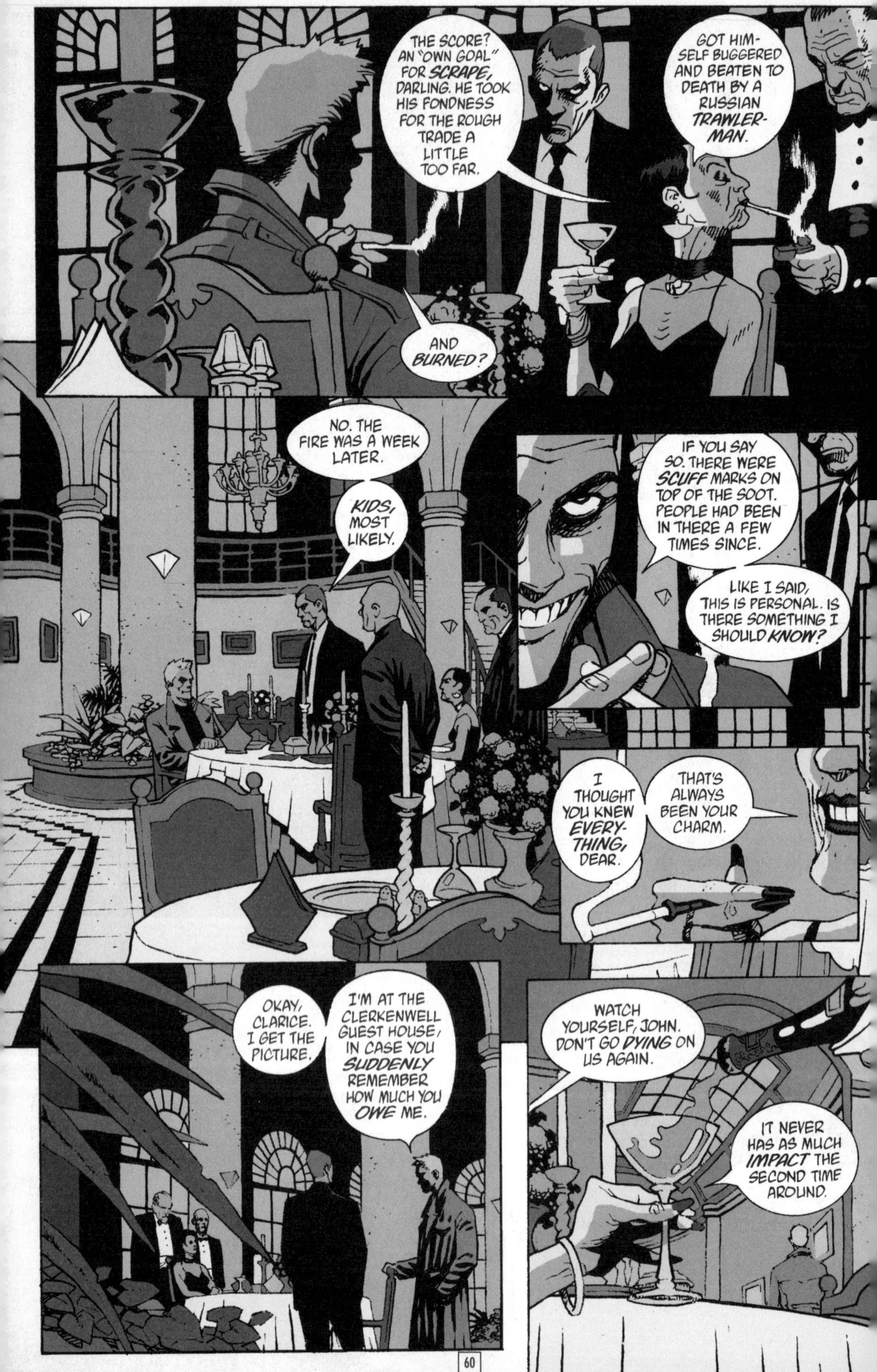
THE SCORE? AN "OWN GOAL" FOR SCRAPE, DARLING. HE TOOK HIS FONDNESS FOR THE ROUGH TRADE A LITTLE TOO FAR.
GOT HIMSELF BUGGERED AND BEATEN TO DEATH BY A RUSSIAN TRAWLERMAN.
AND BURNED?
NO. THE FIRE WAS A WEEK LATER.
KIDS, MOST LIKELY.
IF YOU SAY SO. THERE WERE SCUFF MARKS ON TOP OF THE SOOT. PEOPLE HAD BEEN IN THERE A FEW TIMES SINCE.
LIKE I SAID, THIS IS PERSONAL. IS THERE SOMETHING I SHOULD KNOW?
I THOUGHT YOU KNEW EVERYTHING, DEAR.
THAT'S ALWAYS BEEN YOUR CHARM.
OKAY, CLARICE. I GET THE PICTURE.
I'M AT THE CLERKENWELL GUEST HOUSE, IN CASE YOU SUDDENLY REMEMBER HOW MUCH YOU OWE ME.
WATCH YOURSELF, JOHN. DON'T GO DYING ON US AGAIN.
IT NEVER HAS AS MUCH IMPACT THE SECOND TIME AROUND.

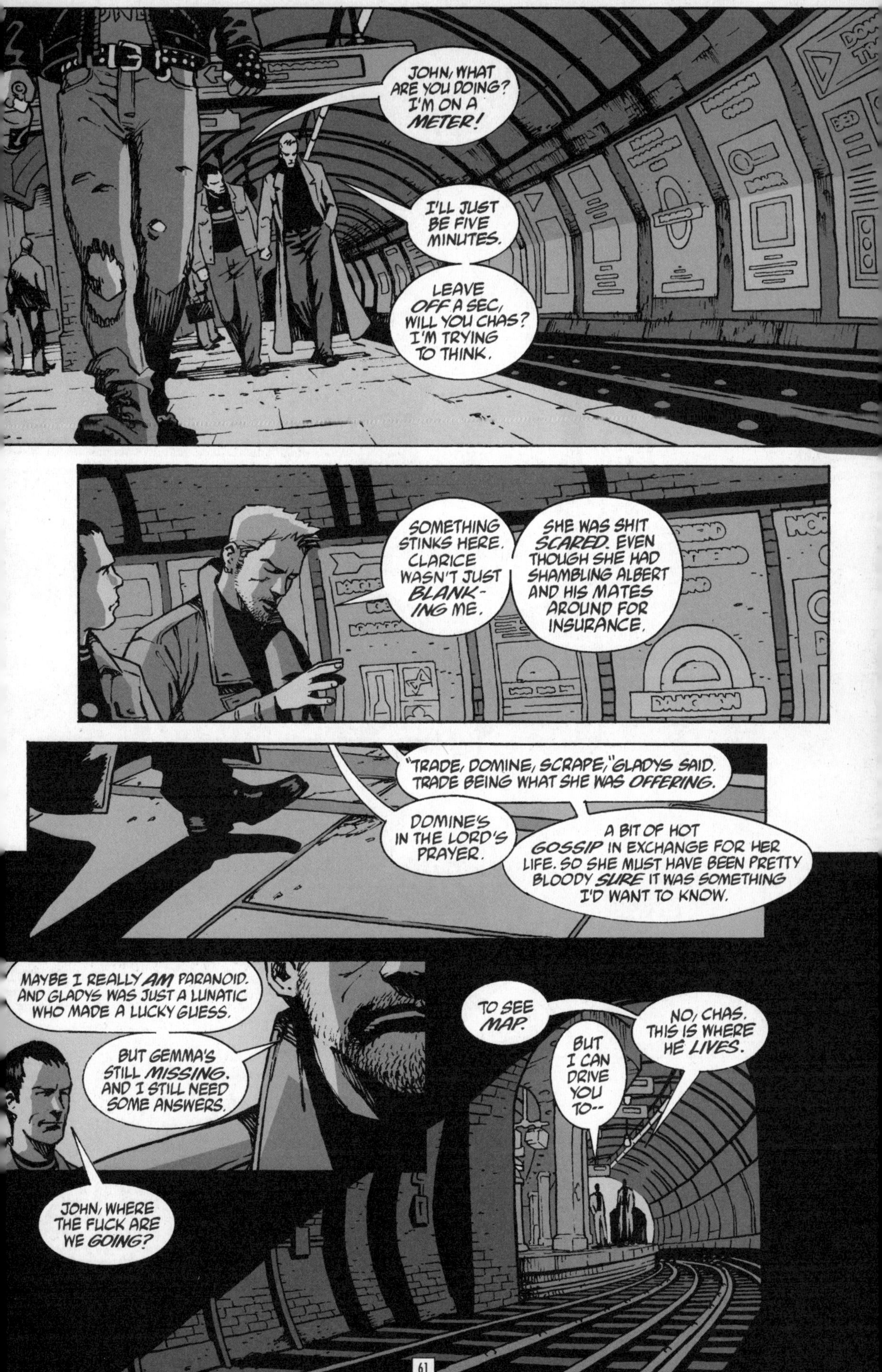

JOHN, WHAT ARE YOU DOING? I'M ON A METER!
I'LL JUST BE FIVE MINUTES.
LEAVE OFF A SEC, WILL YOU CHAS? I'M TRYING TO THINK.
SOMETHING STINKS HERE. CLARICE WASN'T JUST BLANKING ME.
SHE WAS SHIT SCARED. EVEN THOUGH SHE HAD SHAMBLING ALBERT AND HIS MATES AROUND FOR INSURANCE.
"TRADE, DOMINE, SCRAPE," GLADYS SAID. TRADE BEING WHAT SHE WAS OFFERING.
DOMINE'S IN THE LORD'S PRAYER.
A BIT OF HOT GOSSIP IN EXCHANGE FOR HER LIFE. SO SHE MUST HAVE BEEN PRETTY BLOODY SURE IT WAS SOMETHING I'D WANT TO KNOW.
MAYBE I REALLY AM PARANOID. AND GLADYS WAS JUST A LUNATIC WHO MADE A LUCKY GUESS.
BUT GEMMA'S STILL MISSING. AND I STILL NEED SOME ANSWERS.
JOHN, WHERE THE FUCK ARE WE GOING?
TO SEE MAP.
BUT I CAN DRIVE YOU TO--
NO, CHAS. THIS IS WHERE HE LIVES.

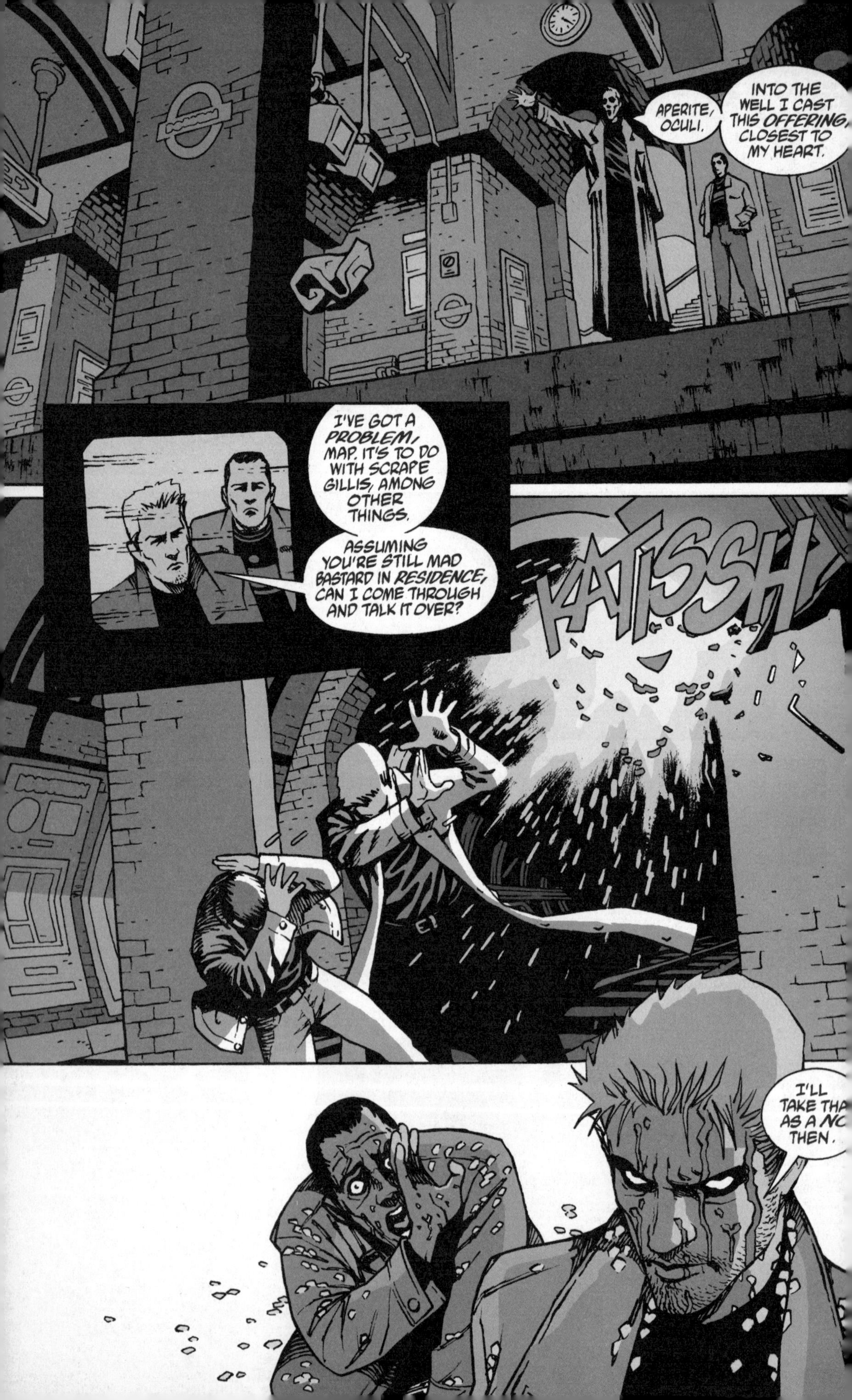
APERITE, OCULI.
INTO THE WELL I CAST THIS OFFERING, CLOSEST TO MY HEART.
I'VE GOT A PROBLEM, MAP. IT'S TO DO WITH SCRAPE GILLIS, AMONG OTHER THINGS.
ASSUMING YOU'RE STILL MAD BASTARD IN RESIDENCE, CAN I COME THROUGH AND TALK IT OVER?
KATISSH
I'LL TAKE THA AS A NO THEN.

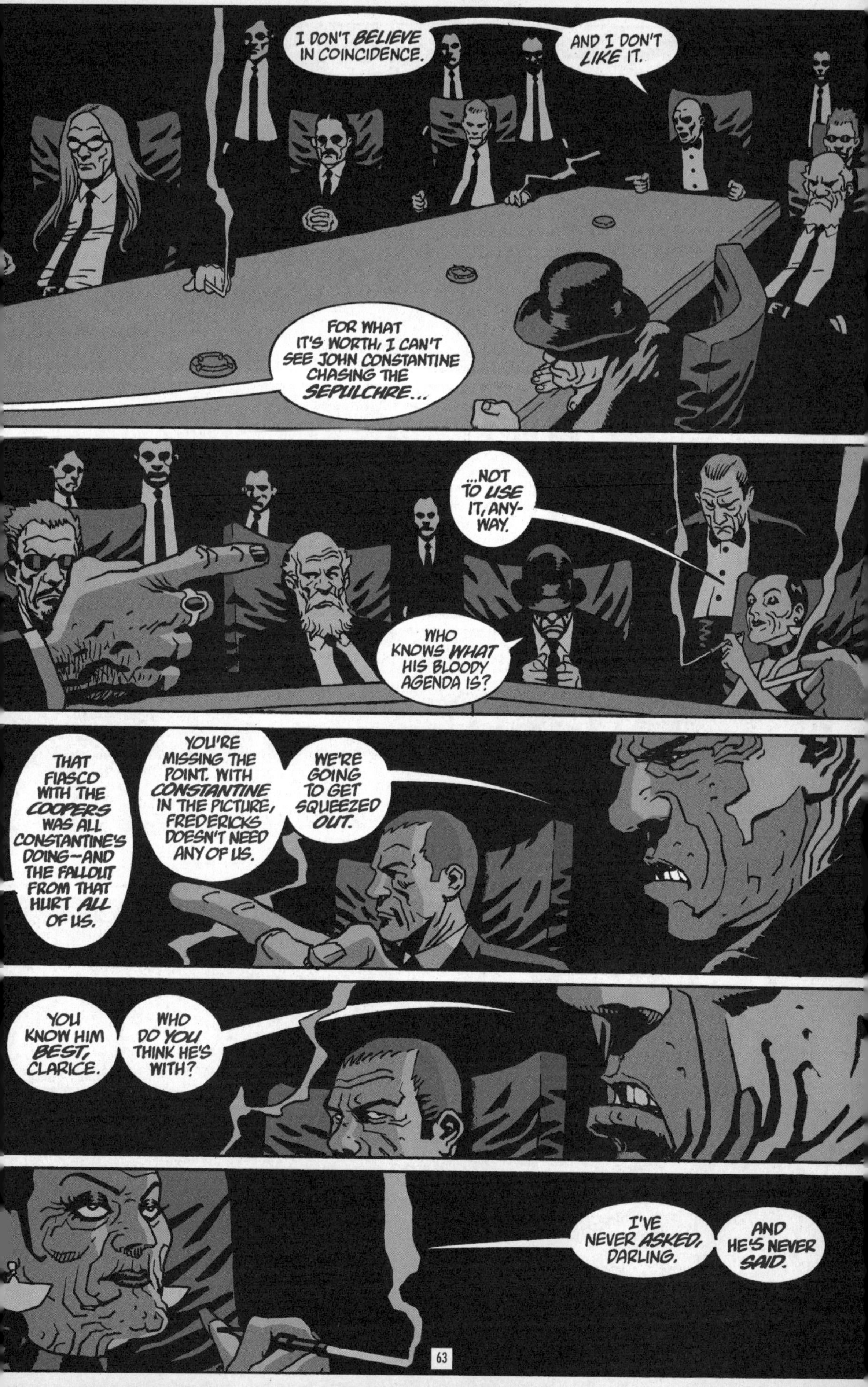
I DON'T BELIEVE IN COINCIDENCE.
AND I DON'T LIKE IT.
FOR WHAT IT'S WORTH, I CAN'T SEE JOHN CONSTANTINE CHASING THE SEPULCHRE...
...NOT TO USE IT, ANYWAY.
WHO KNOWS WHAT HIS BLOODY AGENDA IS?
THAT FIASCO WITH THE COOPERS WAS ALL CONSTANTINE'S DOING--AND THE FALLOUT FROM THAT HURT ALL OF US.
YOU'RE MISSING THE POINT. WITH CONSTANTINE IN THE PICTURE, FREDERICKS DOESN'T NEED ANY OF US.
WE'RE GOING TO GET SQUEEZED OUT.
YOU KNOW HIM BEST, CLARICE.
WHO DO YOU THINK HE'S WITH?
I'VE NEVER ASKED, DARLING.
AND HE'S NEVER SAID.

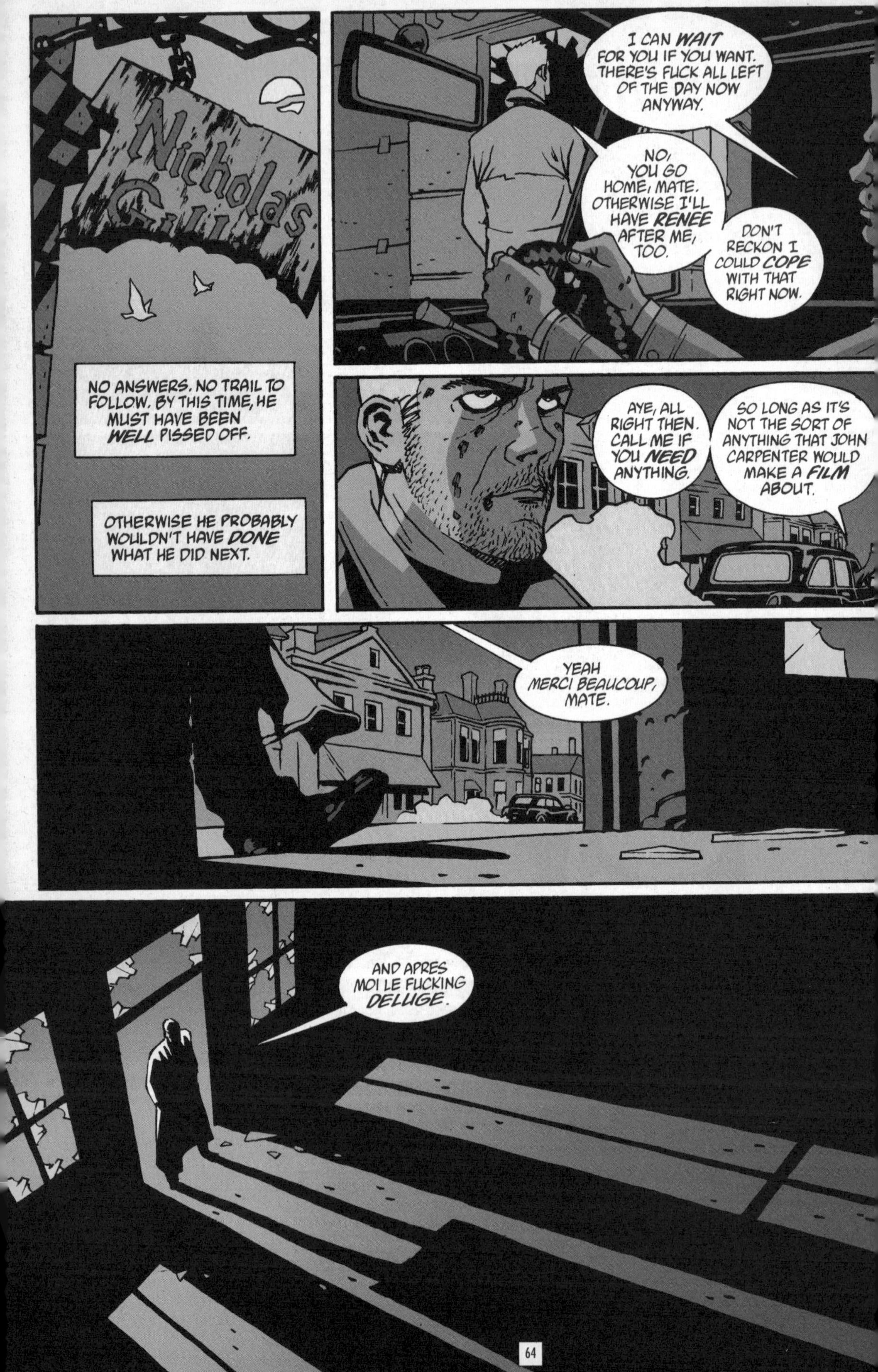
Nicholas
I CAN WAIT FOR YOU IF YOU WANT. THERE'S FUCK ALL LEFT OF THE DAY NOW ANYWAY.
NO, YOU GO HOME, MATE. OTHERWISE I'LL HAVE RENEE AFTER ME, TOO.
DON'T RECKON I COULD COPE WITH THAT RIGHT NOW.
NO ANSWERS. NO TRAIL TO FOLLOW. BY THIS TIME, HE MUST HAVE BEEN WELL PISSED OFF.
OTHERWISE HE PROBABLY WOULDN'T HAVE DONE WHAT HE DID NEXT.
AYE, ALL RIGHT THEN. CALL ME IF YOU NEED ANYTHING.
SO LONG AS IT'S NOT THE SORT OF ANYTHING THAT JOHN CARPENTER WOULD MAKE A FILM ABOUT.
YEAH MERCI BEAUCOUP, MATE.
AND APRES MOI LE FUCKING DELUGE.

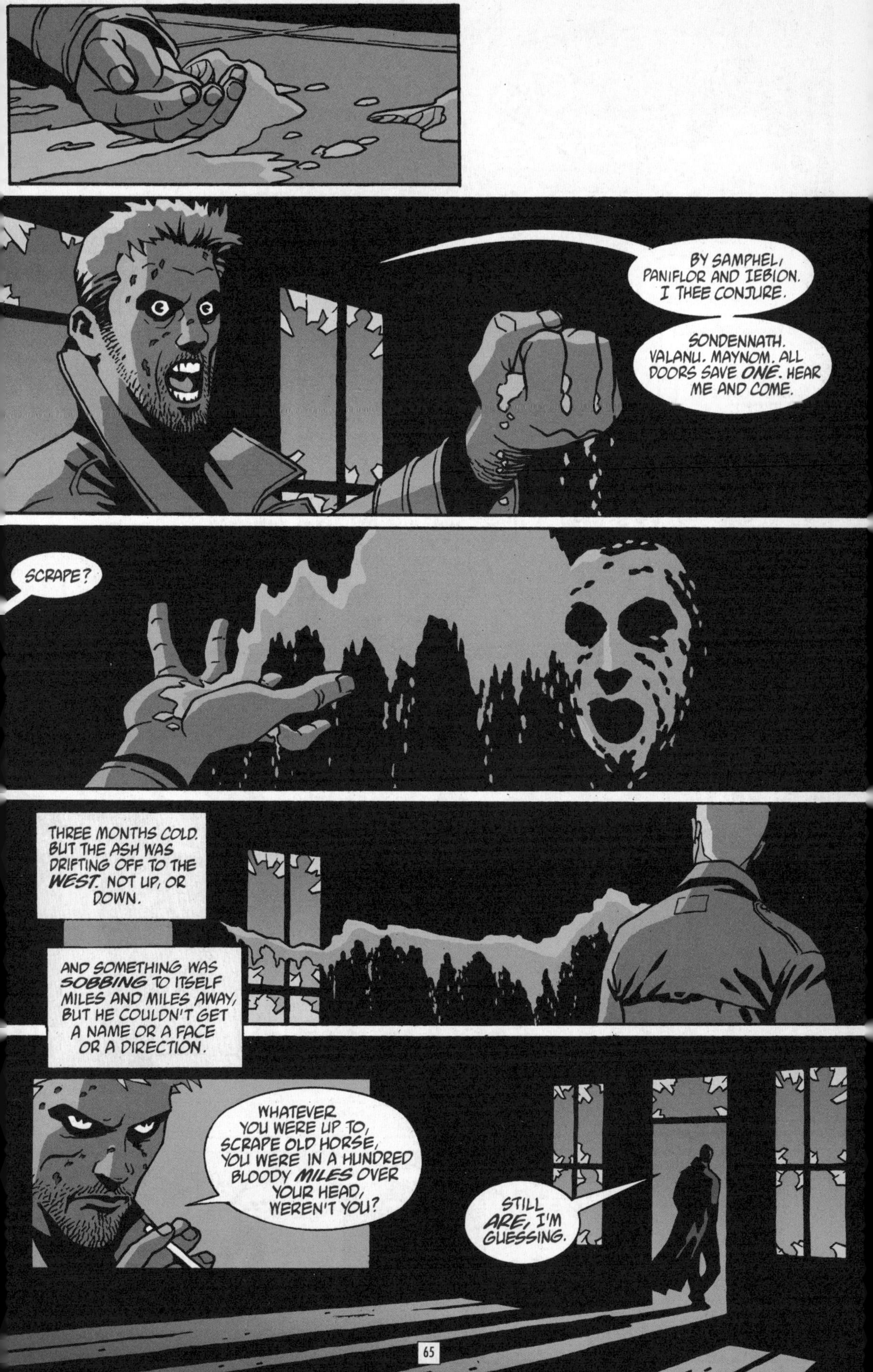
BY SAMPHEL, PANIFLOR AND IEBION. I THEE CONJURE.
SONDENNATH. VALANU. MAYNOM. ALL DOORS SAVE ONE. HEAR ME AND COME.
SCRAPE?
THREE MONTHS COLD. BUT THE ASH WAS DRIFTING OFF TO THE WEST. NOT UP, OR DOWN.
AND SOMETHING WAS SOBBING TO ITSELF MILES AND MILES AWAY, BUT HE COULDN'T GET A NAME OR A FACE OR A DIRECTION.
WHATEVER YOU WERE UP TO, SCRAPE OLD HORSE, YOU WERE IN A HUNDRED BLOODY MILES OVER YOUR HEAD, WEREN'T YOU?
STILL ARE, I'M GUESSING.

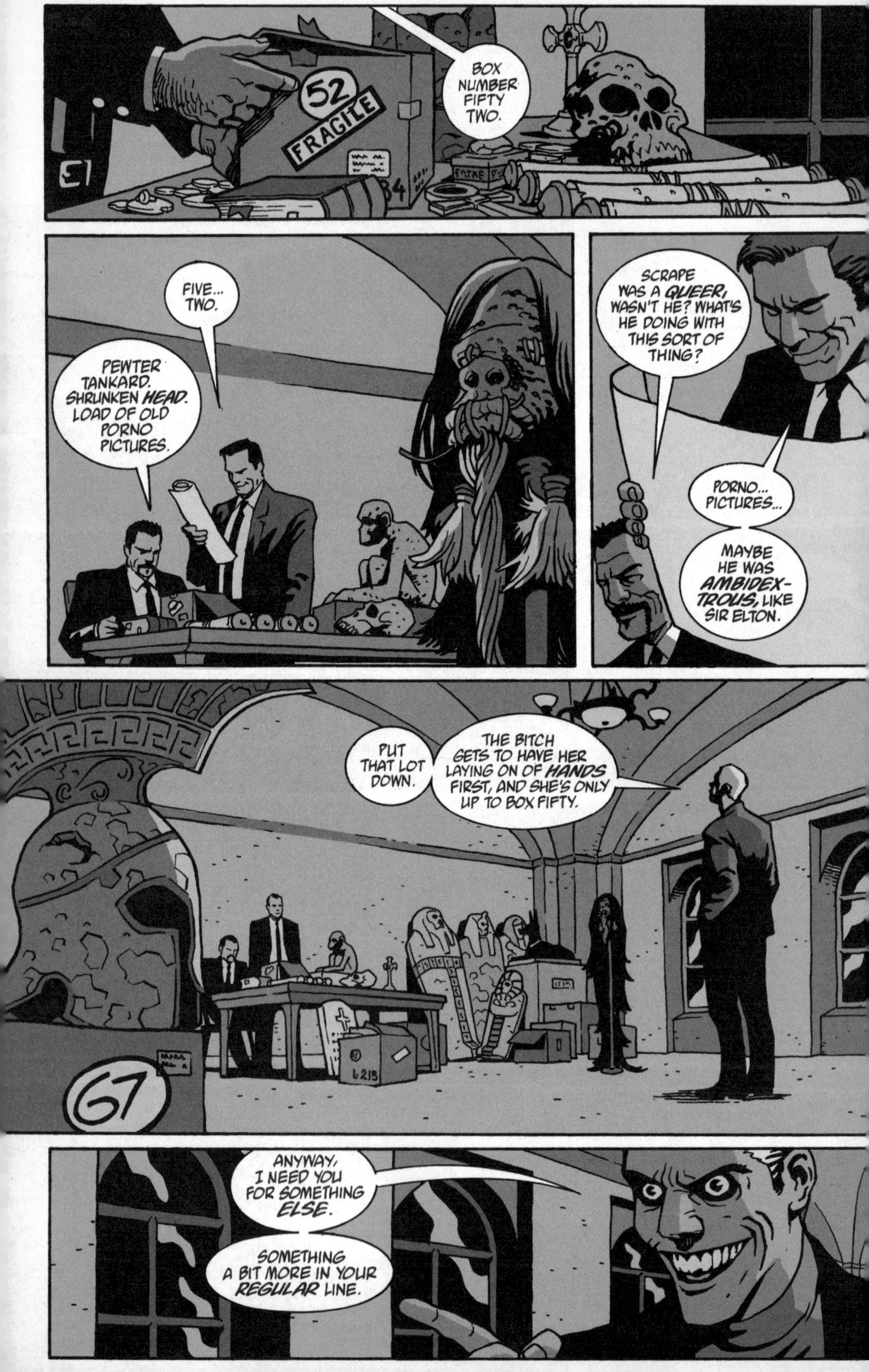

52
FRAGILE
BOX NUMBER FIFTY TWO.
FIVE... TWO.
PEWTER TANKARD. SHRUNKEN HEAD. LOAD OF OLD PORNO PICTURES.
SCRAPE WAS A QUEER, WASN'T HE? WHAT'S HE DOING WITH THIS SORT OF THING?
PORNO... PICTURES...
MAYBE HE WAS AMBIDEX-TROUS, LIKE SIR ELTON.
PUT THAT LOT DOWN.
THE BITCH GETS TO HAVE HER LAYING ON OF HANDS FIRST, AND SHE'S ONLY UP TO BOX FIFTY.
67
ANYWAY, I NEED YOU FOR SOMETHING ELSE.
SOMETHING A BIT MORE IN YOUR REGULAR LINE.

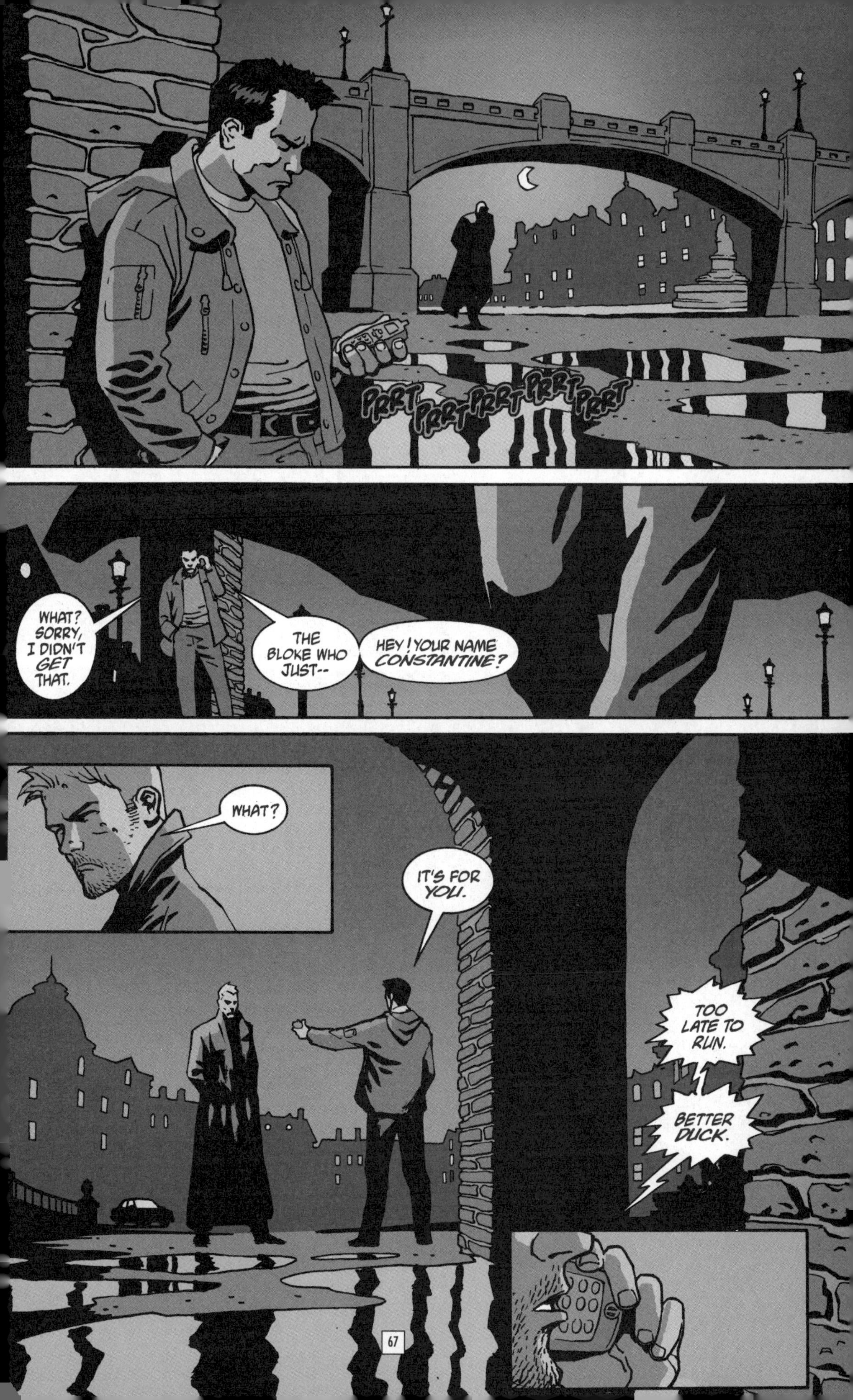
PRRT PRRT PRRT PRRT PRRT
WHAT? SORRY, I DIDN'T GET THAT.
THE BLOKE WHO JUST--
HEY! YOUR NAME CONSTANTINE?
WHAT?
IT'S FOR YOU.
TOO LATE TO RUN.
BETTER DUCK.

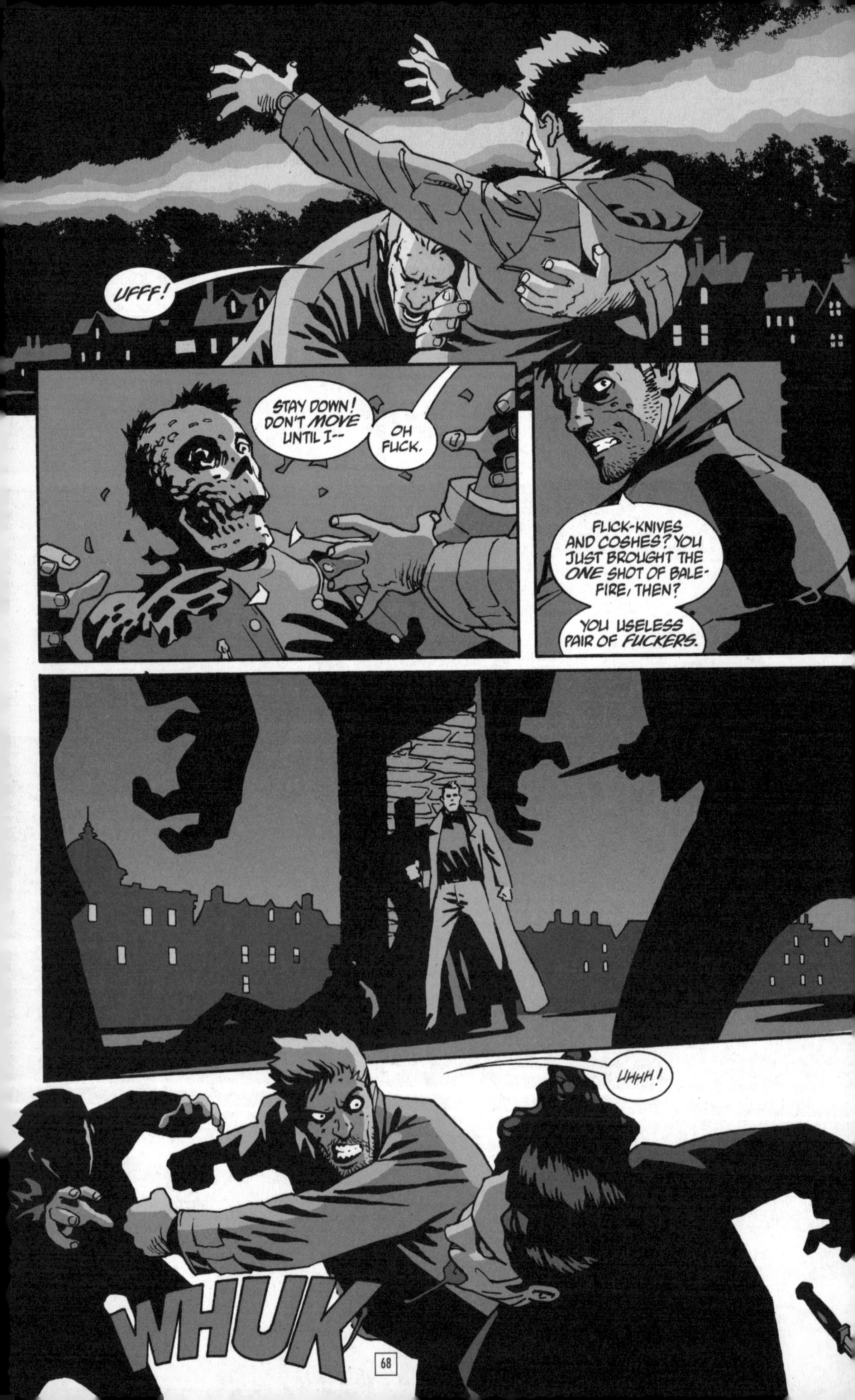
UFFF!
STAY DOWN! DON'T MOVE UNTIL I--
OH FUCK.
FLICK-KNIVES AND COSHES? YOU JUST BROUGHT THE ONE SHOT OF BALE-FIRE, THEN?
YOU USELESS PAIR OF FUCKERS.
UHHH!
WHUK

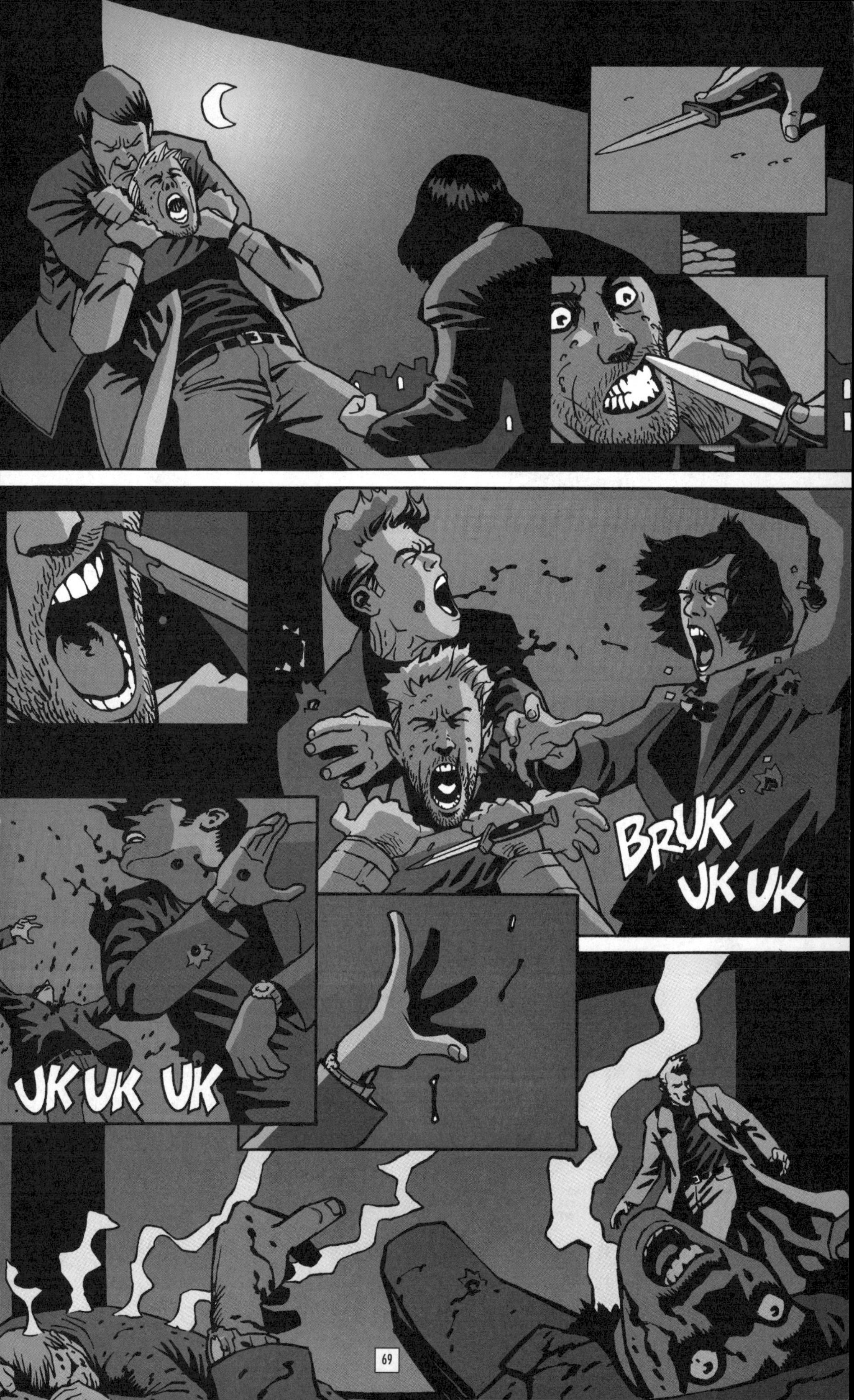
BRUK
UK UK
UK UK UK

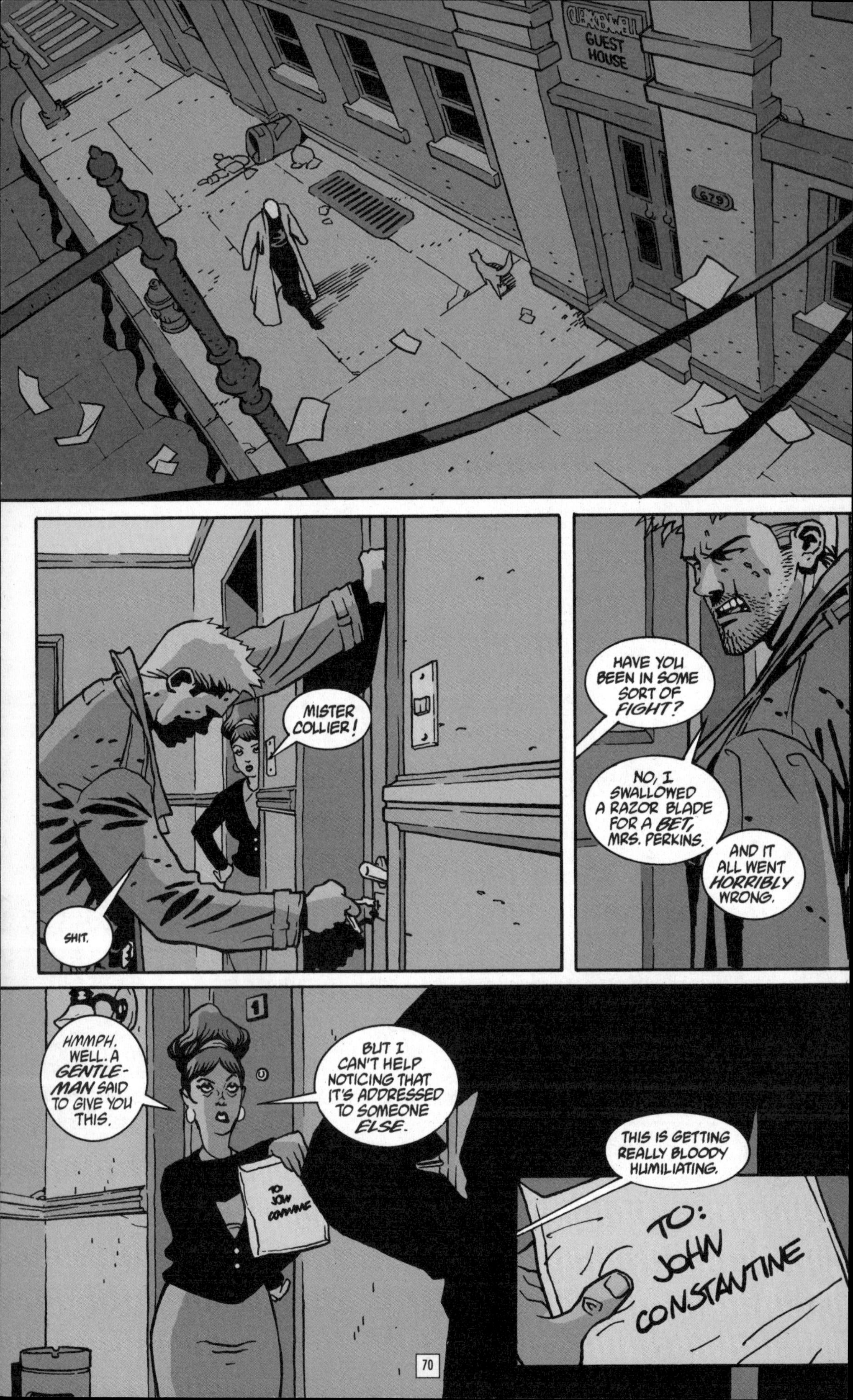
GUEST HOUSE
679
MISTER COLLIER!
SHIT.
HAVE YOU BEEN IN SOME SORT OF FIGHT?
NO, I SWALLOWED A RAZOR BLADE FOR A BET, MRS. PERKINS.
AND IT ALL WENT HORRIBLY WRONG.
HMMPH. WELL. A GENTLE-MAN SAID TO GIVE YOU THIS.
BUT I CAN'T HELP NOTICING THAT IT'S ADDRESSED TO SOMEONE ELSE.
THIS IS GETTING REALLY BLOODY HUMILIATING.
TO: JOHN CONSTANTINE

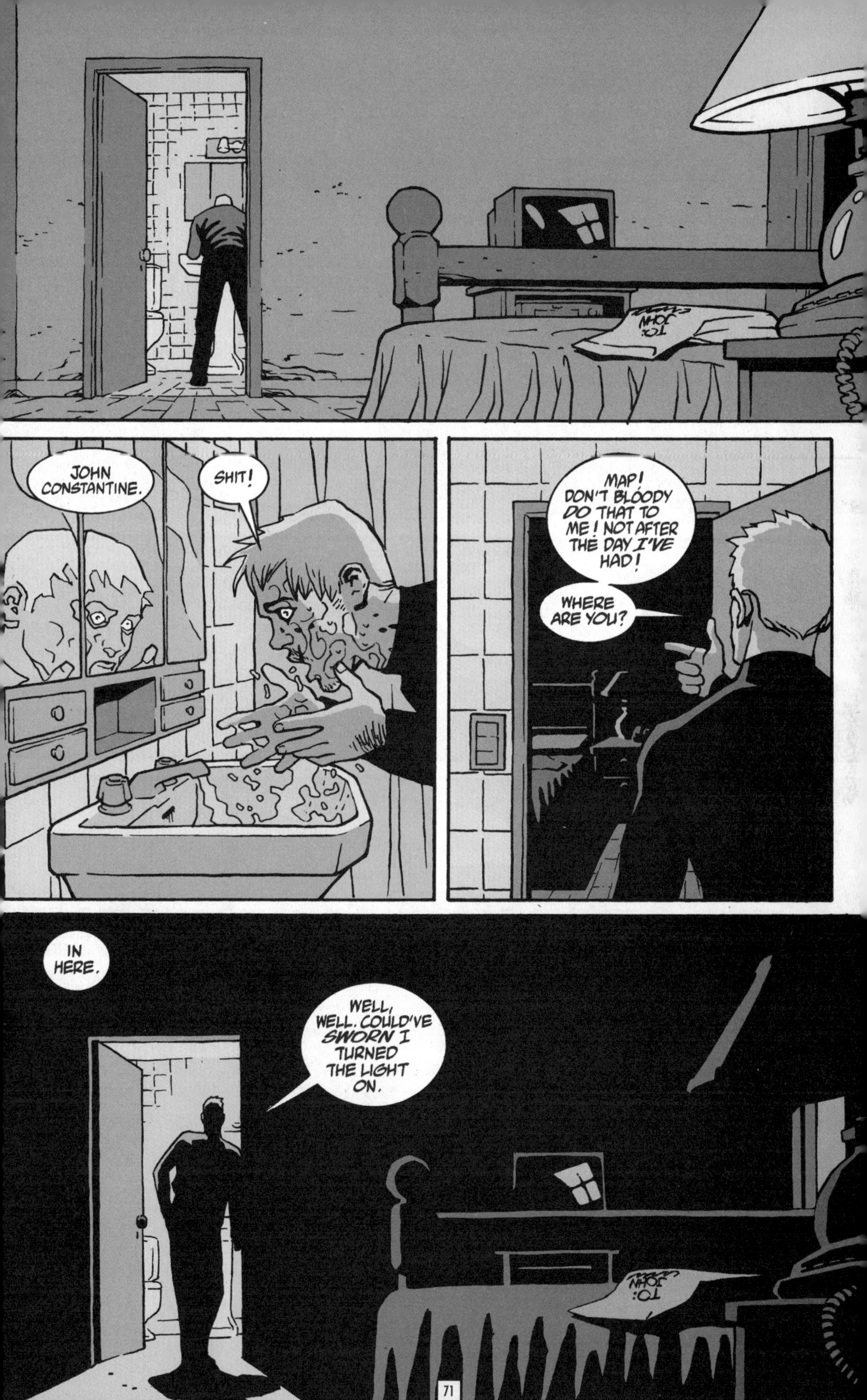
TO: JOHN
JOHN CONSTANTINE.
SHIT!
MAP! DON'T BLOODY DO THAT TO ME! NOT AFTER THE DAY I'VE HAD!
WHERE ARE YOU?
IN HERE.
WELL, WELL. COULD'VE SWORN I TURNED THE LIGHT ON.
TO: JOHN

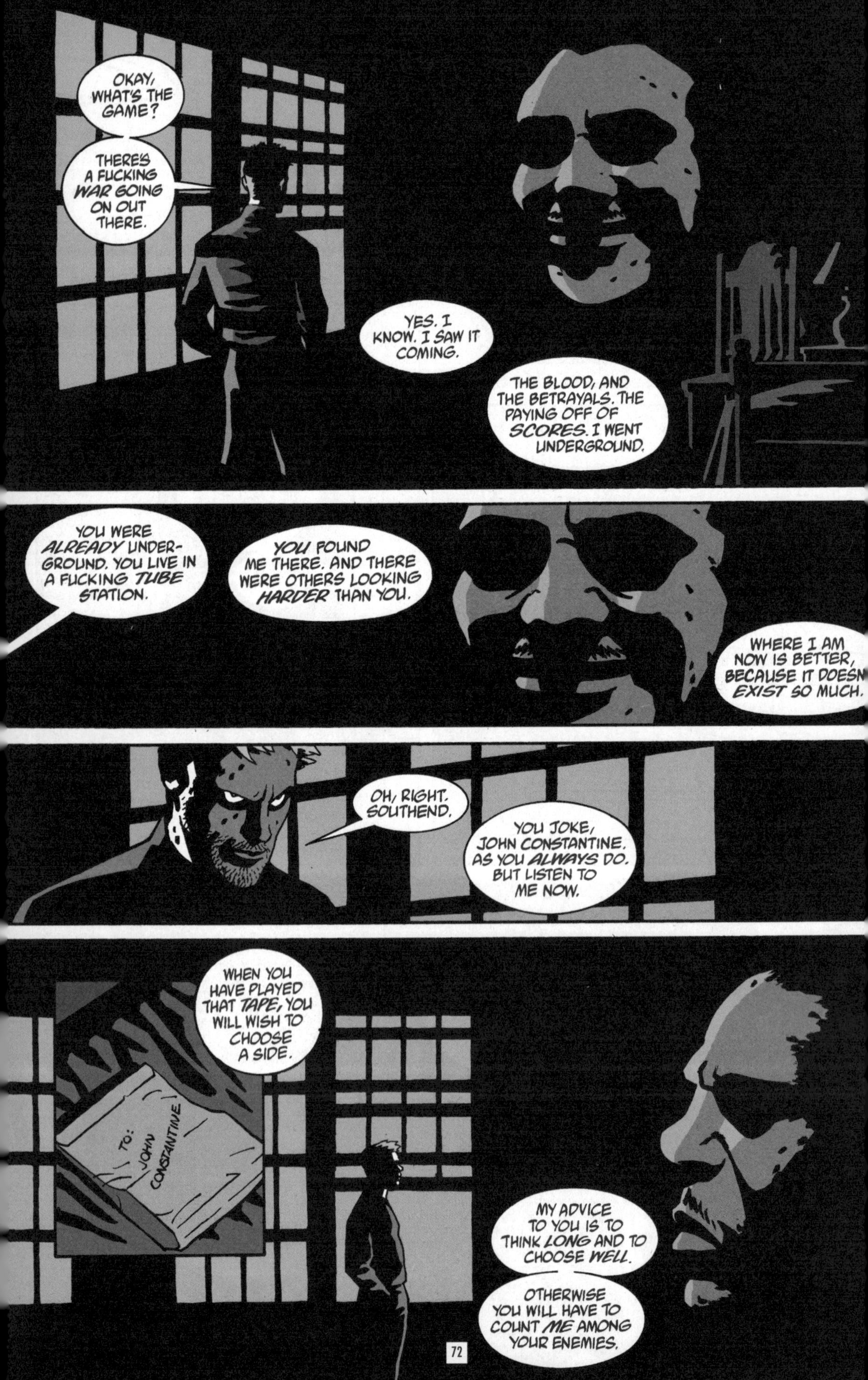
OKAY, WHAT'S THE GAME?
THERE'S A FUCKING WAR GOING ON OUT THERE.
YES. I KNOW. I SAW IT COMING.
THE BLOOD, AND THE BETRAYALS. THE PAYING OFF OF SCORES. I WENT UNDERGROUND.
YOU WERE ALREADY UNDER-GROUND. YOU LIVE IN A FUCKING TUBE STATION.
YOU FOUND ME THERE. AND THERE WERE OTHERS LOOKING HARDER THAN YOU.
WHERE I AM NOW IS BETTER, BECAUSE IT DOESN
EXIST SO MUCH.
OH, RIGHT. SOUTHEND.
YOU JOKE, JOHN CONSTANTINE. AS YOU ALWAYS DO. BUT LISTEN TO ME NOW.
WHEN YOU HAVE PLAYED THAT TAPE, YOU WILL WISH TO CHOOSE A SIDE.
TO: JOHN CONSTANTINE
MY ADVICE TO YOU IS TO THINK LONG AND TO CHOOSE WELL.
OTHERWISE YOU WILL HAVE TO COUNT ME AMONG YOUR ENEMIES.

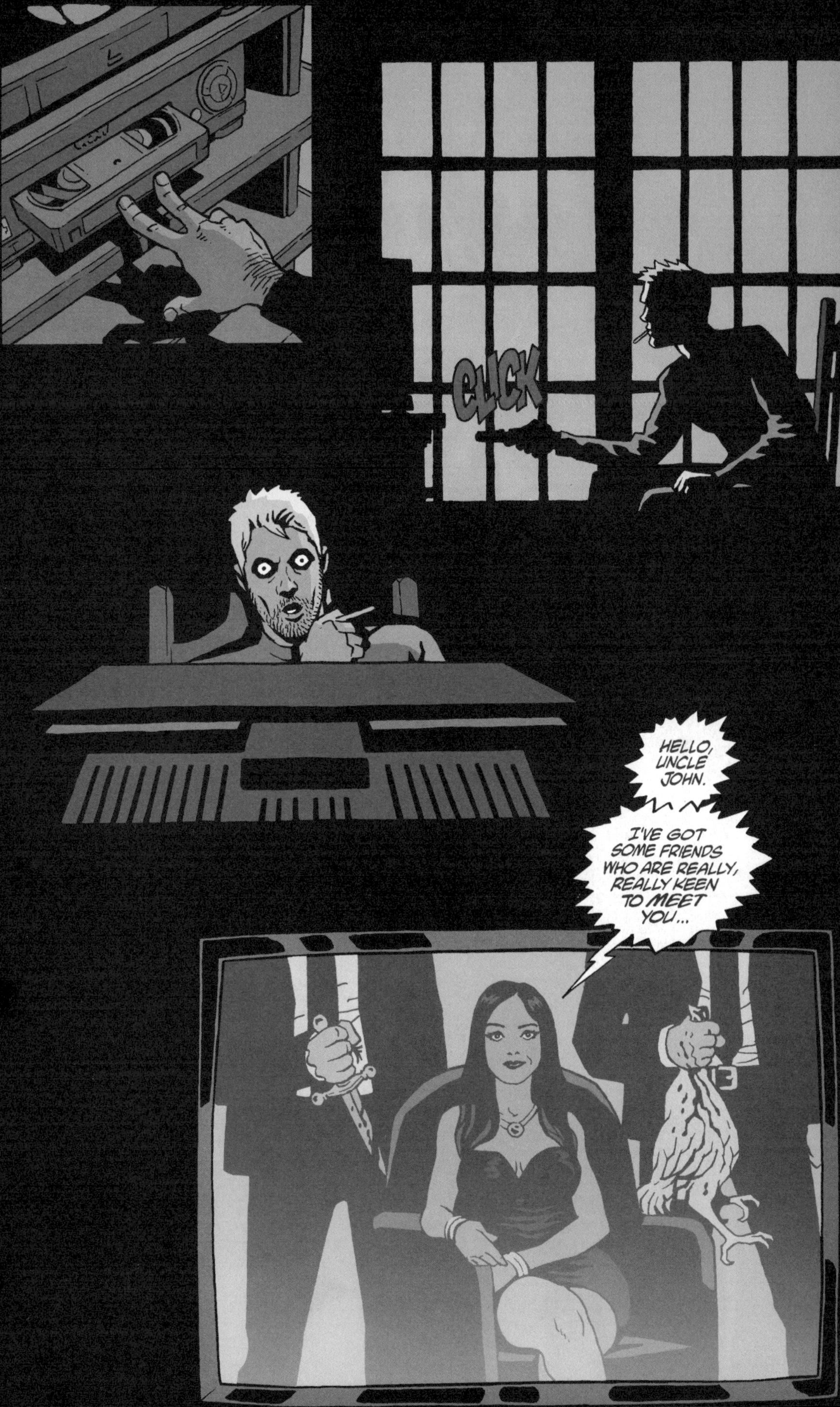
CLICK
HELLO, UNCLE JOHN.
I'VE GOT SOME FRIENDS WHO ARE REALLY, REALLY KEEN TO MEET YOU...

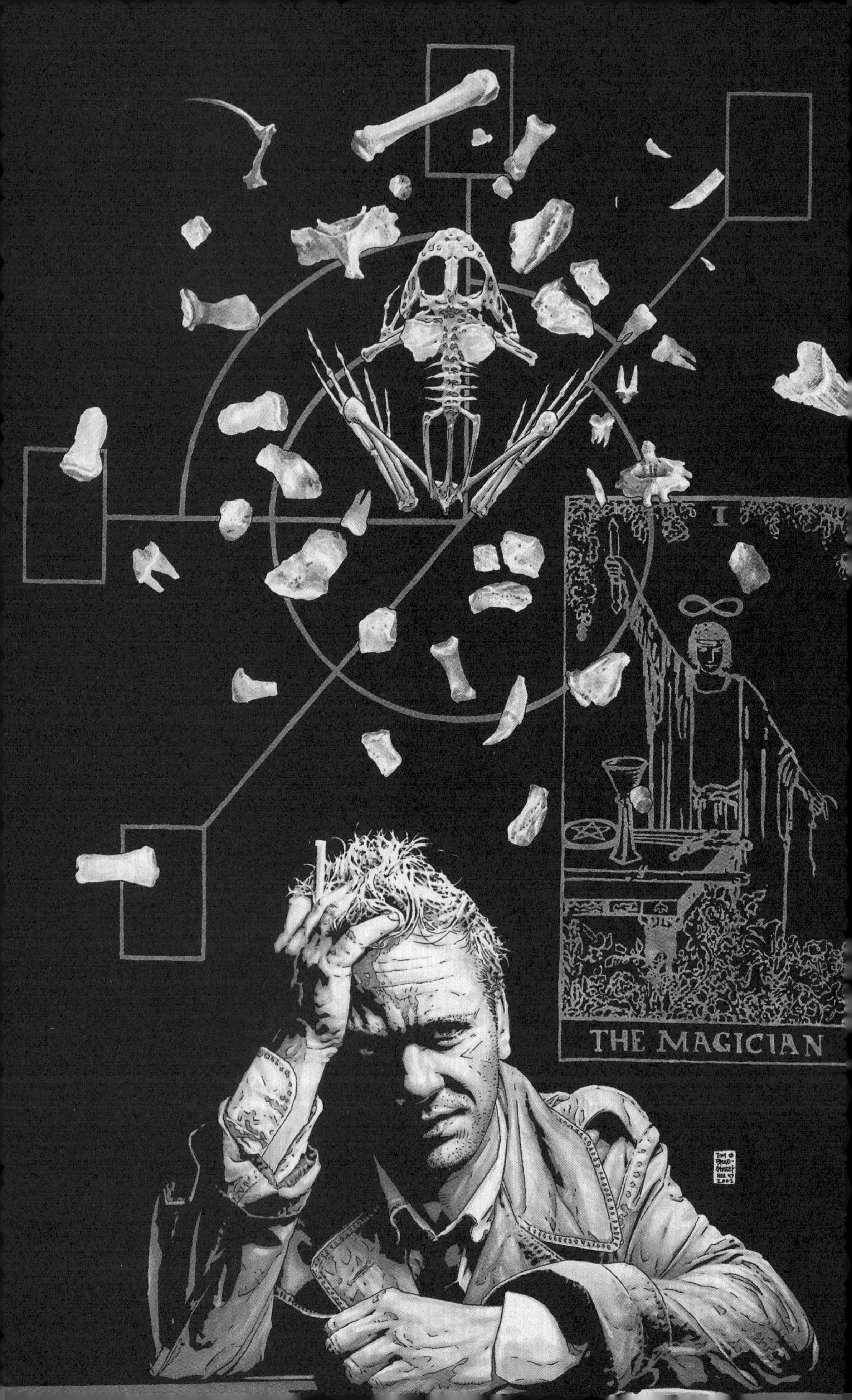
I
THE MAGICIAN
TIM © BRAD-
STREET
2002

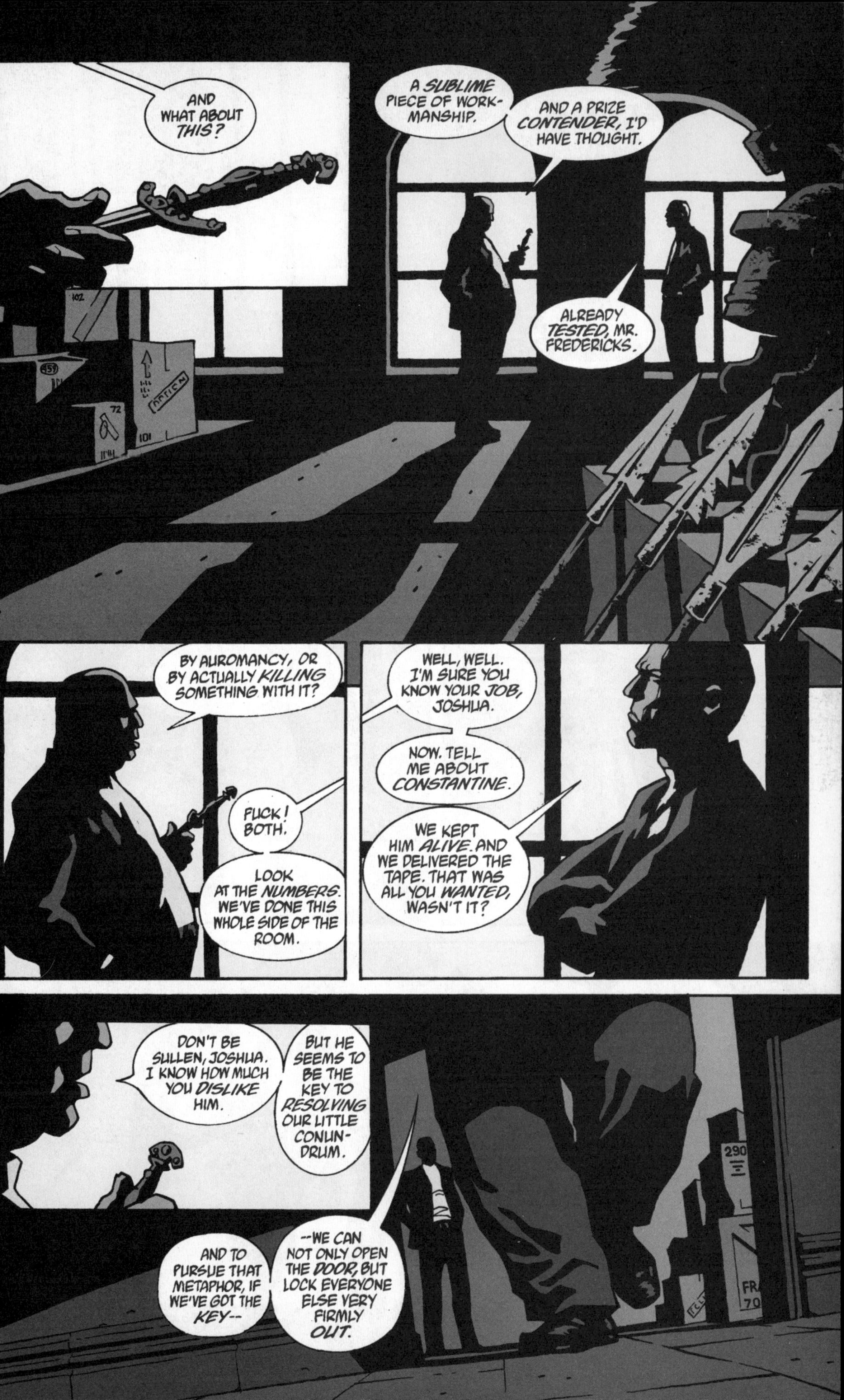
AND WHAT ABOUT THIS?
A SUBLIME PIECE OF WORK-MANSHIP.
AND A PRIZE CONTENDER, I'D HAVE THOUGHT.
ALREADY TESTED, MR. FREDERICKS.
BY AUROMANCY, OR BY ACTUALLY KILLING SOMETHING WITH IT?
FUCK! BOTH.
LOOK AT THE NUMBERS. WE'VE DONE THIS WHOLE SIDE OF THE ROOM.
WELL, WELL. I'M SURE YOU KNOW YOUR JOB, JOSHUA.
NOW. TELL ME ABOUT CONSTANTINE.
WE KEPT HIM ALIVE. AND WE DELIVERED THE TAPE. THAT WAS ALL YOU WANTED, WASN'T IT?
DON'T BE SULLEN, JOSHUA. I KNOW HOW MUCH YOU DISLIKE HIM.
BUT HE SEEMS TO BE THE KEY TO RESOLVING OUR LITTLE CONUN-DRUM.
AND TO PURSUE THAT METAPHOR, IF WE'VE GOT THE KEY--
--WE CAN NOT ONLY OPEN THE DOOR, BUT LOCK EVERYONE ELSE VERY FIRMLY OUT.

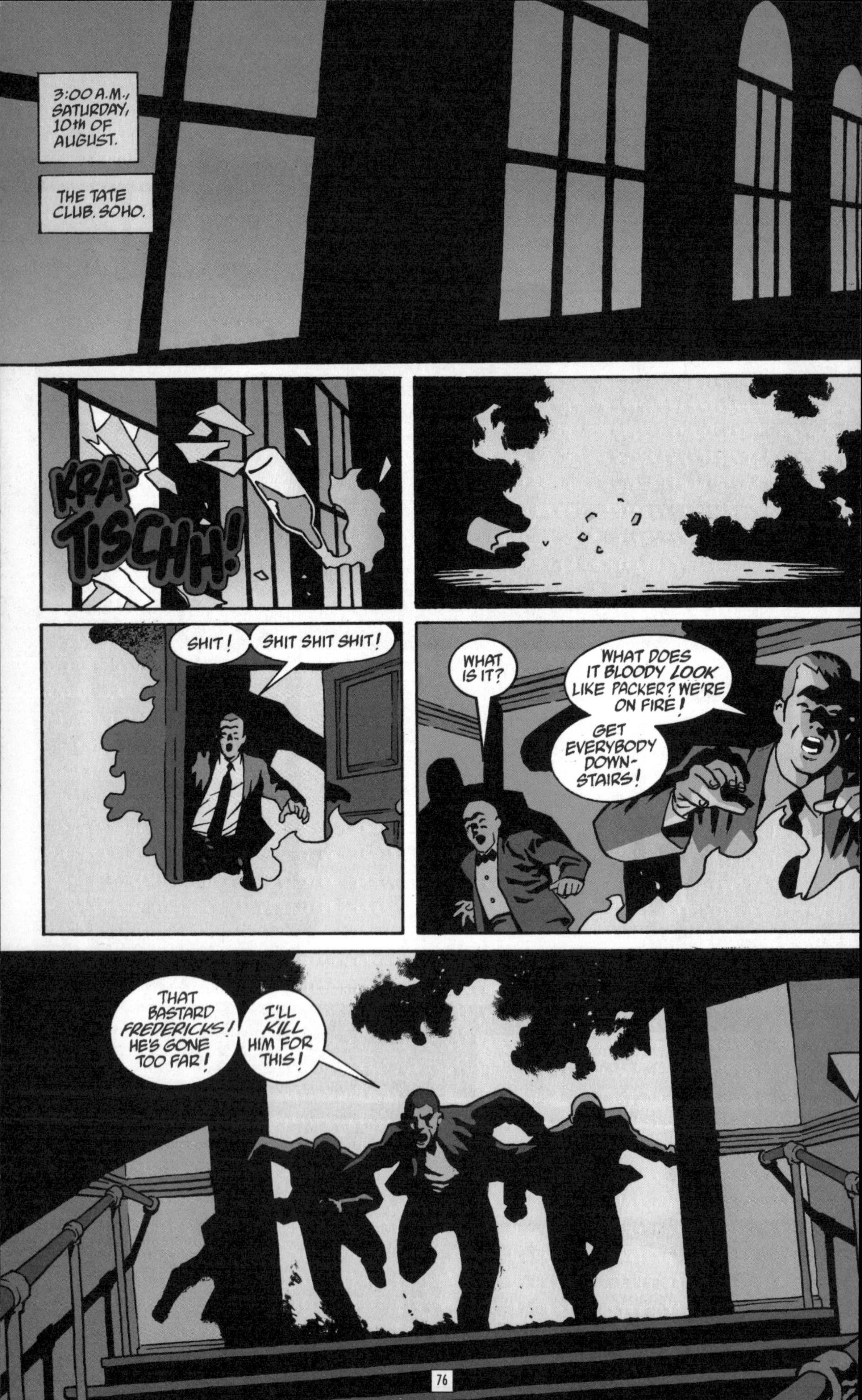
3:00 A.M., SATURDAY, 10th OF AUGUST.
THE TATE CLUB. SOHO.
KRA-TISCHH!
SHIT!
SHIT SHIT SHIT!
WHAT IS IT?
WHAT DOES IT BLOODY LOOK LIKE PACKER? WE'RE ON FIRE!
GET EVERYBODY DOWN-STAIRS!
THAT BASTARD FREDERICKS! HE'S GONE TOO FAR!
I'LL KILL HIM FOR THIS!

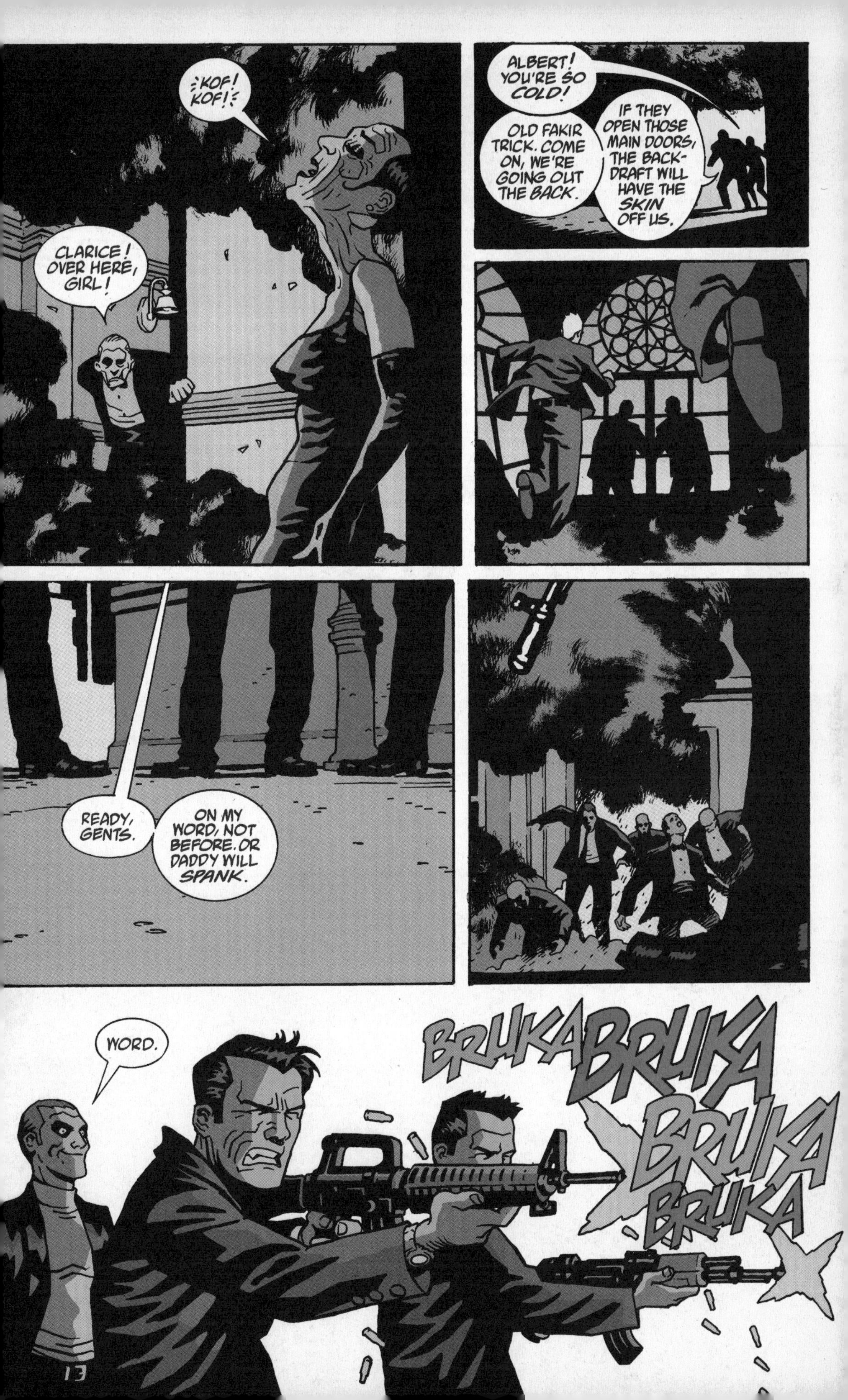

KOF! KOF!
CLARICE! OVER HERE, GIRL!
ALBERT! YOU'RE SO COLD!
OLD FAKIR TRICK. COME ON, WE'RE GOING OUT THE BACK.
IF THEY OPEN THOSE MAIN DOORS, THE BACK-DRAFT WILL HAVE THE SKIN OFF US.
READY, GENTS.
ON MY WORD, NOT BEFORE. OR DADDY WILL SPANK.
WORD.
BRUKA BRUKA
BRUKA
BRUKA

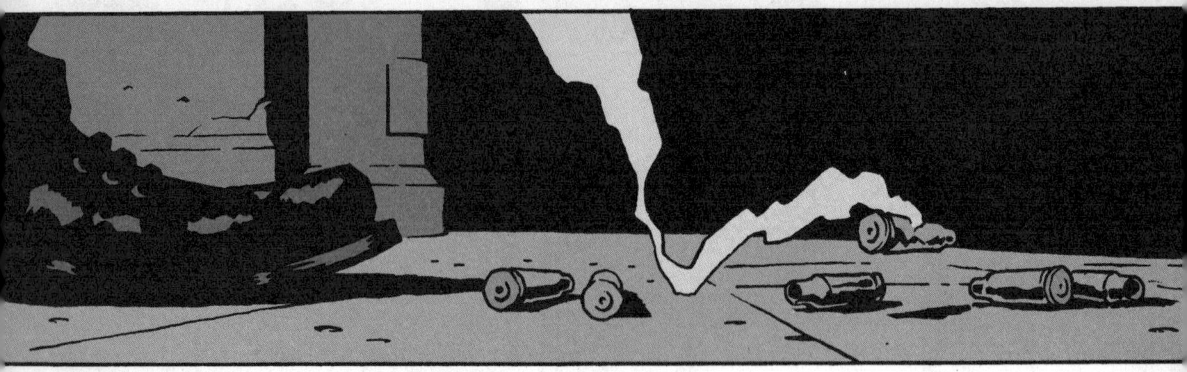

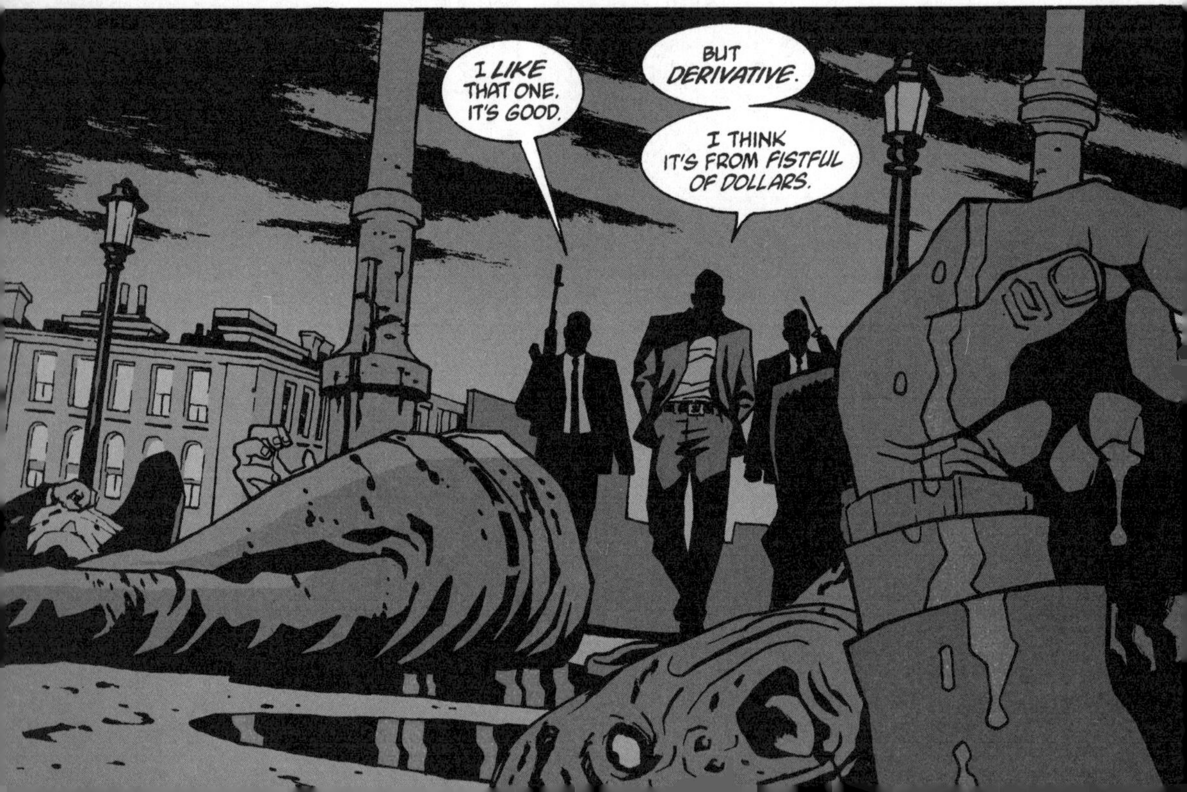
I LIKE THAT ONE. IT'S GOOD.
BUT DERIVATIVE.
I THINK IT'S FROM FISTFUL OF DOLLARS.

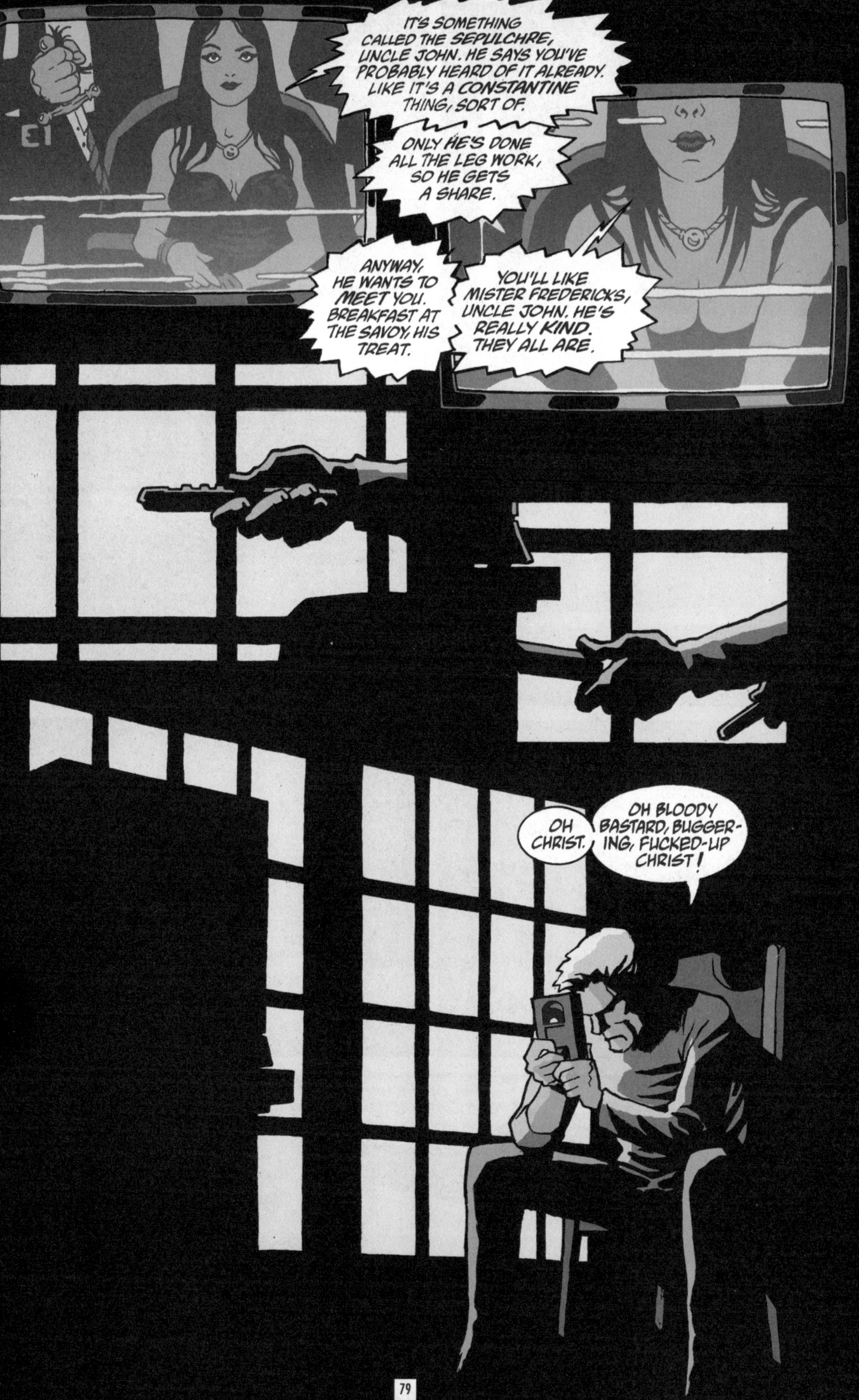
IT'S SOMETHING CALLED THE SEPULCHRE, UNCLE JOHN. HE SAYS YOU'VE PROBABLY HEARD OF IT ALREADY. LIKE IT'S A CONSTANTINE THING, SORT OF.
ONLY HE'S DONE ALL THE LEG WORK, SO HE GETS A SHARE.
ANYWAY, HE WANTS TO MEET YOU. BREAKFAST AT THE SAVOY, HIS TREAT.
YOU'LL LIKE MISTER FREDERICKS, UNCLE JOHN. HE'S REALLY KIND. THEY ALL ARE.
OH CHRIST.
OH BLOODY BASTARD, BUGGER-ING, FUCKED-UP CHRIST!

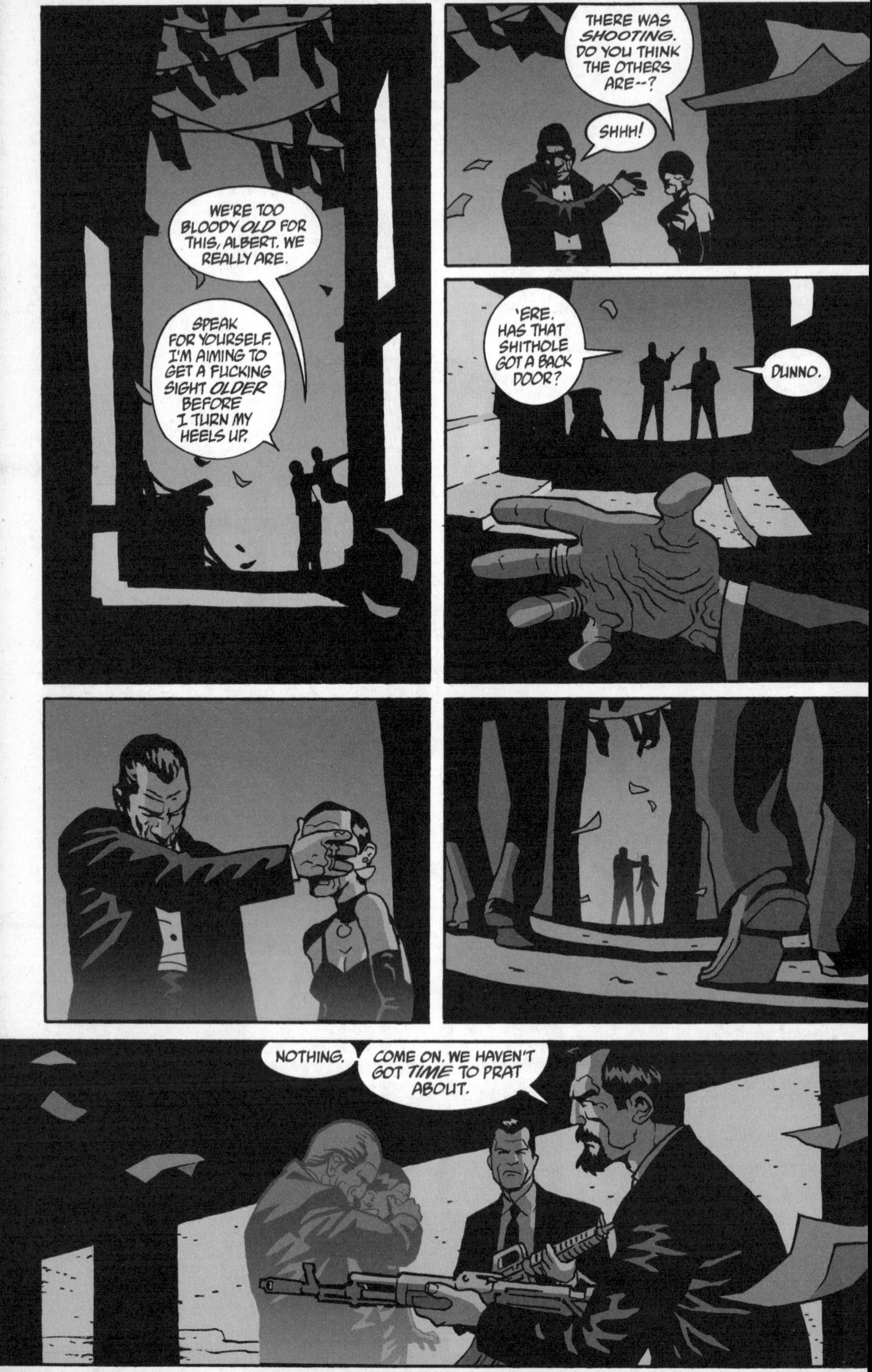
WE'RE TOO BLOODY OLD FOR THIS, ALBERT. WE REALLY ARE.
SPEAK FOR YOURSELF. I'M AIMING TO GET A FUCKING SIGHT OLDER BEFORE I TURN MY HEELS UP.
THERE WAS SHOOTING. DO YOU THINK THE OTHERS ARE--?
SHHH!
'ERE. HAS THAT SHITHOLE GOT A BACK DOOR?
DUNNO.
NOTHING.
COME ON. WE HAVEN'T GOT TIME TO PRAT ABOUT.

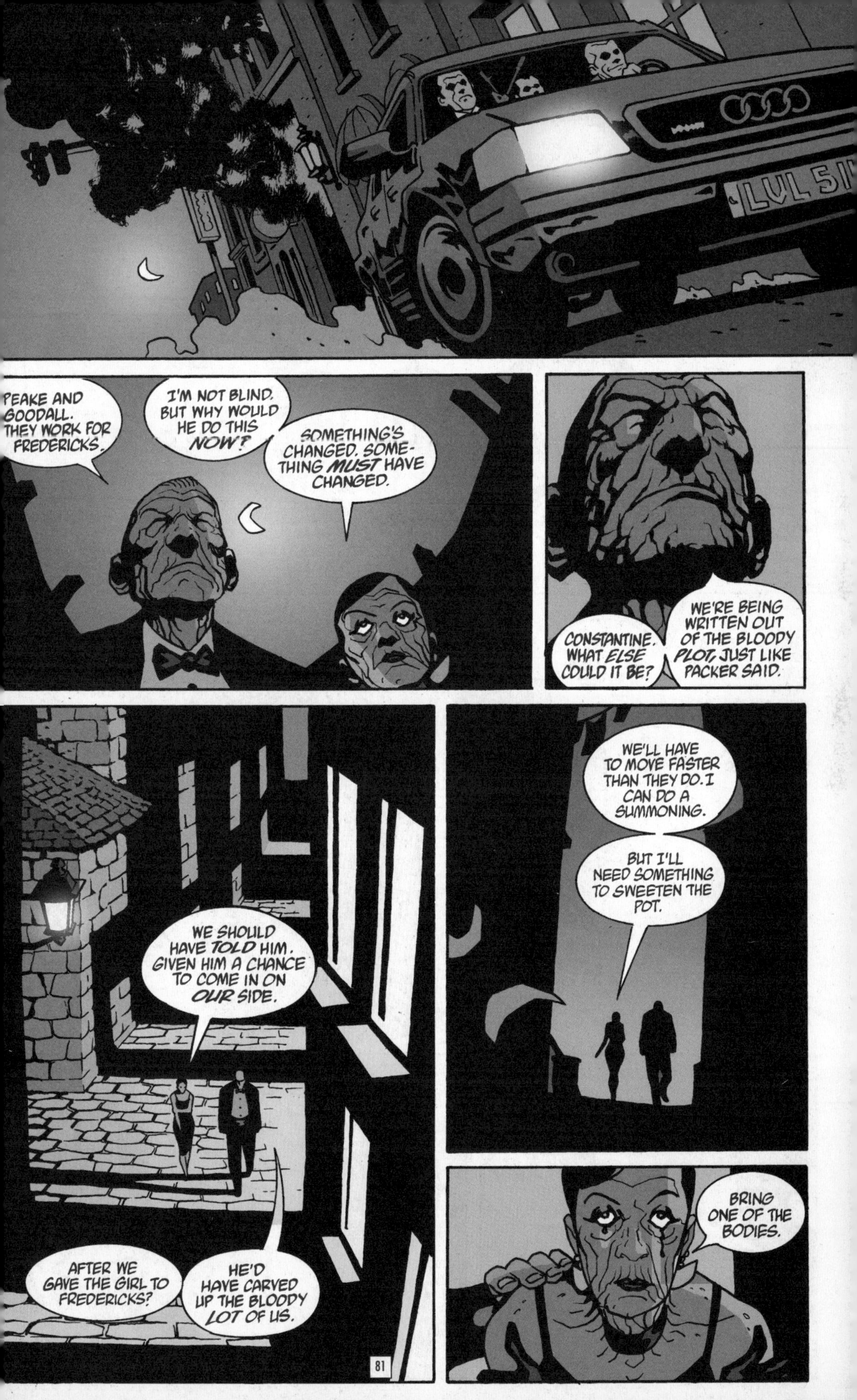
LVL 51
PEAKE AND GOODALL. THEY WORK FOR FREDERICKS.
I'M NOT BLIND. BUT WHY WOULD HE DO THIS NOW?
SOMETHING'S CHANGED. SOMETHING MUST HAVE CHANGED.
CONSTANTINE. WHAT ELSE COULD IT BE?
WE'RE BEING WRITTEN OUT OF THE BLOODY PLOT, JUST LIKE PACKER SAID.
WE SHOULD HAVE TOLD HIM. GIVEN HIM A CHANCE TO COME IN ON OUR SIDE.
AFTER WE GAVE THE GIRL TO FREDERICKS?
HE'D HAVE CARVED UP THE BLOODY LOT OF US.
WE'LL HAVE TO MOVE FASTER THAN THEY DO. I CAN DO A SUMMONING.
BUT I'LL NEED SOMETHING TO SWEETEN THE POT.
BRING ONE OF THE BODIES.

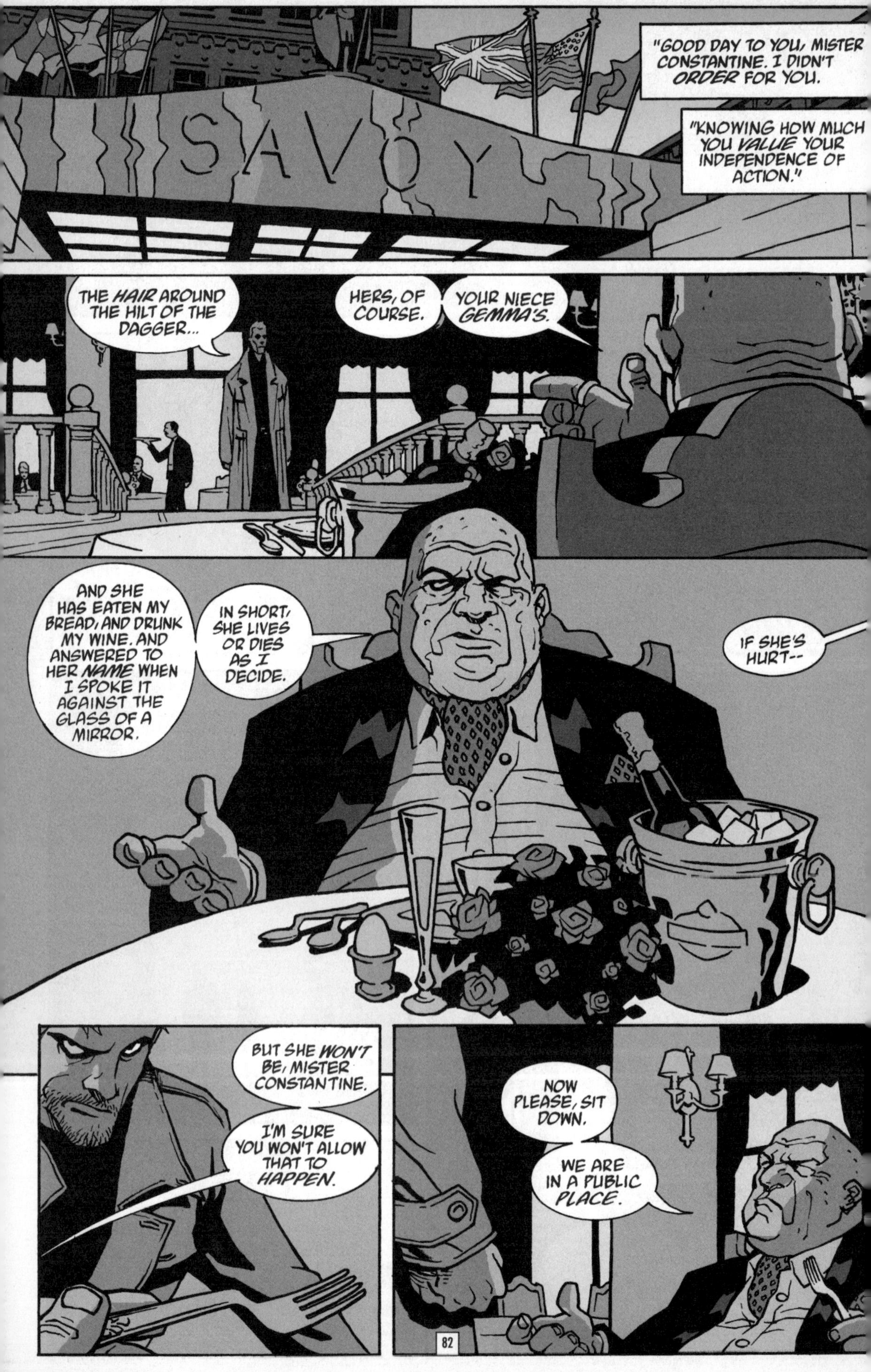
SAVOY
"GOOD DAY TO YOU, MISTER CONSTANTINE. I DIDN'T ORDER FOR YOU.
"KNOWING HOW MUCH YOU VALUE YOUR INDEPENDENCE OF ACTION."
THE HAIR AROUND THE HILT OF THE DAGGER...
HERS, OF COURSE.
YOUR NIECE GEMMA'S.
AND SHE HAS EATEN MY BREAD, AND DRUNK MY WINE. AND ANSWERED TO HER NAME WHEN I SPOKE IT AGAINST THE GLASS OF A MIRROR.
IN SHORT, SHE LIVES OR DIES AS I DECIDE.
IF SHE'S HURT--
BUT SHE WON'T BE, MISTER CONSTANTINE.
I'M SURE YOU WON'T ALLOW THAT TO HAPPEN.
NOW PLEASE, SIT DOWN.
WE ARE IN A PUBLIC PLACE.

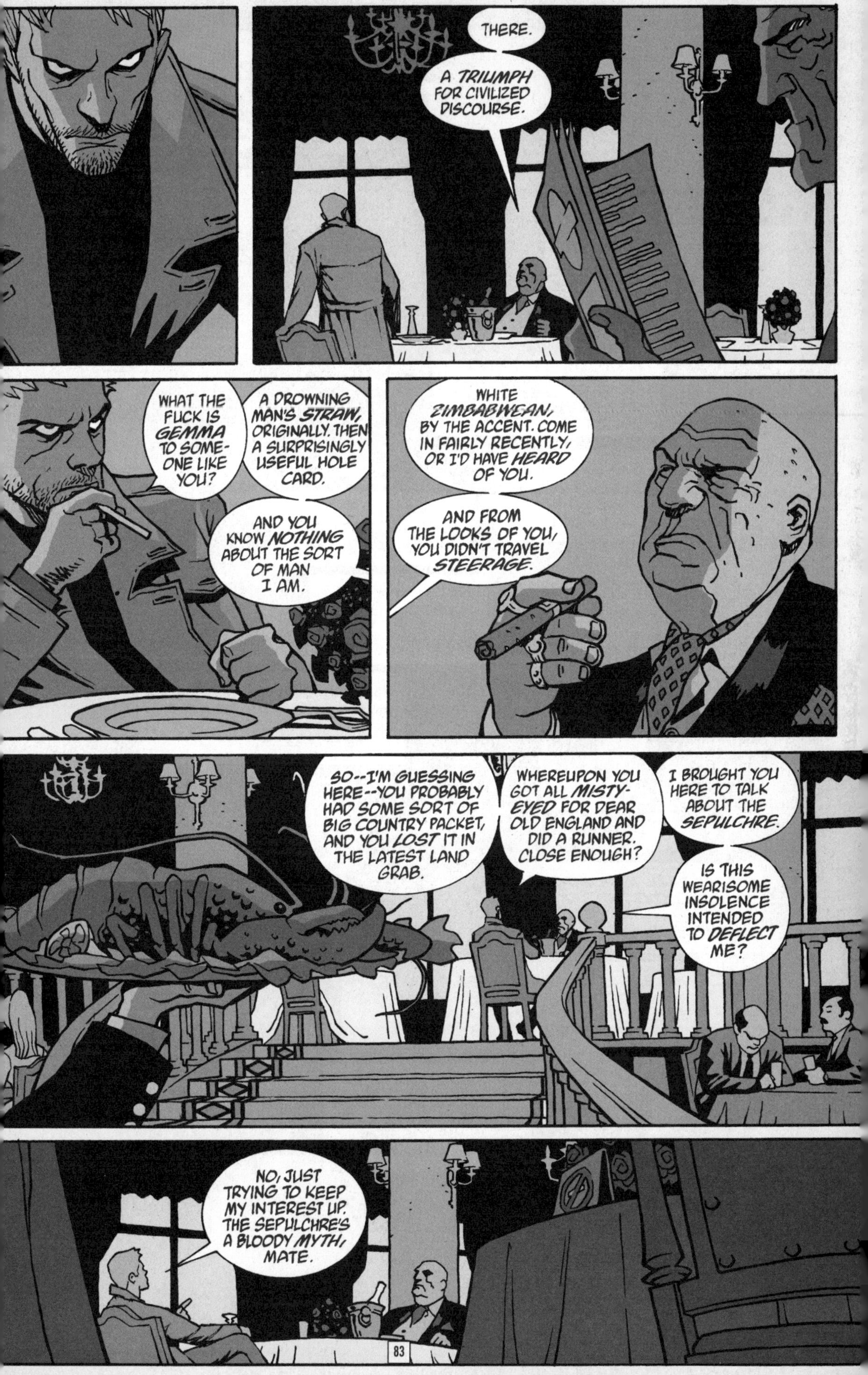
THERE.
A TRIUMPH FOR CIVILIZED DISCOURSE.
WHAT THE FUCK IS GEMMA TO SOMEONE LIKE YOU?
A DROWNING MAN'S STRAW, ORIGINALLY. THEN A SURPRISINGLY USEFUL HOLE CARD.
AND YOU KNOW NOTHING ABOUT THE SORT OF MAN I AM.
WHITE ZIMBABWEAN, BY THE ACCENT. COME IN FAIRLY RECENTLY, OR I'D HAVE HEARD OF YOU.
AND FROM THE LOOKS OF YOU, YOU DIDN'T TRAVEL STEERAGE.
SO--I'M GUESSING HERE--YOU PROBABLY HAD SOME SORT OF BIG COUNTRY PACKET, AND YOU LOST IT IN THE LATEST LAND GRAB.
WHEREUPON YOU GOT ALL MISTY-EYED FOR DEAR OLD ENGLAND AND DID A RUNNER. CLOSE ENOUGH?
I BROUGHT YOU HERE TO TALK ABOUT THE SEPULCHRE.
IS THIS WEARISOME INSOLENCE INTENDED TO DEFLECT ME?
NO, JUST TRYING TO KEEP MY INTEREST UP. THE SEPULCHRE'S A BLOODY MYTH, MATE.

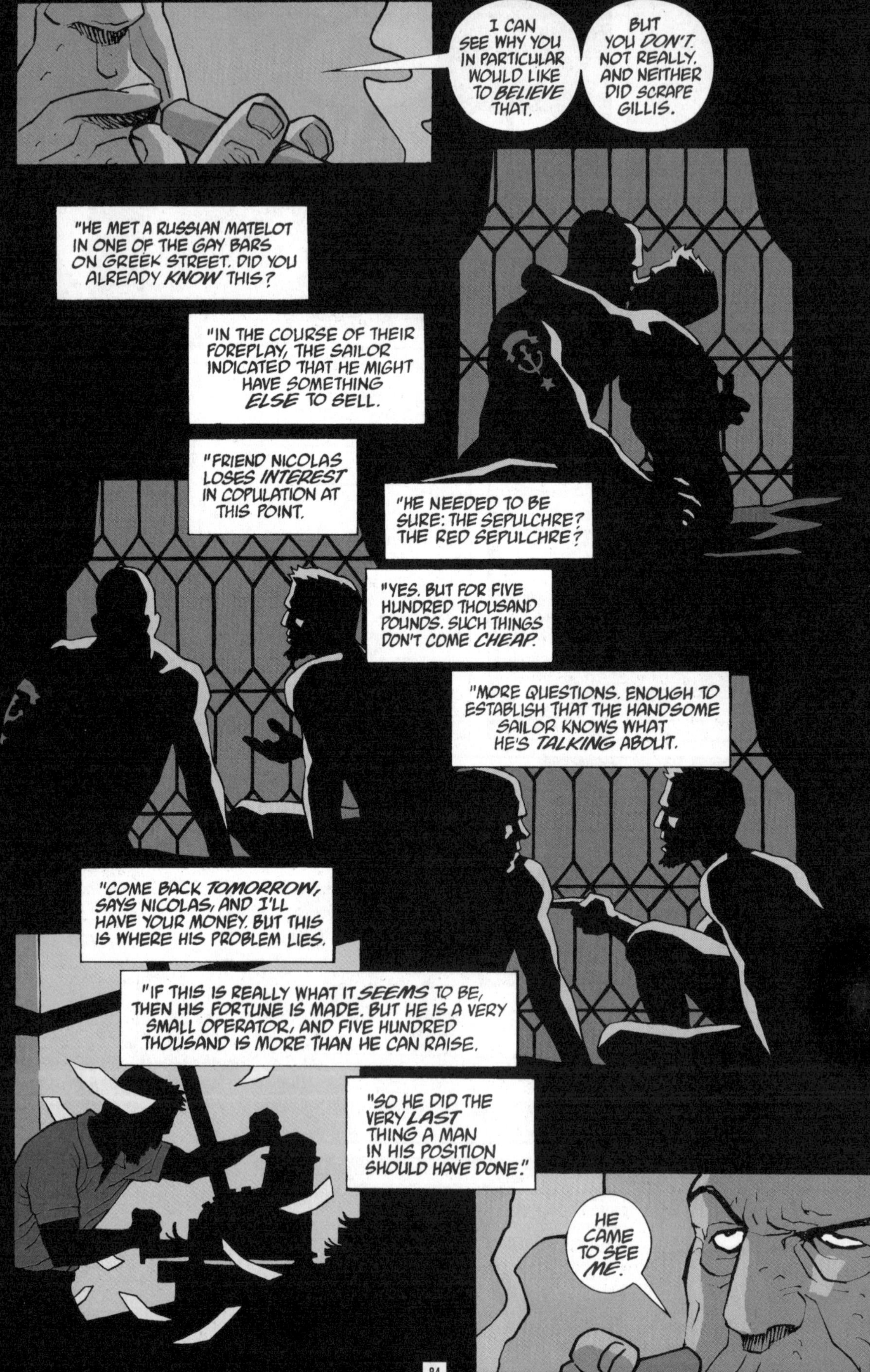
I CAN SEE WHY YOU IN PARTICULAR WOULD LIKE TO *BELIEVE* THAT.
BUT YOU *DON'T*. NOT REALLY. AND NEITHER DID SCRAPE GILLIS.
"HE MET A RUSSIAN MATELOT IN ONE OF THE GAY BARS ON GREEK STREET. DID YOU ALREADY *KNOW* THIS?
"IN THE COURSE OF THEIR FOREPLAY, THE SAILOR INDICATED THAT HE MIGHT HAVE SOMETHING *ELSE* TO SELL.
"FRIEND NICOLAS LOSES *INTEREST* IN COPULATION AT THIS POINT.
"HE NEEDED TO BE SURE: THE SEPULCHRE? THE RED SEPULCHRE?
"YES. BUT FOR FIVE HUNDRED THOUSAND POUNDS. SUCH THINGS DON'T COME *CHEAP*.
"MORE QUESTIONS. ENOUGH TO ESTABLISH THAT THE HANDSOME SAILOR KNOWS WHAT HE'S *TALKING* ABOUT.
"COME BACK *TOMORROW*, SAYS NICOLAS, AND I'LL HAVE YOUR MONEY. BUT THIS IS WHERE HIS PROBLEM LIES.
"IF THIS IS REALLY WHAT IT *SEEMS* TO BE, THEN HIS FORTUNE IS MADE. BUT HE IS A VERY SMALL OPERATOR, AND FIVE HUNDRED THOUSAND IS MORE THAN HE CAN RAISE.
"SO HE DID THE VERY *LAST* THING A MAN IN HIS POSITION SHOULD HAVE DONE."
HE CAME TO SEE *ME*.

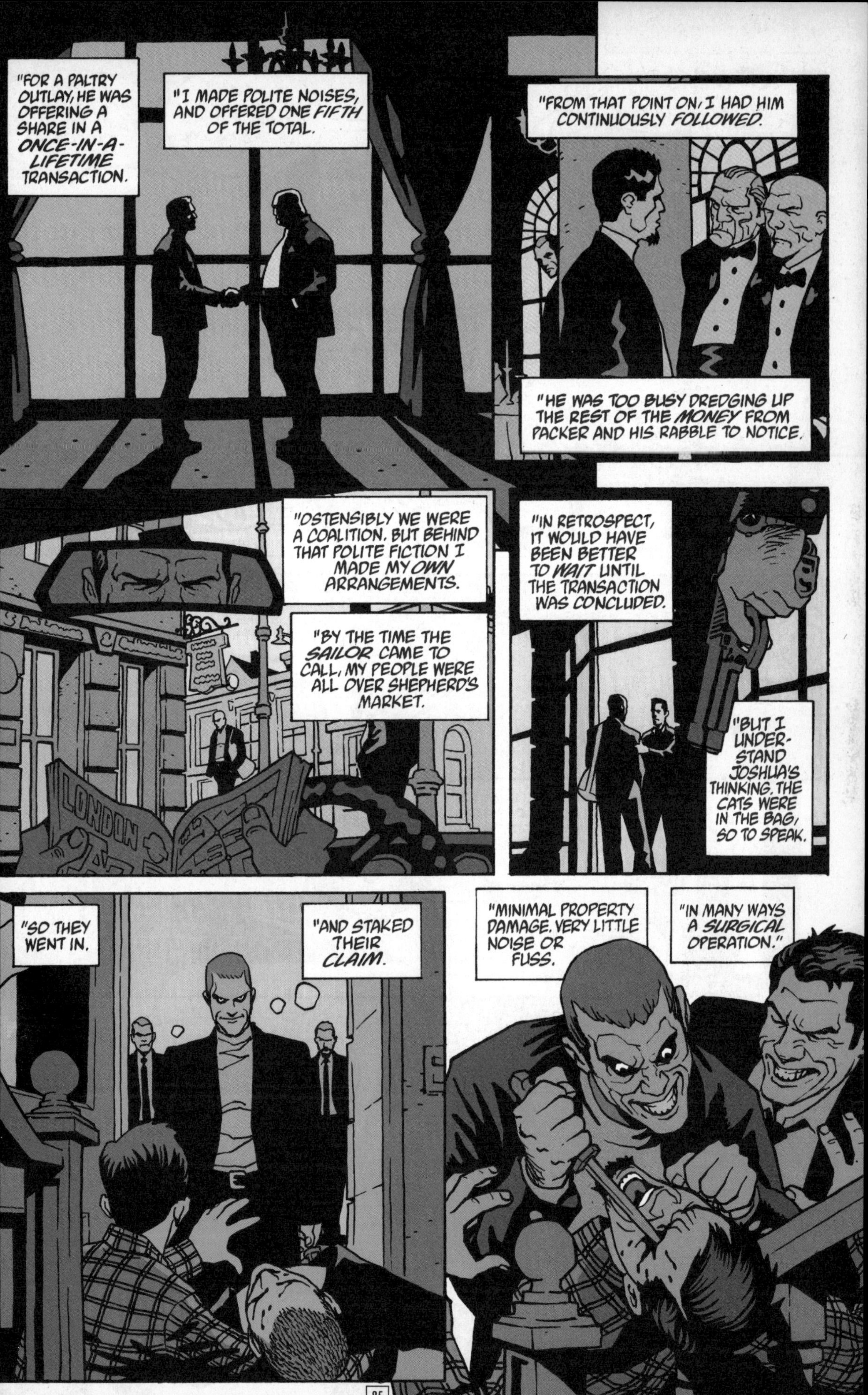

"FOR A PALTRY OUTLAY, HE WAS OFFERING A SHARE IN A *ONCE-IN-A-LIFETIME* TRANSACTION.
"I MADE POLITE NOISES, AND OFFERED ONE *FIFTH* OF THE TOTAL.
"FROM THAT POINT ON, I HAD HIM CONTINUOUSLY *FOLLOWED*.
"HE WAS TOO BUSY DREDGING UP THE REST OF THE *MONEY* FROM PACKER AND HIS RABBLE TO NOTICE.
"OSTENSIBLY WE WERE A *COALITION*. BUT BEHIND THAT POLITE FICTION I MADE MY *OWN* ARRANGEMENTS.
"BY THE TIME THE *SAILOR* CAME TO CALL, MY PEOPLE WERE ALL OVER SHEPHERD'S MARKET.
LONDON
"IN RETROSPECT, IT WOULD HAVE BEEN BETTER TO *WAIT* UNTIL THE TRANSACTION WAS *CONCLUDED*.
"BUT I UNDERSTAND JOSHUA'S THINKING. THE CATS WERE IN THE BAG, SO TO SPEAK.
"SO THEY WENT IN.
"AND STAKED THEIR *CLAIM*.
"MINIMAL PROPERTY DAMAGE. VERY LITTLE NOISE OR FUSS.
"IN MANY WAYS A *SURGICAL* OPERATION."

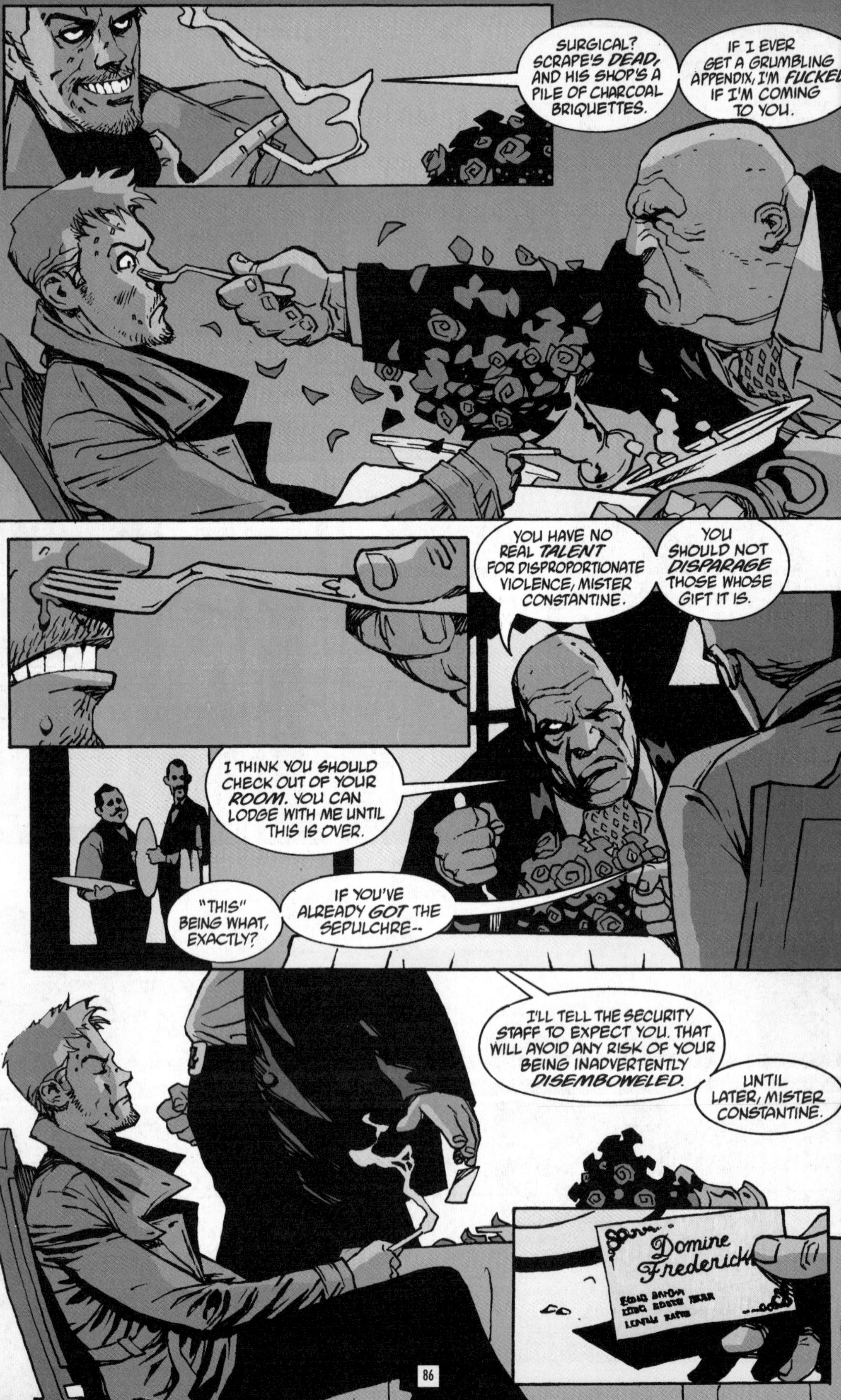
SURGICAL? SCRAPE'S DEAD, AND HIS SHOP'S A PILE OF CHARCOAL BRIQUETTES.
IF I EVER GET A GRUMBLING APPENDIX, I'M FUCKED IF I'M COMING TO YOU.
YOU HAVE NO REAL TALENT FOR DISPROPORTIONATE VIOLENCE, MISTER CONSTANTINE.
YOU SHOULD NOT DISPARAGE THOSE WHOSE GIFT IT IS.
I THINK YOU SHOULD CHECK OUT OF YOUR ROOM. YOU CAN LODGE WITH ME UNTIL THIS IS OVER.
"THIS" BEING WHAT, EXACTLY?
IF YOU'VE ALREADY GOT THE SEPULCHRE--
I'LL TELL THE SECURITY STAFF TO EXPECT YOU. THAT WILL AVOID ANY RISK OF YOUR BEING INADVERTENTLY DISEMBOWELED.
UNTIL LATER, MISTER CONSTANTINE.
Domine Frederick

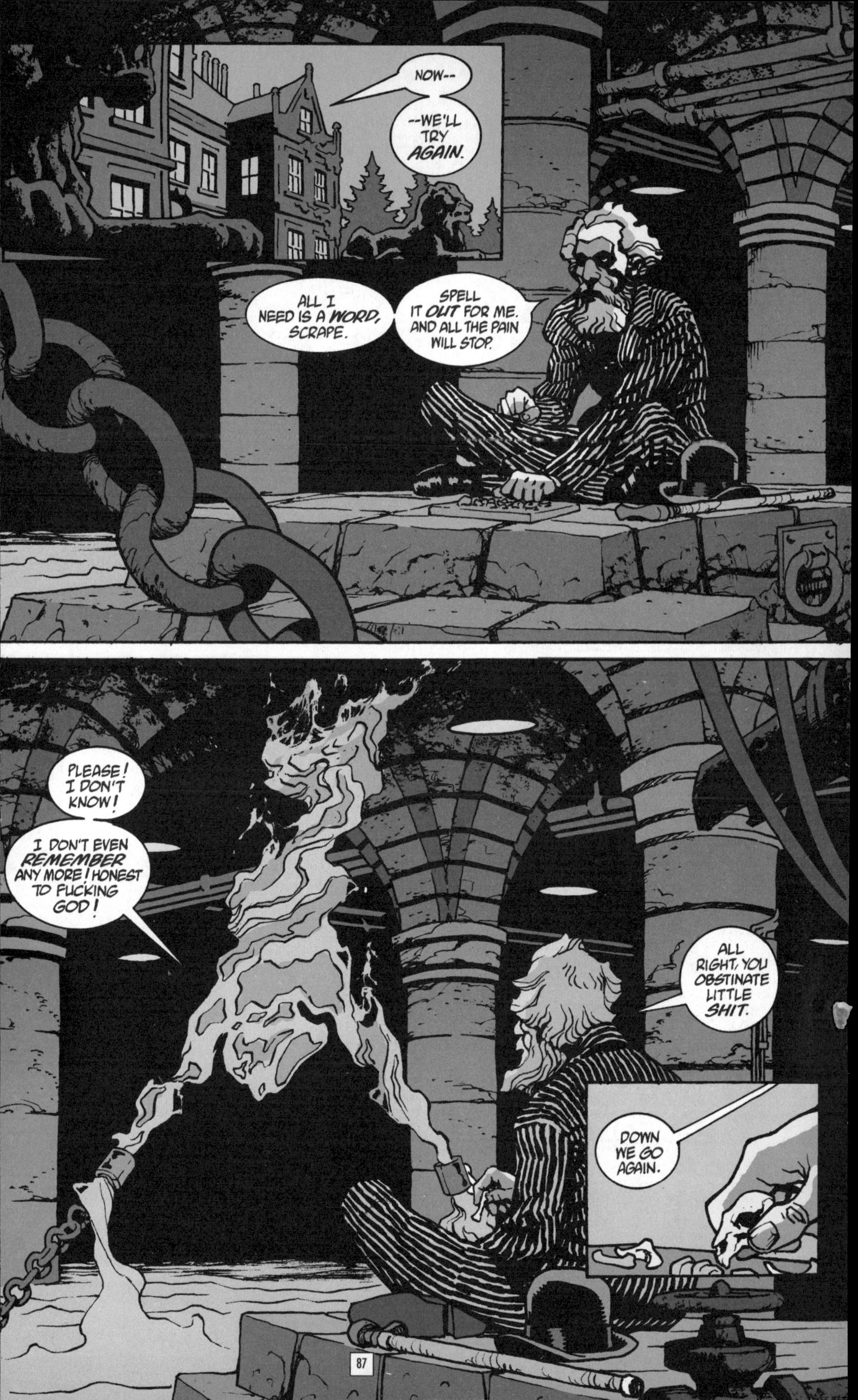
NOW--
--WE'LL TRY AGAIN.
ALL I NEED IS A WORD, SCRAPE.
SPELL IT OUT FOR ME. AND ALL THE PAIN WILL STOP.
PLEASE! I DON'T KNOW!
I DON'T EVEN REMEMBER ANY MORE! HONEST TO FUCKING GOD!
ALL RIGHT, YOU OBSTINATE LITTLE SHIT.
DOWN WE GO AGAIN.

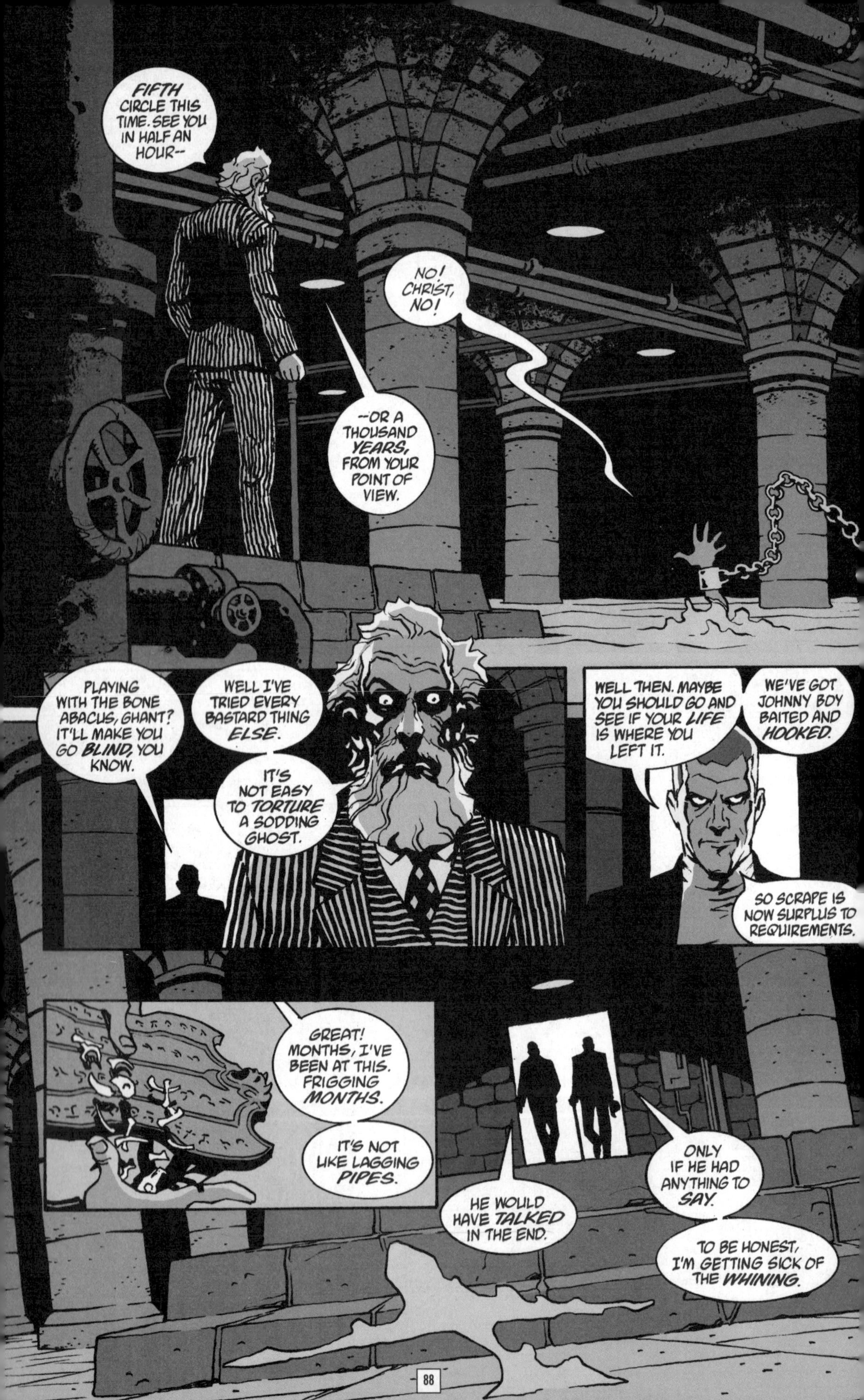

FIFTH CIRCLE THIS TIME. SEE YOU IN HALF AN HOUR--
NO! CHRIST, NO!
--OR A THOUSAND YEARS, FROM YOUR POINT OF VIEW.
PLAYING WITH THE BONE ABACUS, GHANT? IT'LL MAKE YOU GO BLIND, YOU KNOW.
WELL I'VE TRIED EVERY BASTARD THING ELSE.
IT'S NOT EASY TO TORTURE A SODDING GHOST.
WELL THEN. MAYBE YOU SHOULD GO AND SEE IF YOUR LIFE IS WHERE YOU LEFT IT.
WE'VE GOT JOHNNY BOY BAITED AND HOOKED.
SO SCRAPE IS NOW SURPLUS TO REQUIREMENTS.
GREAT! MONTHS, I'VE BEEN AT THIS. FRIGGING MONTHS.
IT'S NOT LIKE LAGGING PIPES.
HE WOULD HAVE TALKED IN THE END.
ONLY IF HE HAD ANYTHING TO SAY.
TO BE HONEST, I'M GETTING SICK OF THE WHINING.

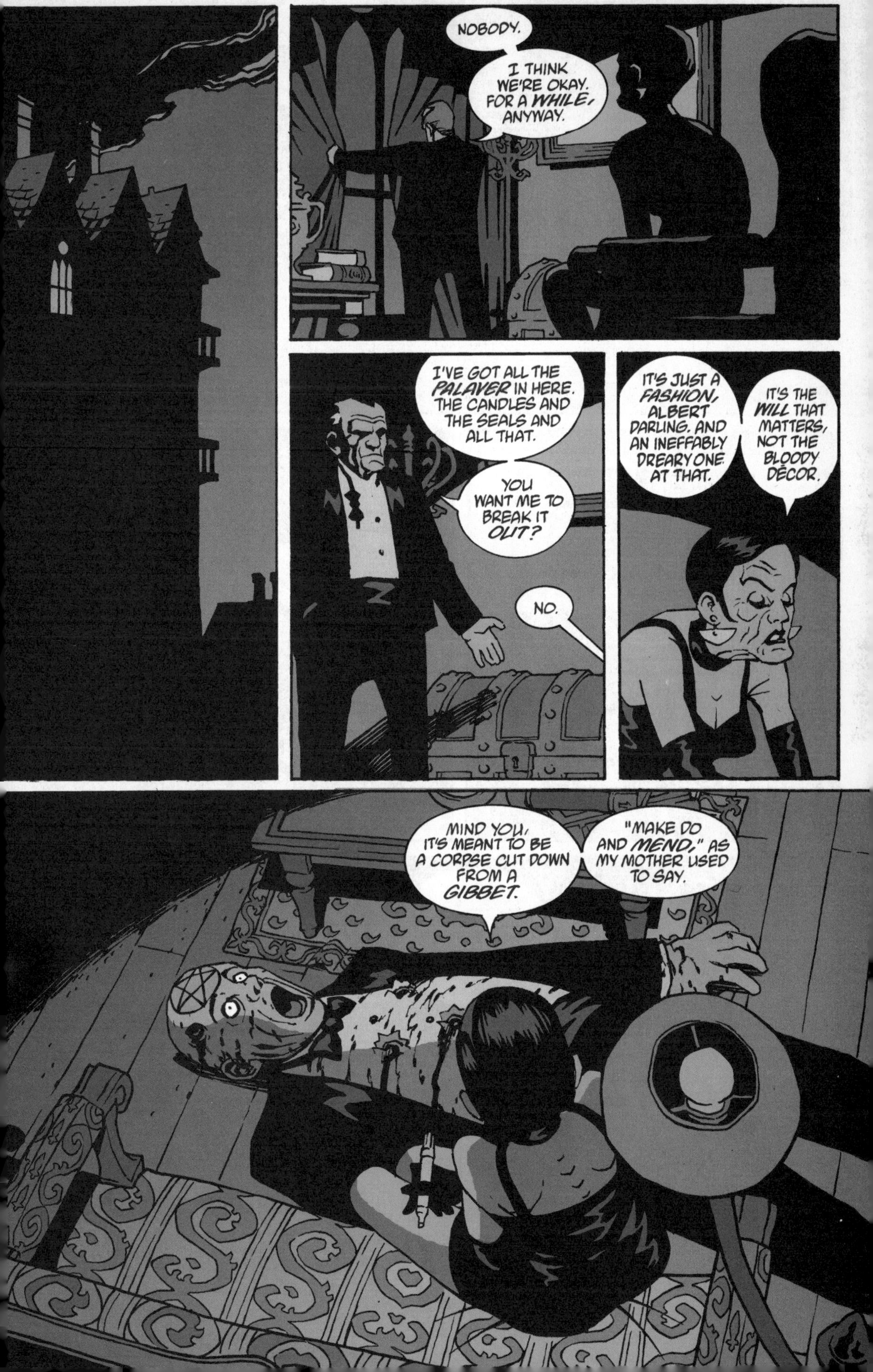
NOBODY.
I THINK WE'RE OKAY. FOR A WHILE, ANYWAY.
I'VE GOT ALL THE PALAVER IN HERE. THE CANDLES AND THE SEALS AND ALL THAT.
YOU WANT ME TO BREAK IT OUT?
NO.
IT'S JUST A FASHION, ALBERT DARLING. AND AN INEFFABLY DREARY ONE AT THAT.
IT'S THE WILL THAT MATTERS, NOT THE BLOODY DÉCOR.
MIND YOU, IT'S MEANT TO BE A CORPSE CUT DOWN FROM A GIBBET.
"MAKE DO AND MEND," AS MY MOTHER USED TO SAY.

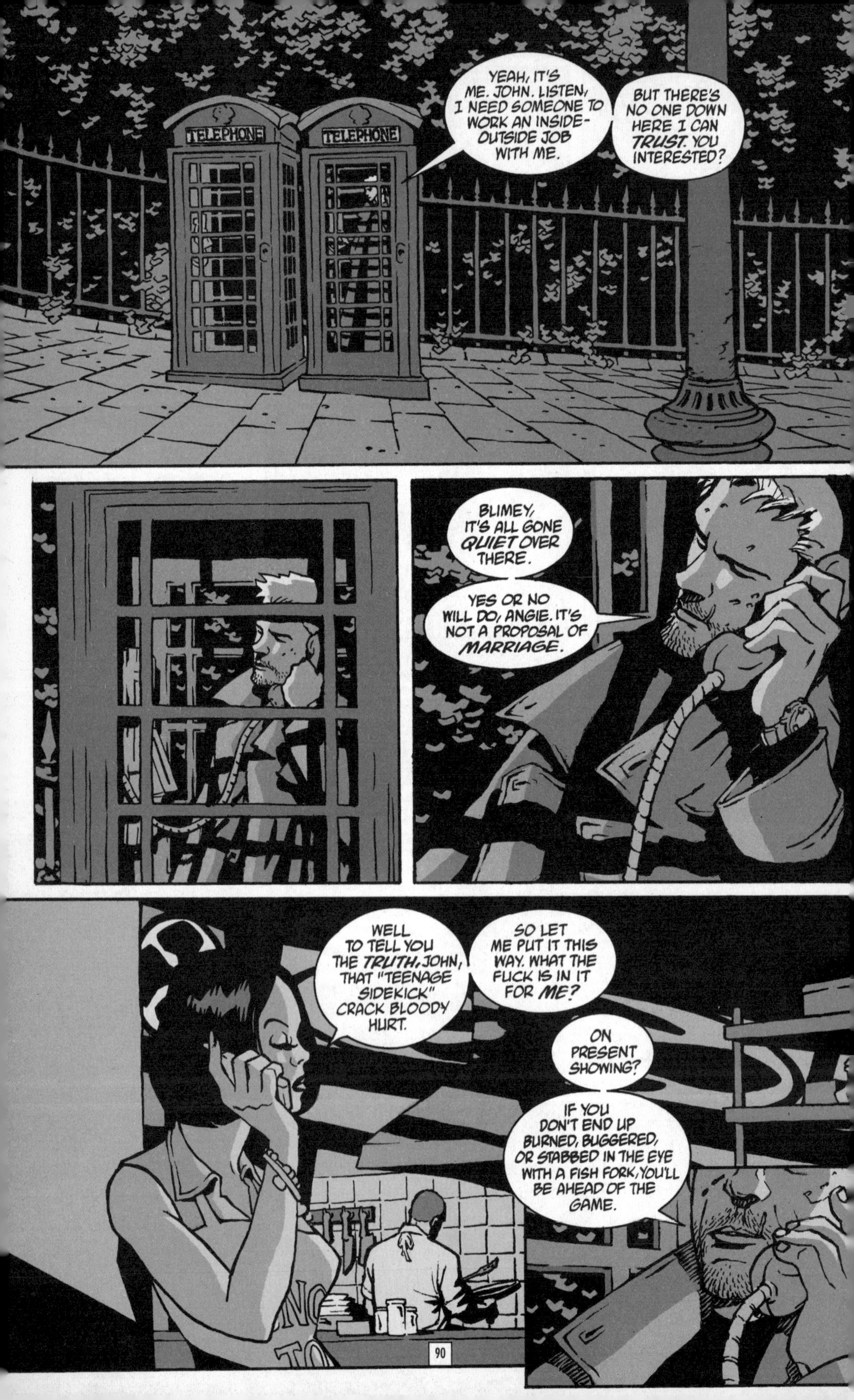
TELEPHONE
TELEPHONE
YEAH, IT'S ME. JOHN. LISTEN, I NEED SOMEONE TO WORK AN INSIDE-OUTSIDE JOB WITH ME.
BUT THERE'S NO ONE DOWN HERE I CAN TRUST. YOU INTERESTED?
BLIMEY, IT'S ALL GONE QUIET OVER THERE.
YES OR NO WILL DO, ANGIE. IT'S NOT A PROPOSAL OF MARRIAGE.
WELL TO TELL YOU THE TRUTH, JOHN, THAT "TEENAGE SIDEKICK" CRACK BLOODY HURT.
SO LET ME PUT IT THIS WAY. WHAT THE FUCK IS IN IT FOR ME?
ON PRESENT SHOWING?
IF YOU DON'T END UP BURNED, BUGGERED, OR STABBED IN THE EYE WITH A FISH FORK, YOU'LL BE AHEAD OF THE GAME.

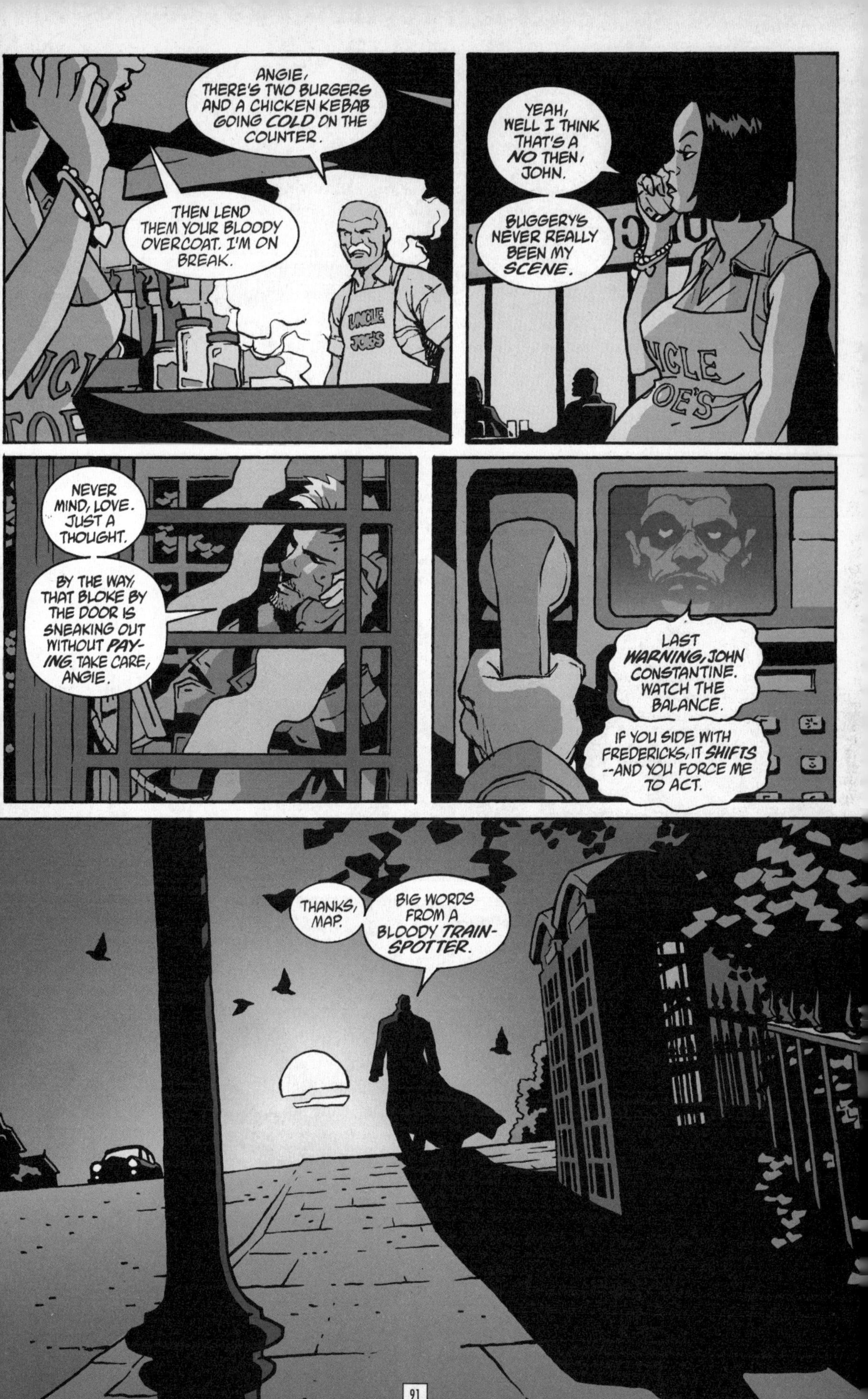

ANGIE, THERE'S TWO BURGERS AND A CHICKEN KEBAB GOING *COLD* ON THE COUNTER.
THEN LEND THEM YOUR BLOODY OVERCOAT. I'M ON BREAK.
UNCLE JOE'S
YEAH, WELL I THINK THAT'S A *NO* THEN, JOHN.
BUGGERY'S NEVER REALLY BEEN MY *SCENE*.
UNCLE JOE'S
NEVER MIND, LOVE. JUST A THOUGHT.
BY THE WAY, THAT BLOKE BY THE DOOR IS SNEAKING OUT WITHOUT *PAYING*. TAKE CARE, ANGIE.
LAST *WARNING*, JOHN CONSTANTINE. WATCH THE BALANCE.
IF YOU SIDE WITH FREDERICKS, IT *SHIFTS* --AND YOU FORCE ME TO ACT.
THANKS, MAP.
BIG WORDS FROM A BLOODY *TRAIN-SPOTTER*.

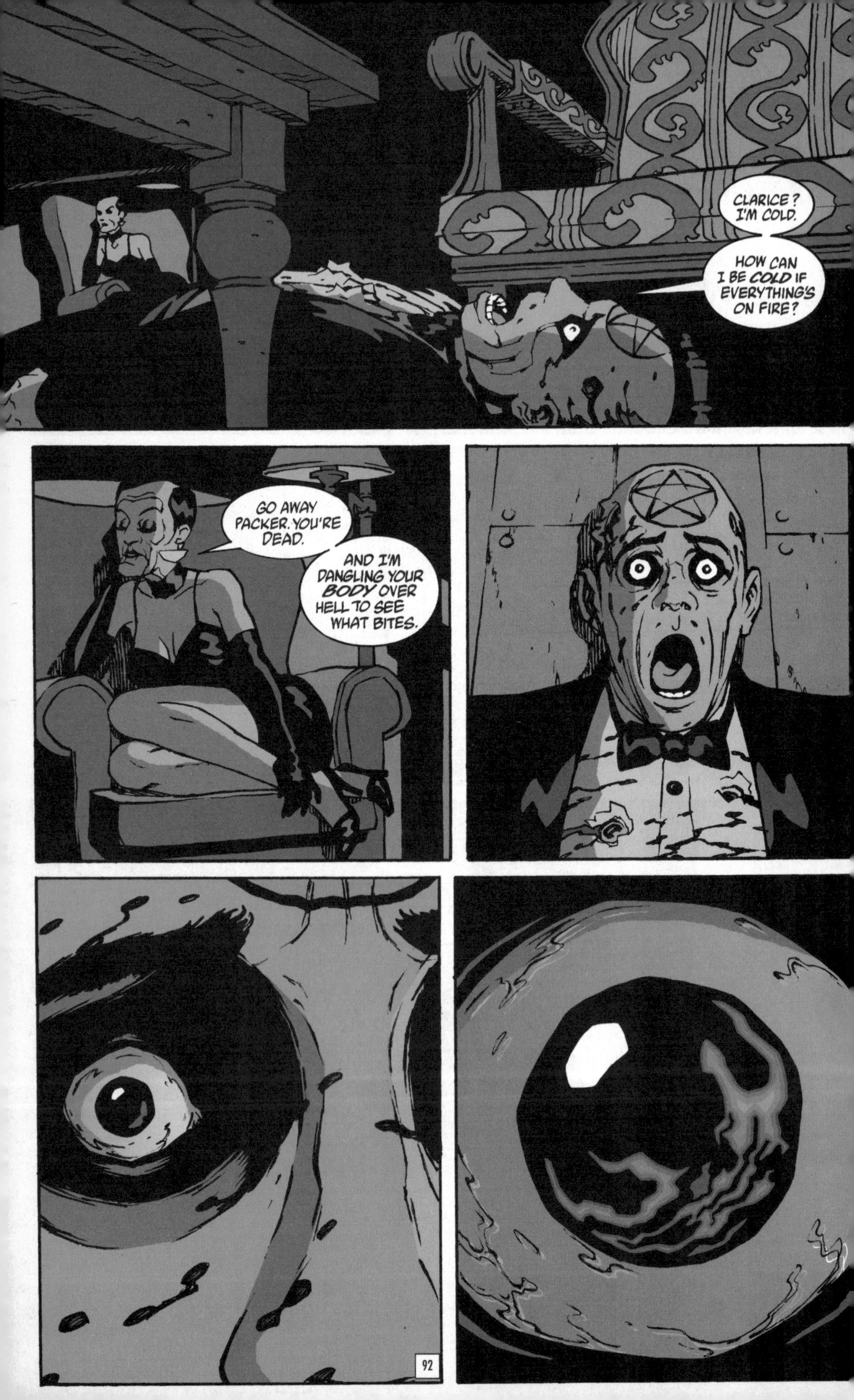
CLARICE? I'M COLD.
HOW CAN I BE COLD IF EVERYTHING'S ON FIRE?
GO AWAY PACKER. YOU'RE DEAD.
AND I'M DANGLING YOUR BODY OVER HELL TO SEE WHAT BITES.

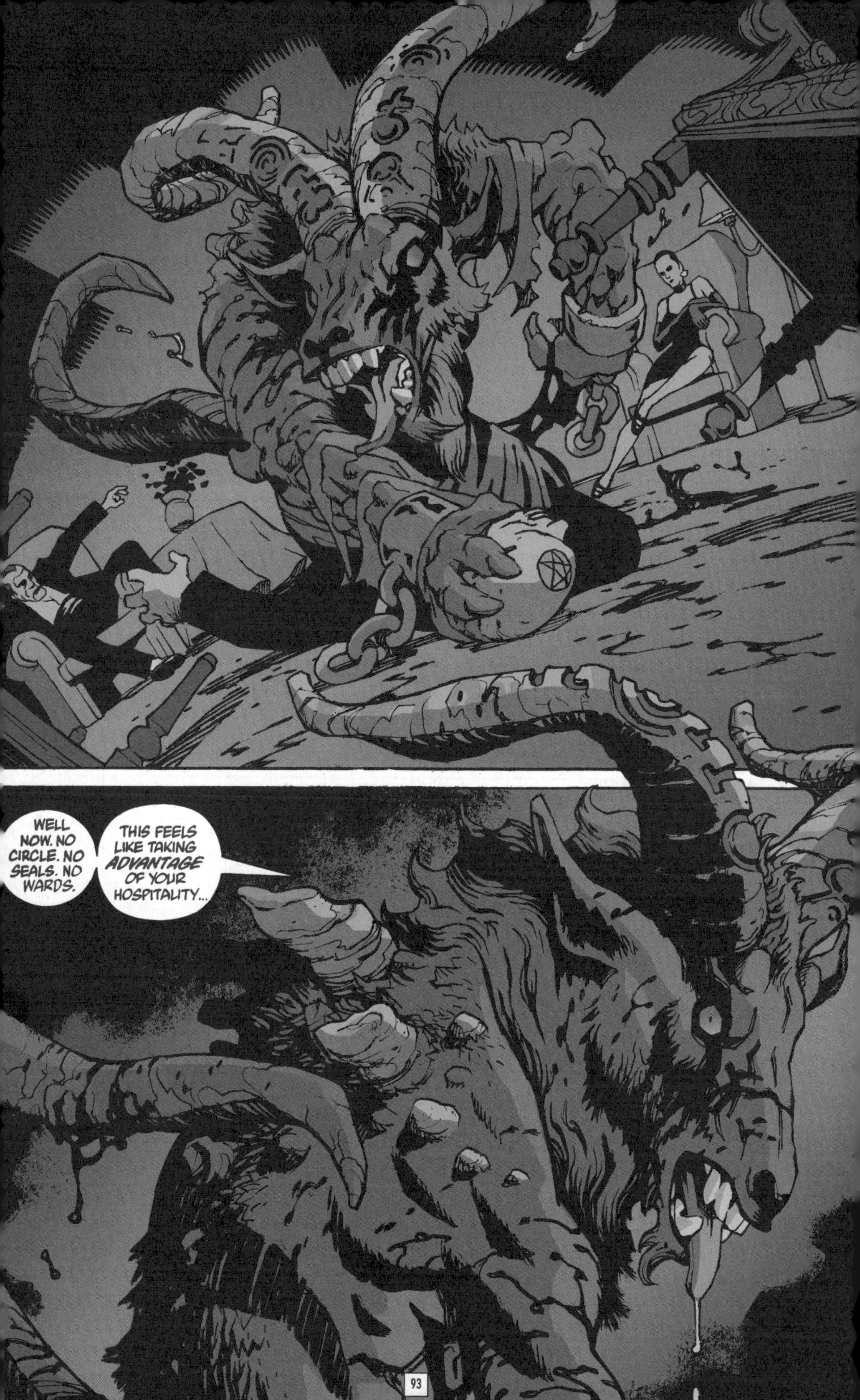
WELL NOW. NO CIRCLE. NO SEALS. NO WARDS.
THIS FEELS LIKE TAKING ADVANTAGE OF YOUR HOSPITALITY...

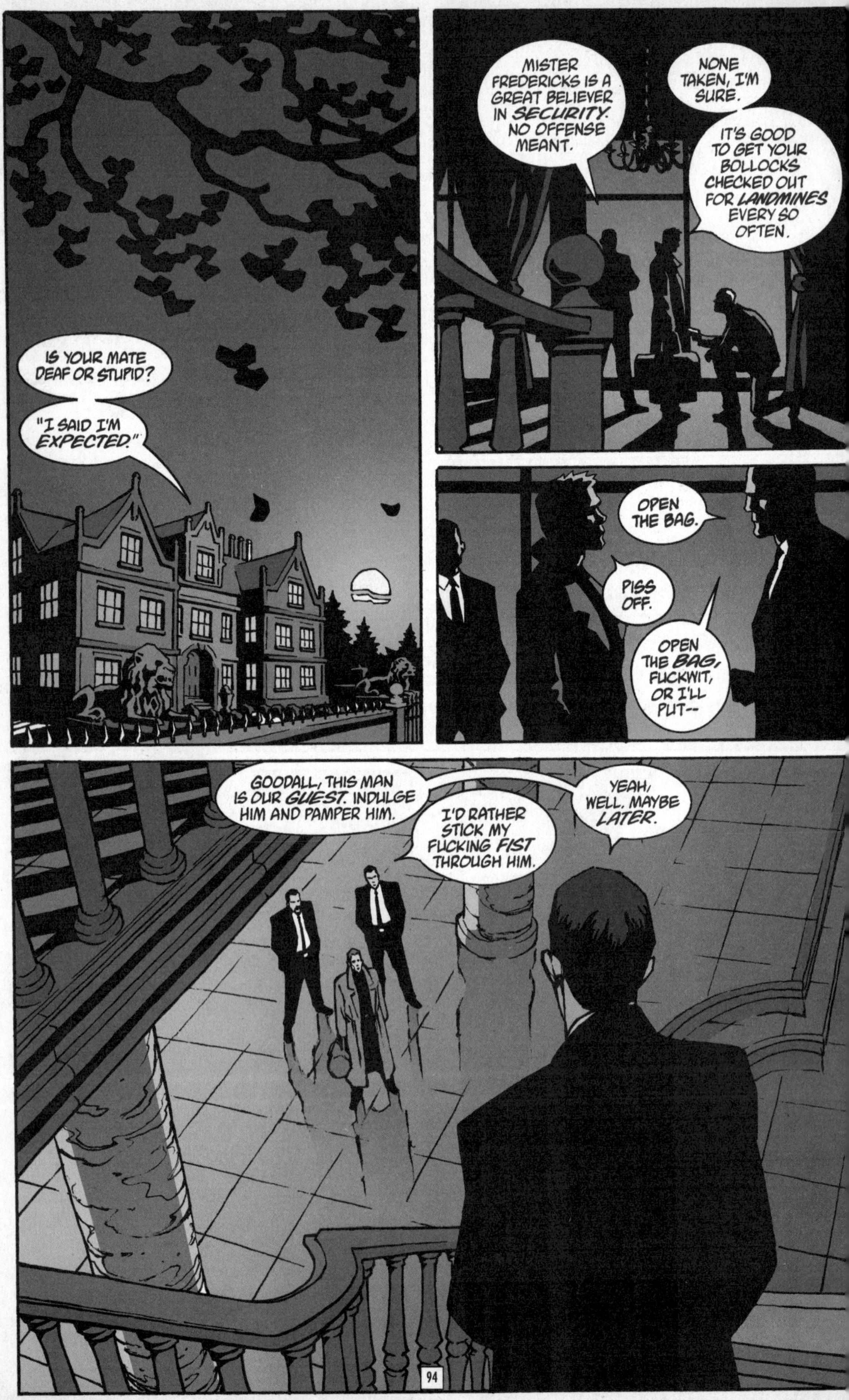
IS YOUR MATE DEAF OR STUPID?
"I SAID I'M EXPECTED."
MISTER FREDERICKS IS A GREAT BELIEVER IN SECURITY. NO OFFENSE MEANT.
NONE TAKEN, I'M SURE.
IT'S GOOD TO GET YOUR BOLLOCKS CHECKED OUT FOR LANDMINES EVERY SO OFTEN.
OPEN THE BAG.
PISS OFF.
OPEN THE BAG, FUCKWIT, OR I'LL PUT--
GOODALL, THIS MAN IS OUR GUEST. INDULGE HIM AND PAMPER HIM.
I'D RATHER STICK MY FUCKING FIST THROUGH HIM.
YEAH, WELL. MAYBE LATER.

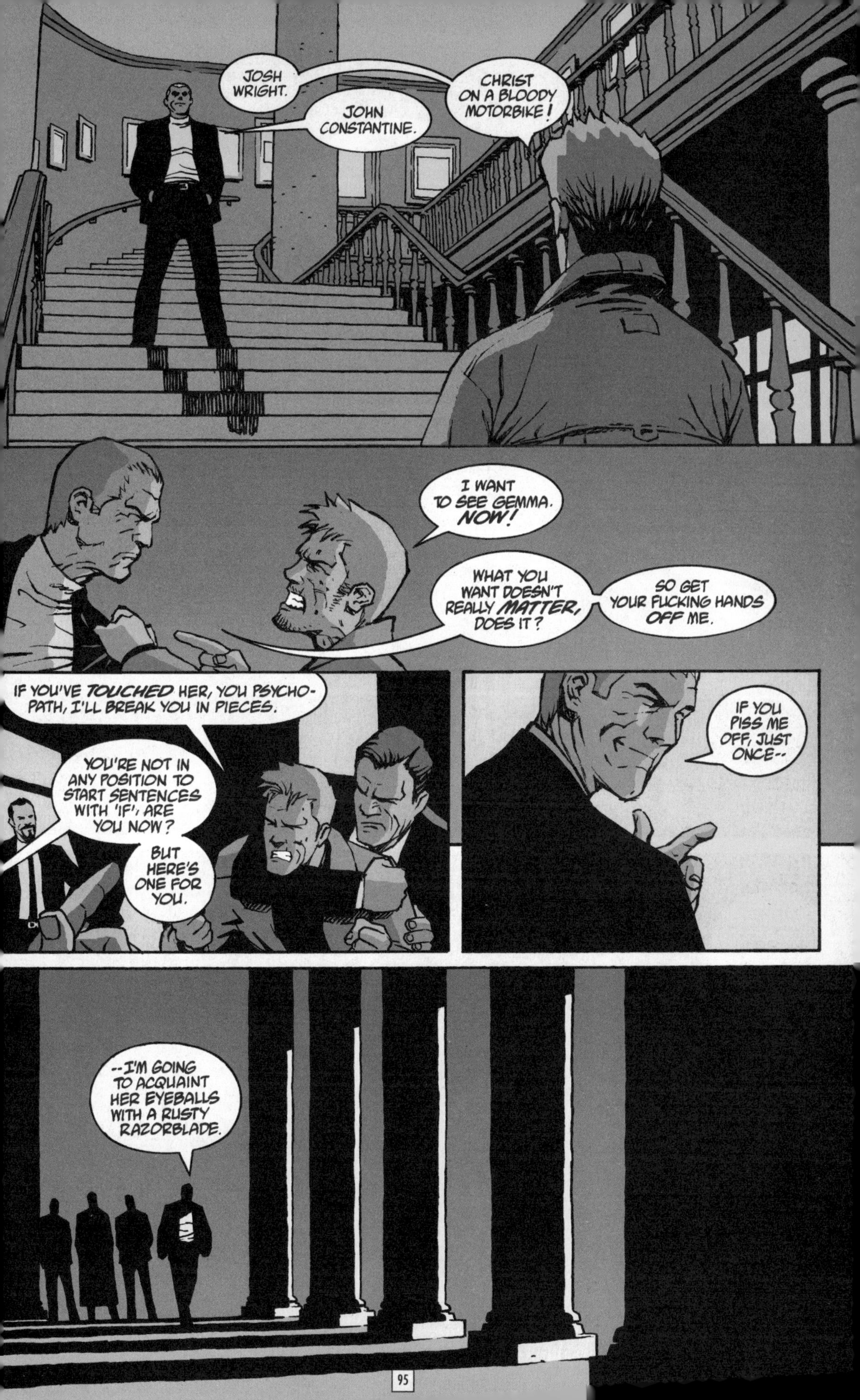
JOSH WRIGHT.
CHRIST ON A BLOODY MOTORBIKE!
JOHN CONSTANTINE.
I WANT TO SEE GEMMA. NOW!
WHAT YOU WANT DOESN'T REALLY MATTER, DOES IT?
SO GET YOUR FUCKING HANDS OFF ME.
IF YOU'VE TOUCHED HER, YOU PSYCHO-PATH, I'LL BREAK YOU IN PIECES.
YOU'RE NOT IN ANY POSITION TO START SENTENCES WITH 'IF', ARE YOU NOW?
BUT HERE'S ONE FOR YOU.
IF YOU PISS ME OFF, JUST ONCE--
--I'M GOING TO ACQUAINT HER EYEBALLS WITH A RUSTY RAZORBLADE.

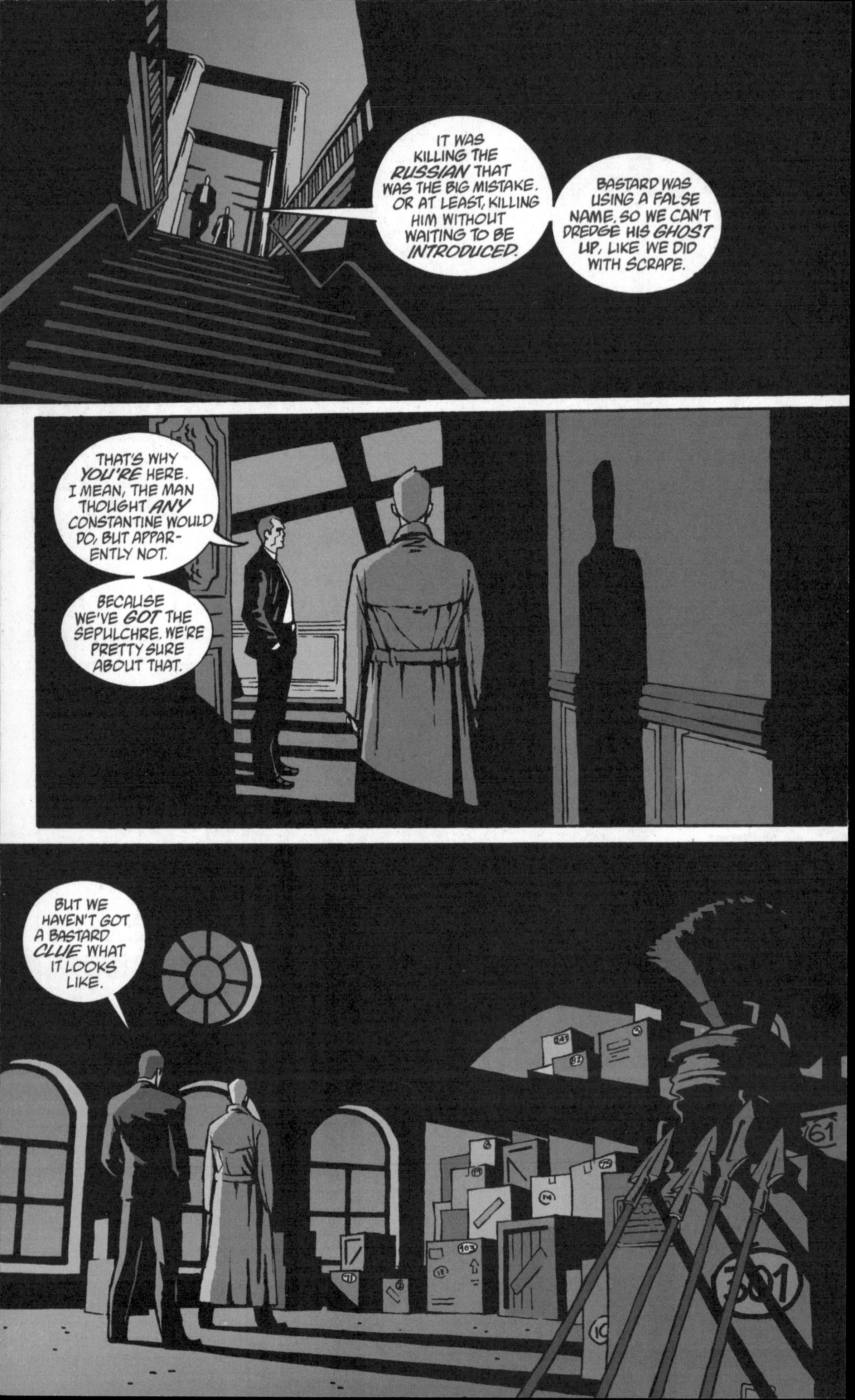
IT WAS KILLING THE RUSSIAN THAT WAS THE BIG MISTAKE. OR AT LEAST, KILLING HIM WITHOUT WAITING TO BE INTRODUCED.
BASTARD WAS USING A FALSE NAME. SO WE CAN'T DREDGE HIS GHOST UP, LIKE WE DID WITH SCRAPE.
THAT'S WHY YOU'RE HERE. I MEAN, THE MAN THOUGHT ANY CONSTANTINE WOULD DO, BUT APPARENTLY NOT.
BECAUSE WE'VE GOT THE SEPULCHRE. WE'RE PRETTY SURE ABOUT THAT.
BUT WE HAVEN'T GOT A BASTARD CLUE WHAT IT LOOKS LIKE.

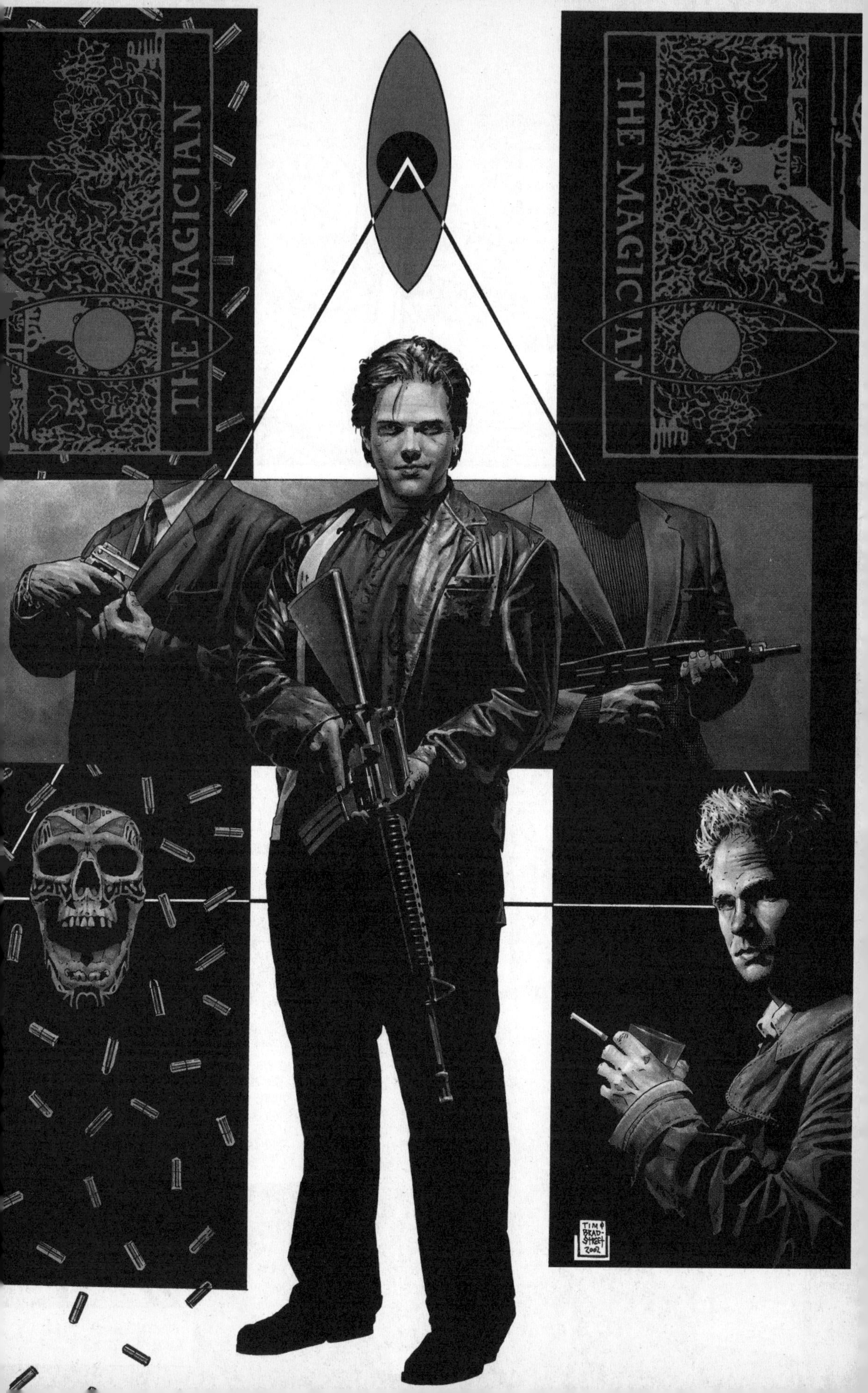
THE MAGICIAN
THE MAGICIAN
TIM BRAD-STREET 2002

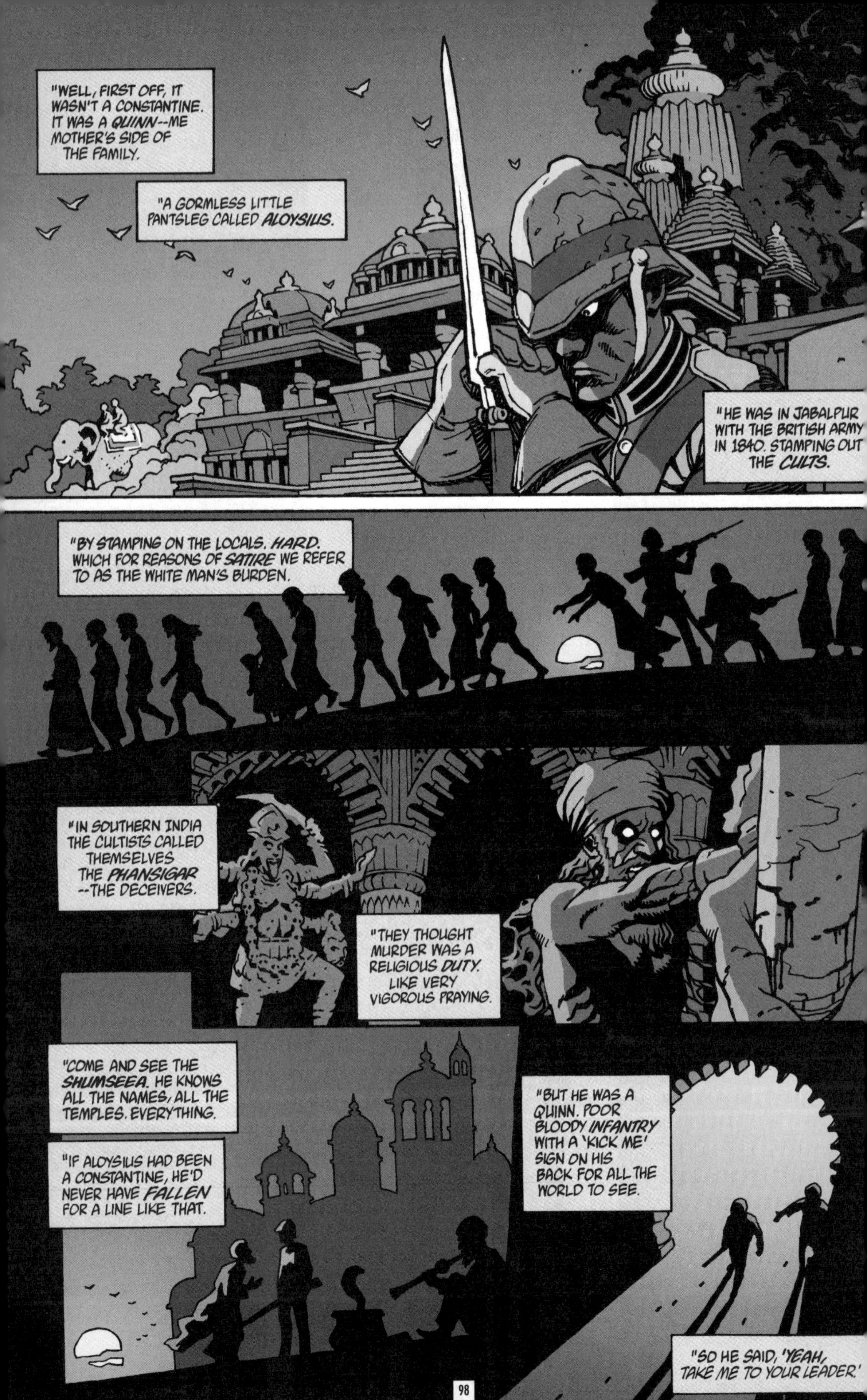
"WELL, FIRST OFF, IT WASN'T A CONSTANTINE. IT WAS A QUINN--ME MOTHER'S SIDE OF THE FAMILY.
"A GORMLESS LITTLE PANTSLEG CALLED ALOYSIUS.
"HE WAS IN JABALPUR WITH THE BRITISH ARMY IN 1840. STAMPING OUT THE CULTS.
"BY STAMPING ON THE LOCALS. HARD. WHICH FOR REASONS OF SATIRE WE REFER TO AS THE WHITE MAN'S BURDEN.
"IN SOUTHERN INDIA THE CULTISTS CALLED THEMSELVES THE PHANSIGAR --THE DECEIVERS.
"THEY THOUGHT MURDER WAS A RELIGIOUS DUTY. LIKE VERY VIGOROUS PRAYING.
"COME AND SEE THE SHUMSEEA. HE KNOWS ALL THE NAMES, ALL THE TEMPLES. EVERYTHING.
"IF ALOYSIUS HAD BEEN A CONSTANTINE, HE'D NEVER HAVE FALLEN FOR A LINE LIKE THAT.
"BUT HE WAS A QUINN. POOR BLOODY INFANTRY WITH A 'KICK ME' SIGN ON HIS BACK FOR ALL THE WORLD TO SEE.
"SO HE SAID, 'YEAH, TAKE ME TO YOUR LEADER.'

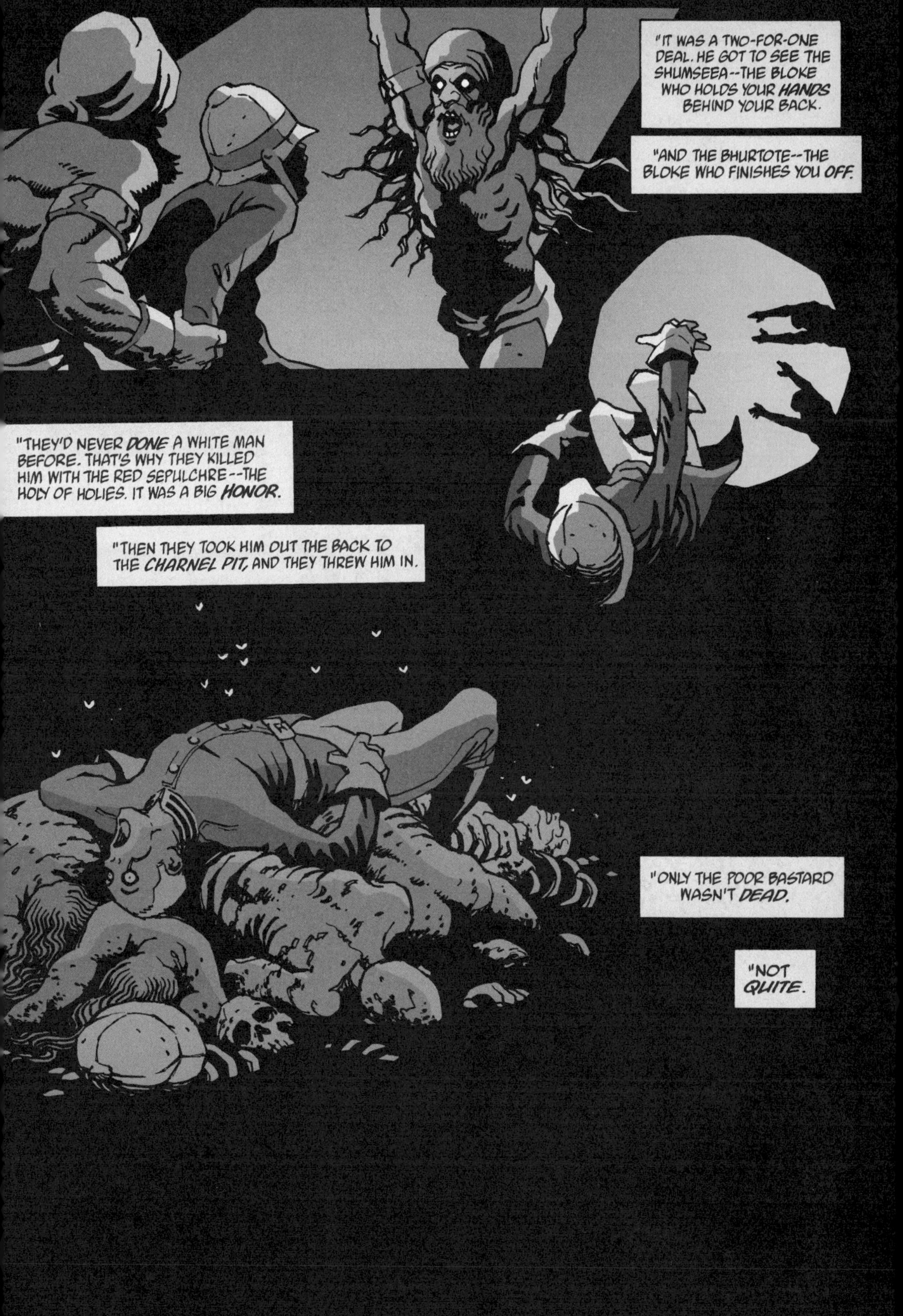
"IT WAS A TWO-FOR-ONE DEAL. HE GOT TO SEE THE SHUMSEEA--THE BLOKE WHO HOLDS YOUR *HANDS* BEHIND YOUR BACK.
"AND THE BHURTOTE--THE BLOKE WHO FINISHES YOU *OFF*.
"THEY'D NEVER *DONE* A WHITE MAN BEFORE. THAT'S WHY THEY KILLED HIM WITH THE RED SEPULCHRE--THE HOLY OF HOLIES. IT WAS A BIG *HONOR*.
"THEN THEY TOOK HIM OUT THE BACK TO THE *CHARNEL PIT,* AND THEY THREW HIM IN.
"ONLY THE POOR BASTARD WASN'T *DEAD*.
"NOT *QUITE*.

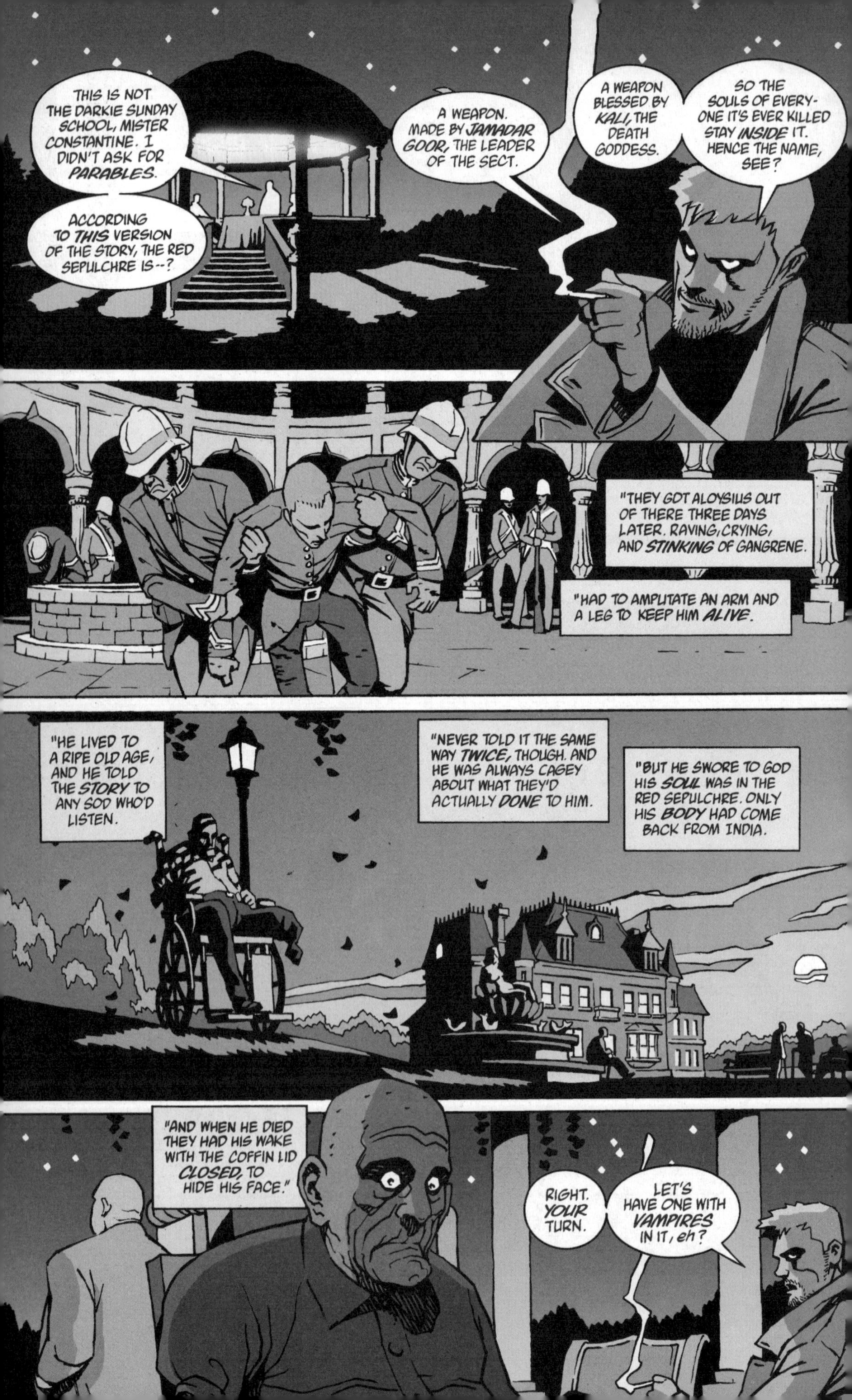
THIS IS NOT THE DARKIE SUNDAY SCHOOL, MISTER CONSTANTINE. I DIDN'T ASK FOR PARABLES.
ACCORDING TO THIS VERSION OF THE STORY, THE RED SEPULCHRE IS--?
A WEAPON. MADE BY JAMADAR GOOR, THE LEADER OF THE SECT.
A WEAPON BLESSED BY KALI, THE DEATH GODDESS.
SO THE SOULS OF EVERY-ONE IT'S EVER KILLED STAY INSIDE IT. HENCE THE NAME, SEE?
"THEY GOT ALOYSIUS OUT OF THERE THREE DAYS LATER. RAVING, CRYING, AND STINKING OF GANGRENE.
"HAD TO AMPUTATE AN ARM AND A LEG TO KEEP HIM ALIVE.
"HE LIVED TO A RIPE OLD AGE, AND HE TOLD THE STORY TO ANY SOD WHO'D LISTEN.
"NEVER TOLD IT THE SAME WAY TWICE, THOUGH. AND HE WAS ALWAYS CAGEY ABOUT WHAT THEY'D ACTUALLY DONE TO HIM.
"BUT HE SWORE TO GOD HIS SOUL WAS IN THE RED SEPULCHRE. ONLY HIS BODY HAD COME BACK FROM INDIA.
"AND WHEN HE DIED THEY HAD HIS WAKE WITH THE COFFIN LID CLOSED, TO HIDE HIS FACE."
RIGHT. YOUR TURN.
LET'S HAVE ONE WITH VAMPIRES IN IT, eh?

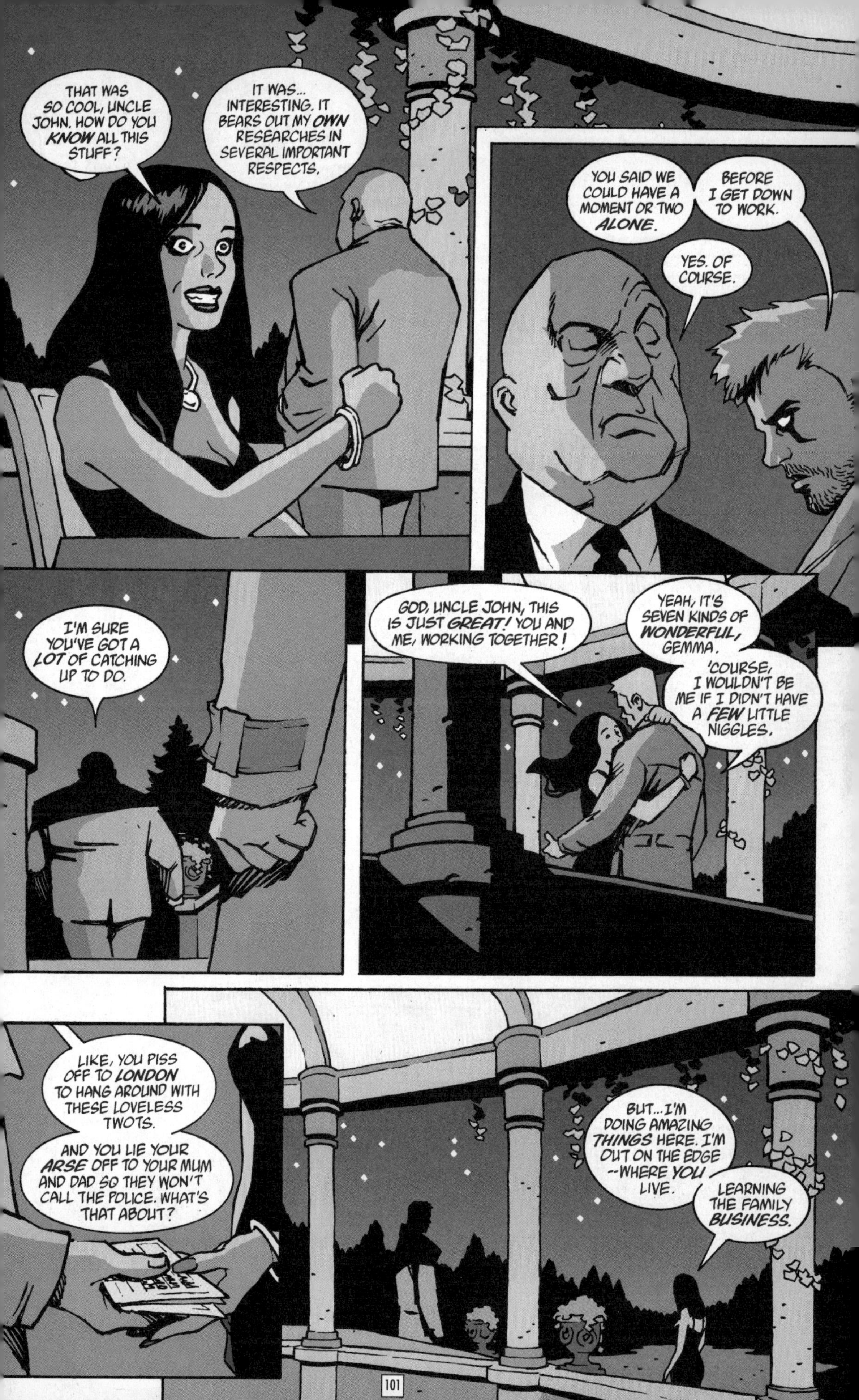
THAT WAS SO COOL, UNCLE JOHN. HOW DO YOU KNOW ALL THIS STUFF?
IT WAS... INTERESTING. IT BEARS OUT MY OWN RESEARCHES IN SEVERAL IMPORTANT RESPECTS.
YOU SAID WE COULD HAVE A MOMENT OR TWO ALONE.
BEFORE I GET DOWN TO WORK.
YES. OF COURSE.
I'M SURE YOU'VE GOT A LOT OF CATCHING UP TO DO.
GOD, UNCLE JOHN, THIS IS JUST GREAT! YOU AND ME, WORKING TOGETHER!
YEAH, IT'S SEVEN KINDS OF WONDERFUL, GEMMA.
'COURSE, I WOULDN'T BE ME IF I DIDN'T HAVE A FEW LITTLE NIGGLES.
LIKE, YOU PISS OFF TO LONDON TO HANG AROUND WITH THESE LOVELESS TWOTS.
AND YOU LIE YOUR ARSE OFF TO YOUR MUM AND DAD SO THEY WON'T CALL THE POLICE. WHAT'S THAT ABOUT?
BUT... I'M DOING AMAZING THINGS HERE. I'M OUT ON THE EDGE --WHERE YOU LIVE.
LEARNING THE FAMILY BUSINESS.

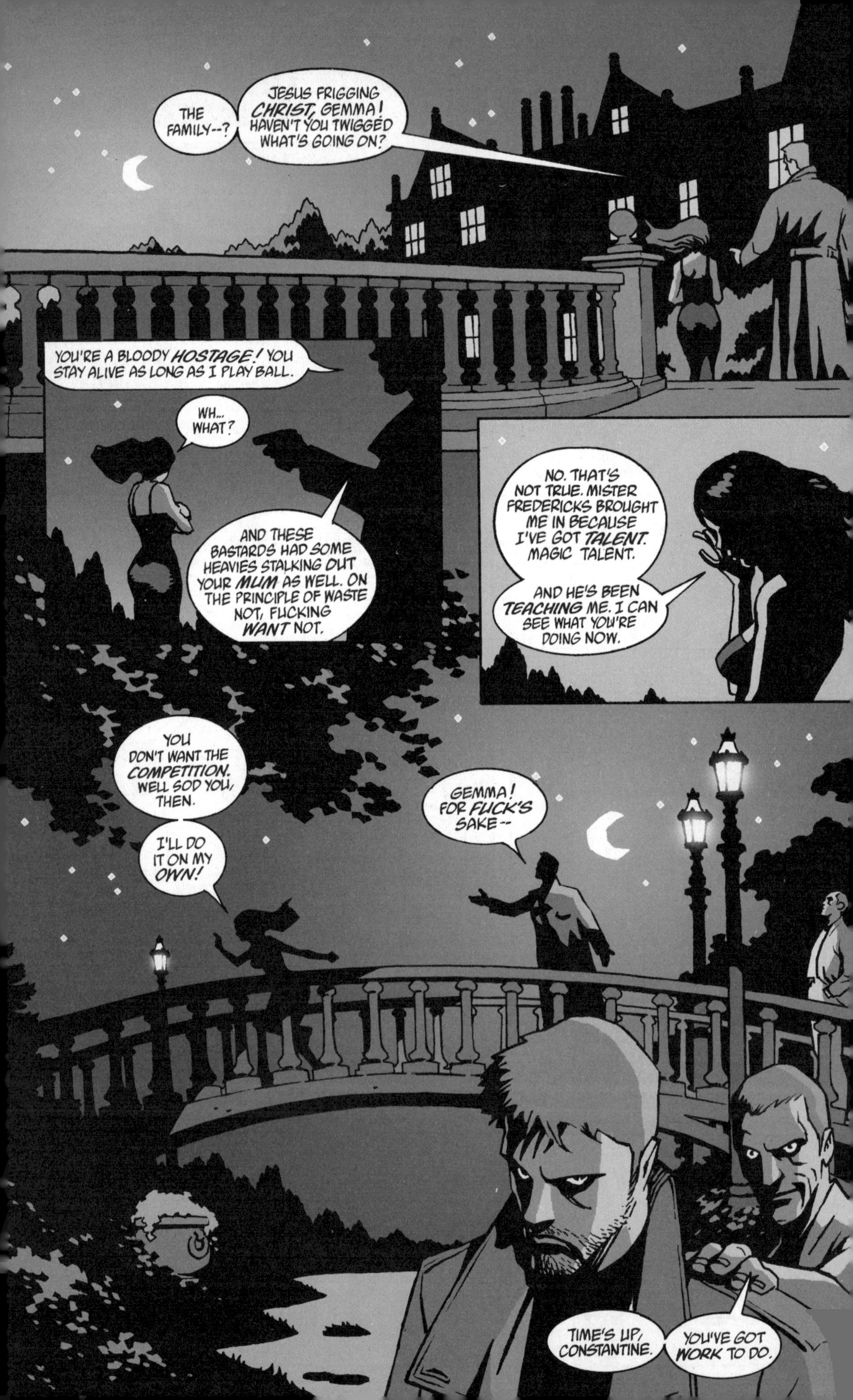
THE FAMILY--?
JESUS FRIGGING CHRIST, GEMMA! HAVEN'T YOU TWIGGED WHAT'S GOING ON?
YOU'RE A BLOODY HOSTAGE! YOU STAY ALIVE AS LONG AS I PLAY BALL.
WH... WHAT?
AND THESE BASTARDS HAD SOME HEAVIES STALKING OUT YOUR MUM AS WELL. ON THE PRINCIPLE OF WASTE NOT, FUCKING WANT NOT.
NO. THAT'S NOT TRUE. MISTER FREDERICKS BROUGHT ME IN BECAUSE I'VE GOT TALENT. MAGIC TALENT.
AND HE'S BEEN TEACHING ME. I CAN SEE WHAT YOU'RE DOING NOW.
YOU DON'T WANT THE COMPETITION. WELL SOD YOU, THEN.
I'LL DO IT ON MY OWN!
GEMMA! FOR FUCK'S SAKE--
TIME'S UP, CONSTANTINE.
YOU'VE GOT WORK TO DO.

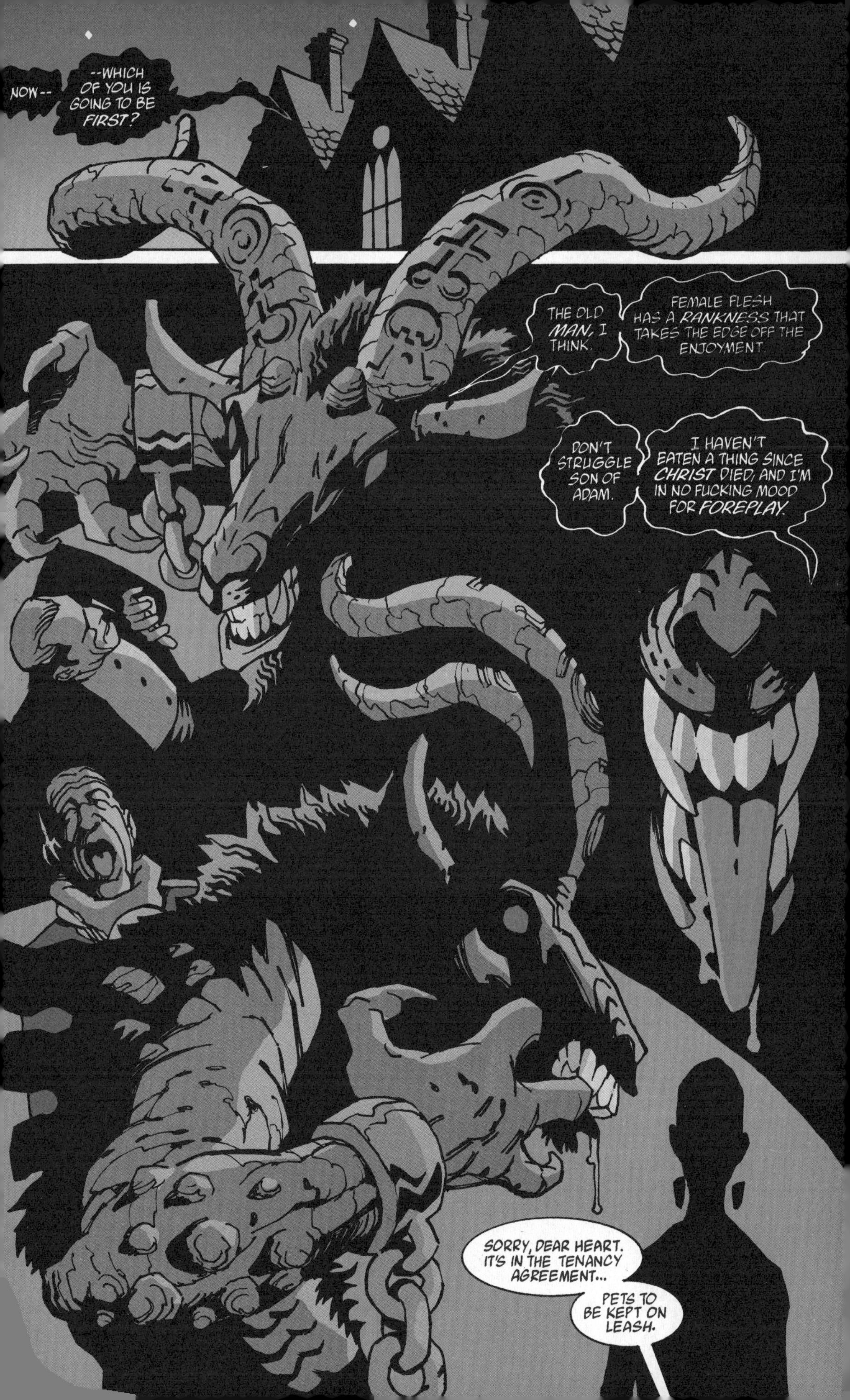
NOW--
--WHICH OF YOU IS GOING TO BE FIRST?
THE OLD MAN, I THINK.
FEMALE FLESH HAS A RANKNESS THAT TAKES THE EDGE OFF THE ENJOYMENT.
DON'T STRUGGLE SON OF ADAM.
I HAVEN'T EATEN A THING SINCE CHRIST DIED, AND I'M IN NO FUCKING MOOD FOR FOREPLAY.
SORRY, DEAR HEART. IT'S IN THE TENANCY AGREEMENT...
PETS TO BE KEPT ON LEASH.

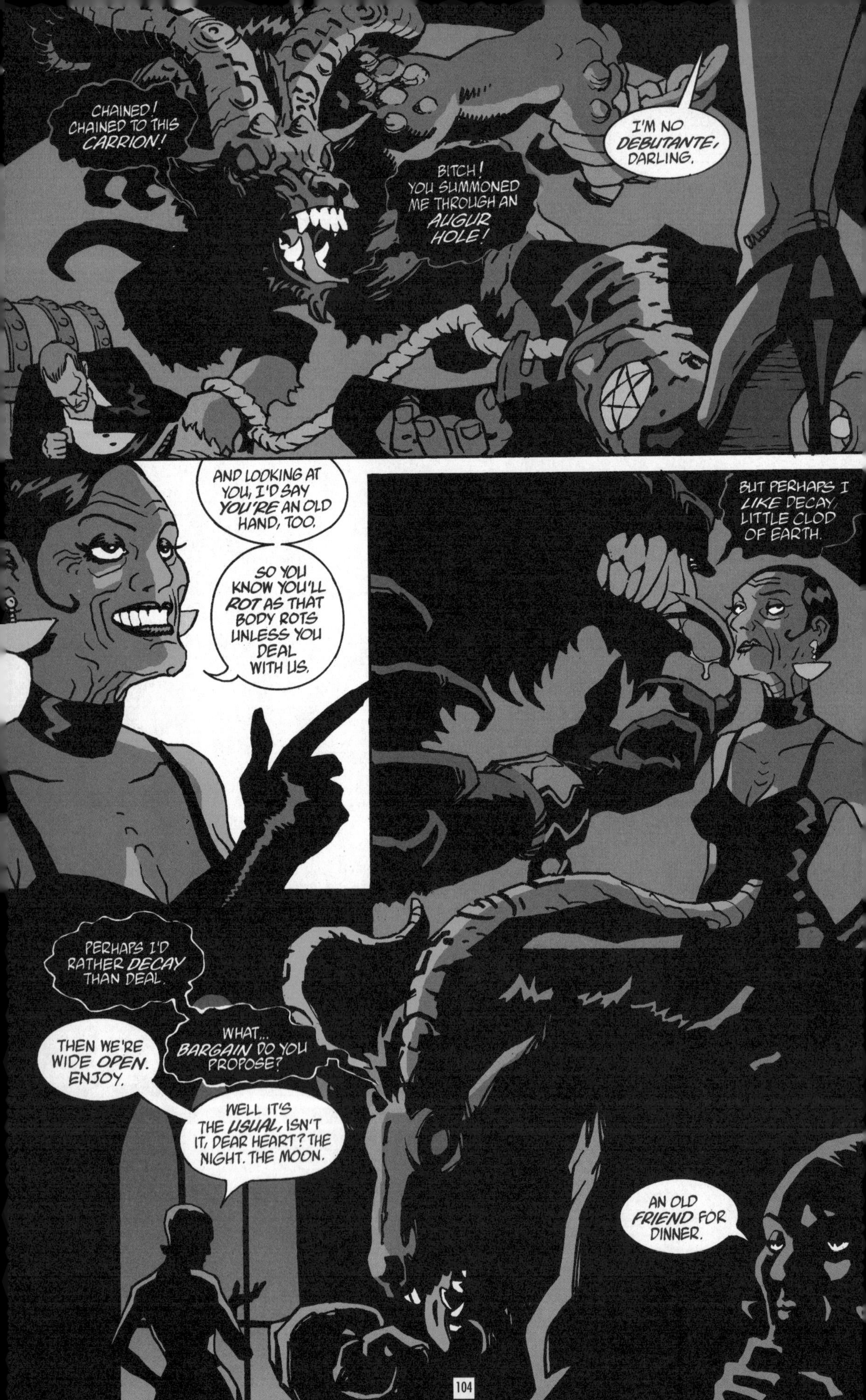

CHAINED! CHAINED TO THIS CARRION!
BITCH! YOU SUMMONED ME THROUGH AN AUGUR HOLE!
I'M NO DEBUTANTE, DARLING.
AND LOOKING AT YOU, I'D SAY YOU'RE AN OLD HAND, TOO.
SO YOU KNOW YOU'LL ROT AS THAT BODY ROTS UNLESS YOU DEAL WITH US.
BUT PERHAPS I LIKE DECAY, LITTLE CLOD OF EARTH.
PERHAPS I'D RATHER DECAY THAN DEAL.
THEN WE'RE WIDE OPEN. ENJOY.
WHAT... BARGAIN DO YOU PROPOSE?
WELL IT'S THE USUAL, ISN'T IT, DEAR HEART? THE NIGHT. THE MOON.
AN OLD FRIEND FOR DINNER.

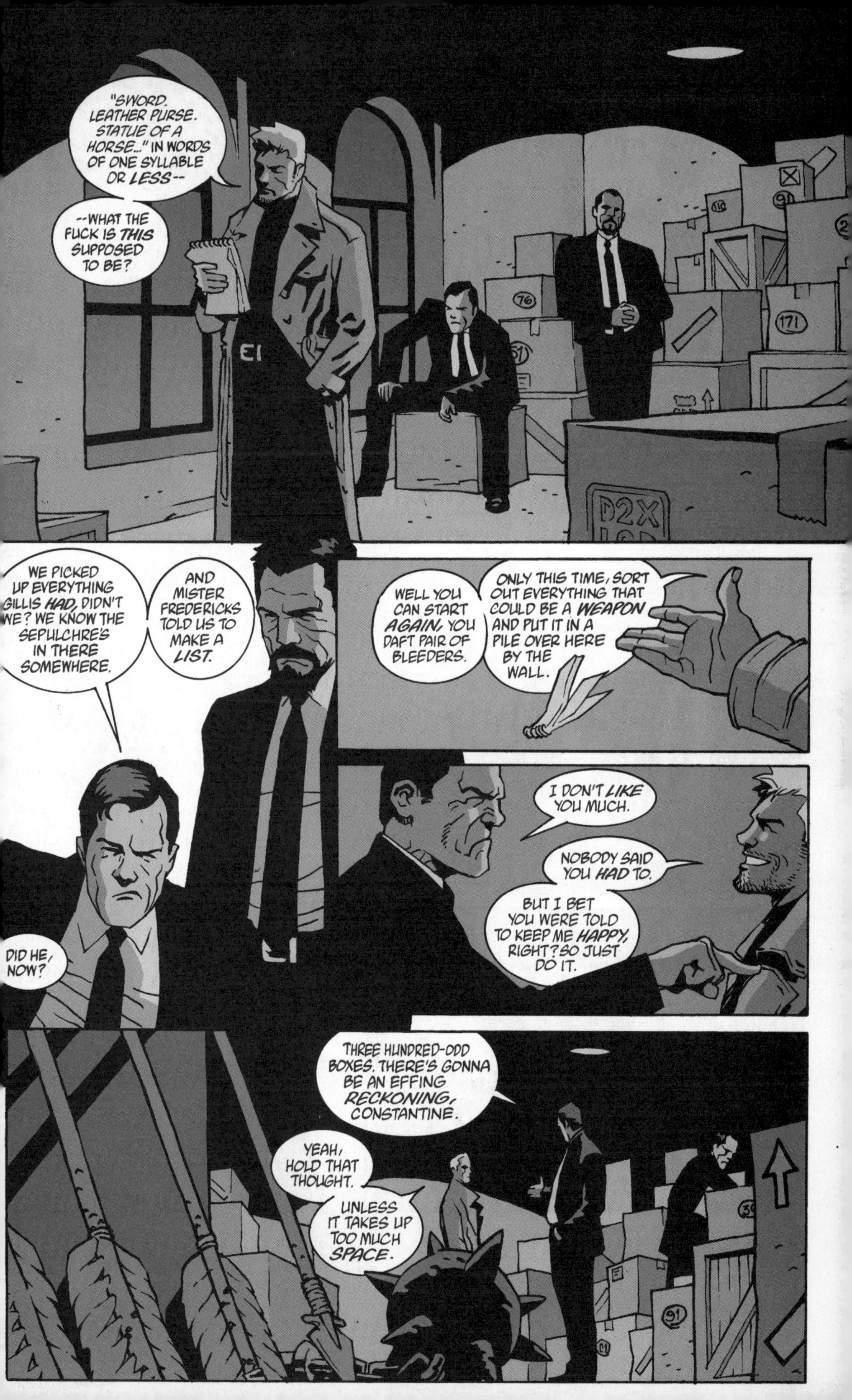

"SWORD. LEATHER PURSE. STATUE OF A HORSE..." IN WORDS OF ONE SYLLABLE OR LESS--
--WHAT THE FUCK IS THIS SUPPOSED TO BE?
WE PICKED UP EVERYTHING GILLIS HAD, DIDN'T WE? WE KNOW THE SEPULCHRE'S IN THERE SOMEWHERE.
AND MISTER FREDERICKS TOLD US TO MAKE A LIST.
DID HE, NOW?
WELL YOU CAN START AGAIN, YOU DAFT PAIR OF BLEEDERS.
ONLY THIS TIME, SORT OUT EVERYTHING THAT COULD BE A WEAPON AND PUT IT IN A PILE OVER HERE BY THE WALL.
I DON'T LIKE YOU MUCH.
NOBODY SAID YOU HAD TO.
BUT I BET YOU WERE TOLD TO KEEP ME HAPPY, RIGHT? SO JUST DO IT.
THREE HUNDRED-ODD BOXES. THERE'S GONNA BE AN EFFING RECKONING, CONSTANTINE.
YEAH, HOLD THAT THOUGHT.
UNLESS IT TAKES UP TOO MUCH SPACE.

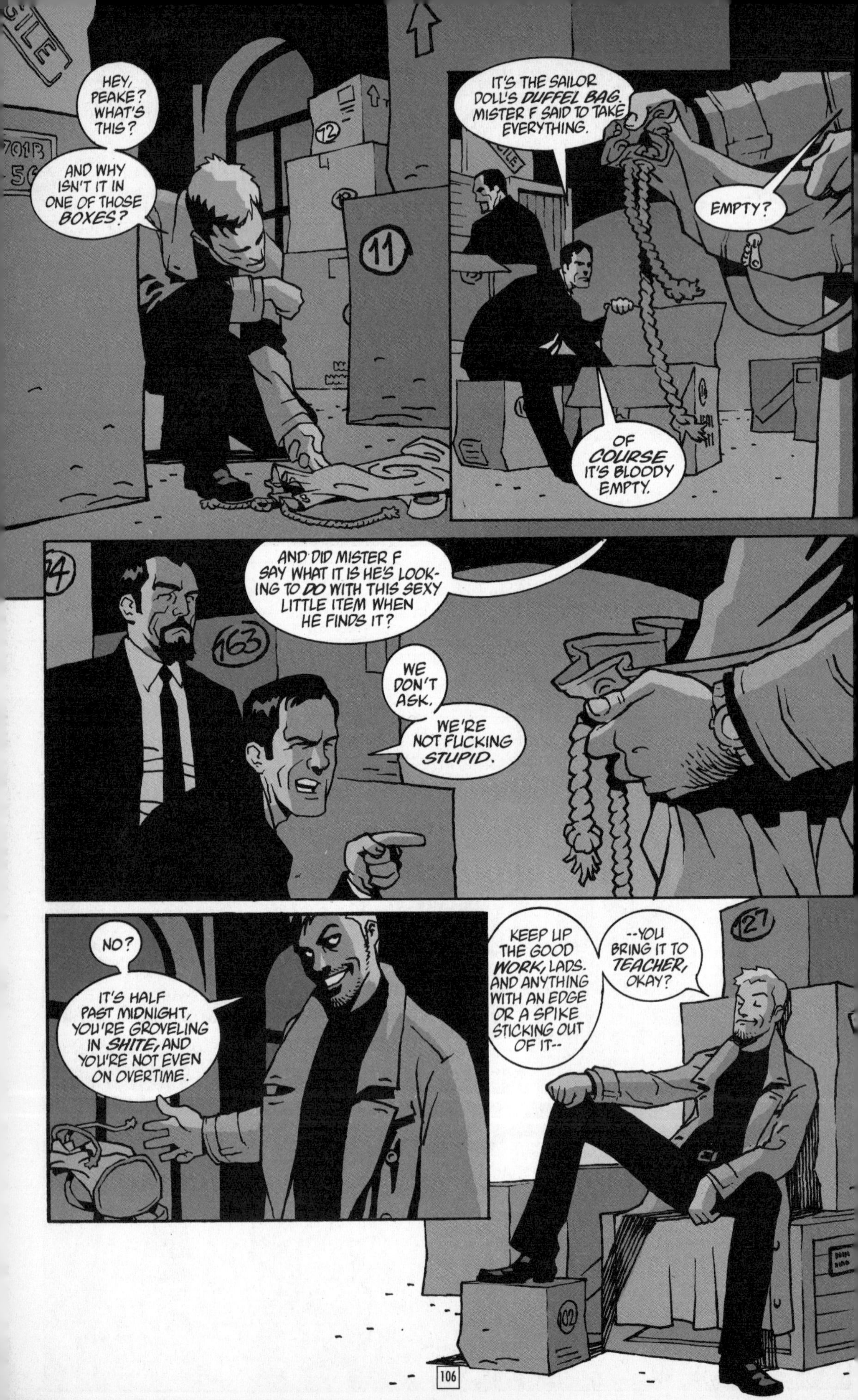
HEY, PEAKE? WHAT'S THIS?
AND WHY ISN'T IT IN ONE OF THOSE BOXES?
IT'S THE SAILOR DOLL'S DUFFEL BAG. MISTER F SAID TO TAKE EVERYTHING.
EMPTY?
OF COURSE IT'S BLOODY EMPTY.
AND DID MISTER F SAY WHAT IT IS HE'S LOOKING TO DO WITH THIS SEXY LITTLE ITEM WHEN HE FINDS IT?
WE DON'T ASK.
WE'RE NOT FUCKING STUPID.
NO?
IT'S HALF PAST MIDNIGHT, YOU'RE GROVELING IN SHITE, AND YOU'RE NOT EVEN ON OVERTIME.
KEEP UP THE GOOD WORK, LADS. AND ANYTHING WITH AN EDGE OR A SPIKE STICKING OUT OF IT--
--YOU BRING IT TO TEACHER, OKAY?

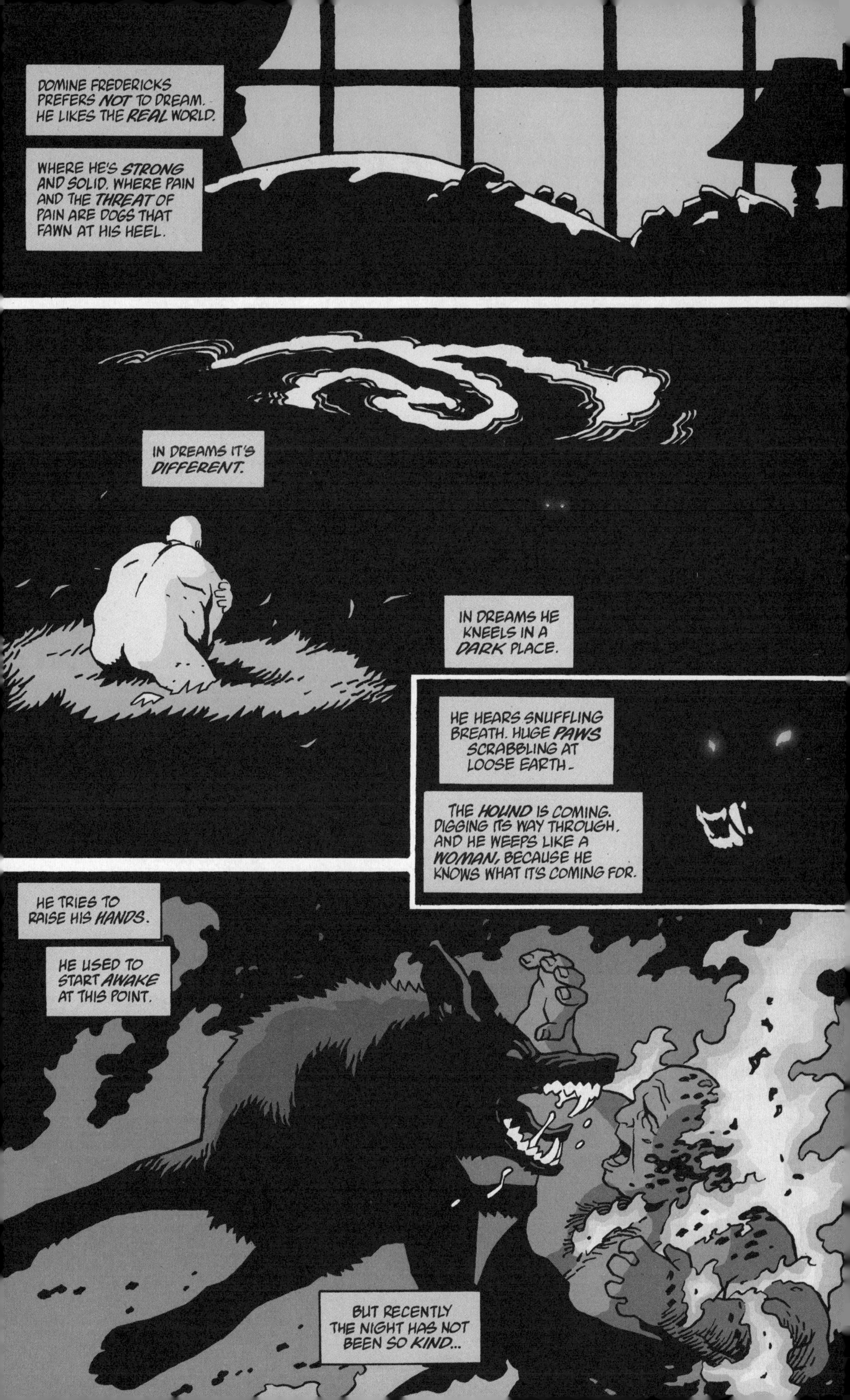
DOMINE FREDERICKS PREFERS *NOT* TO DREAM. HE LIKES THE *REAL* WORLD.
WHERE HE'S *STRONG* AND SOLID. WHERE PAIN AND THE *THREAT* OF PAIN ARE DOGS THAT FAWN AT HIS HEEL.
IN DREAMS IT'S *DIFFERENT*.
IN DREAMS HE KNEELS IN A *DARK* PLACE.
HE HEARS SNUFFLING BREATH. HUGE *PAWS* SCRABBLING AT LOOSE EARTH -
THE *HOUND* IS COMING. DIGGING ITS WAY THROUGH. AND HE WEEPS LIKE A *WOMAN,* BECAUSE HE KNOWS WHAT IT'S COMING FOR.
HE TRIES TO RAISE HIS *HANDS*.
HE USED TO START *AWAKE* AT THIS POINT.
BUT RECENTLY THE NIGHT HAS NOT BEEN SO *KIND*...

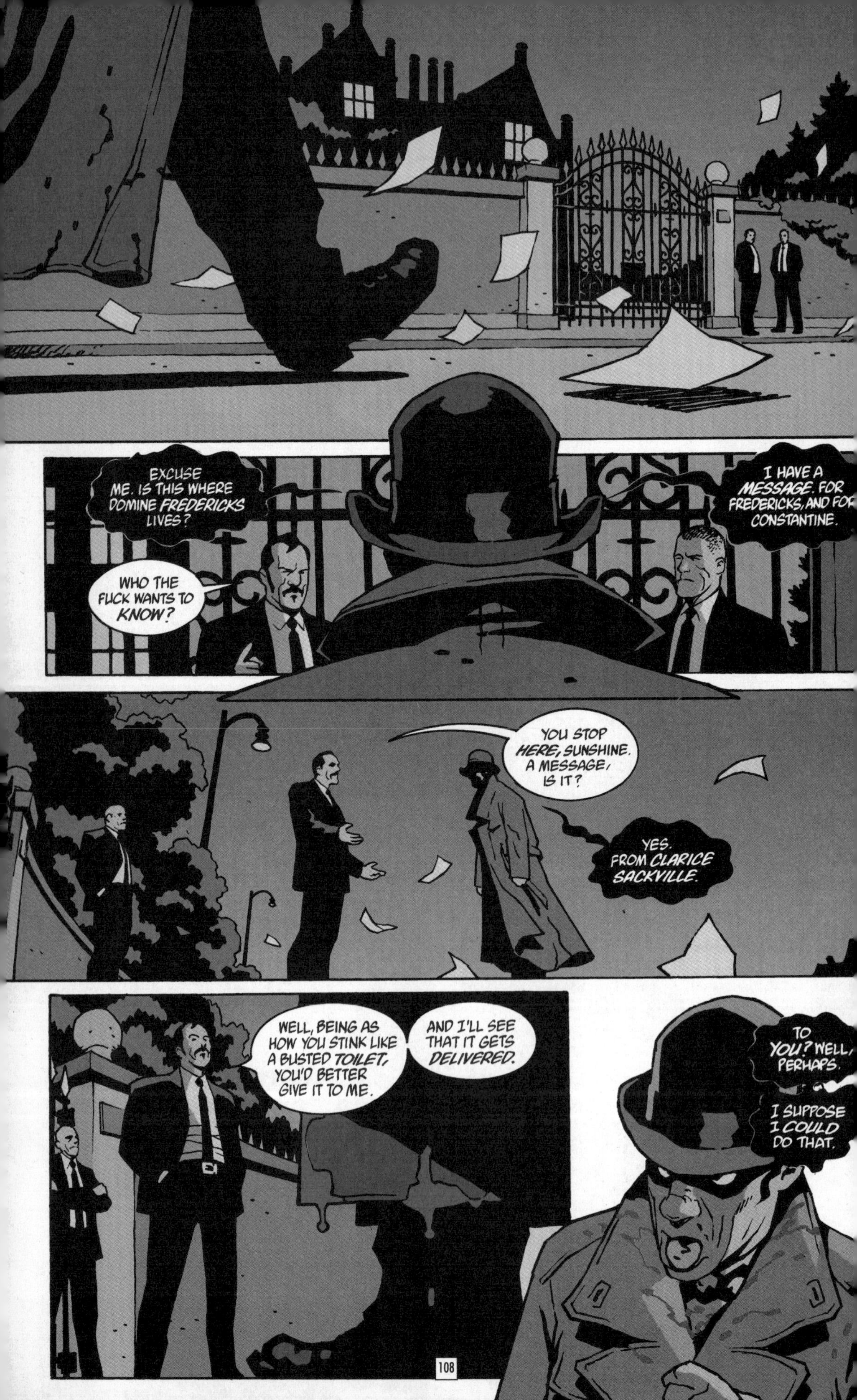
EXCUSE ME. IS THIS WHERE DOMINE FREDERICKS LIVES?
I HAVE A MESSAGE. FOR FREDERICKS, AND FOR CONSTANTINE.
WHO THE FUCK WANTS TO KNOW?
YOU STOP HERE, SUNSHINE. A MESSAGE, IS IT?
YES. FROM CLARICE SACKVILLE.
WELL, BEING AS HOW YOU STINK LIKE A BUSTED TOILET, YOU'D BETTER GIVE IT TO ME.
AND I'LL SEE THAT IT GETS DELIVERED.
TO YOU? WELL, PERHAPS.
I SUPPOSE I COULD DO THAT.

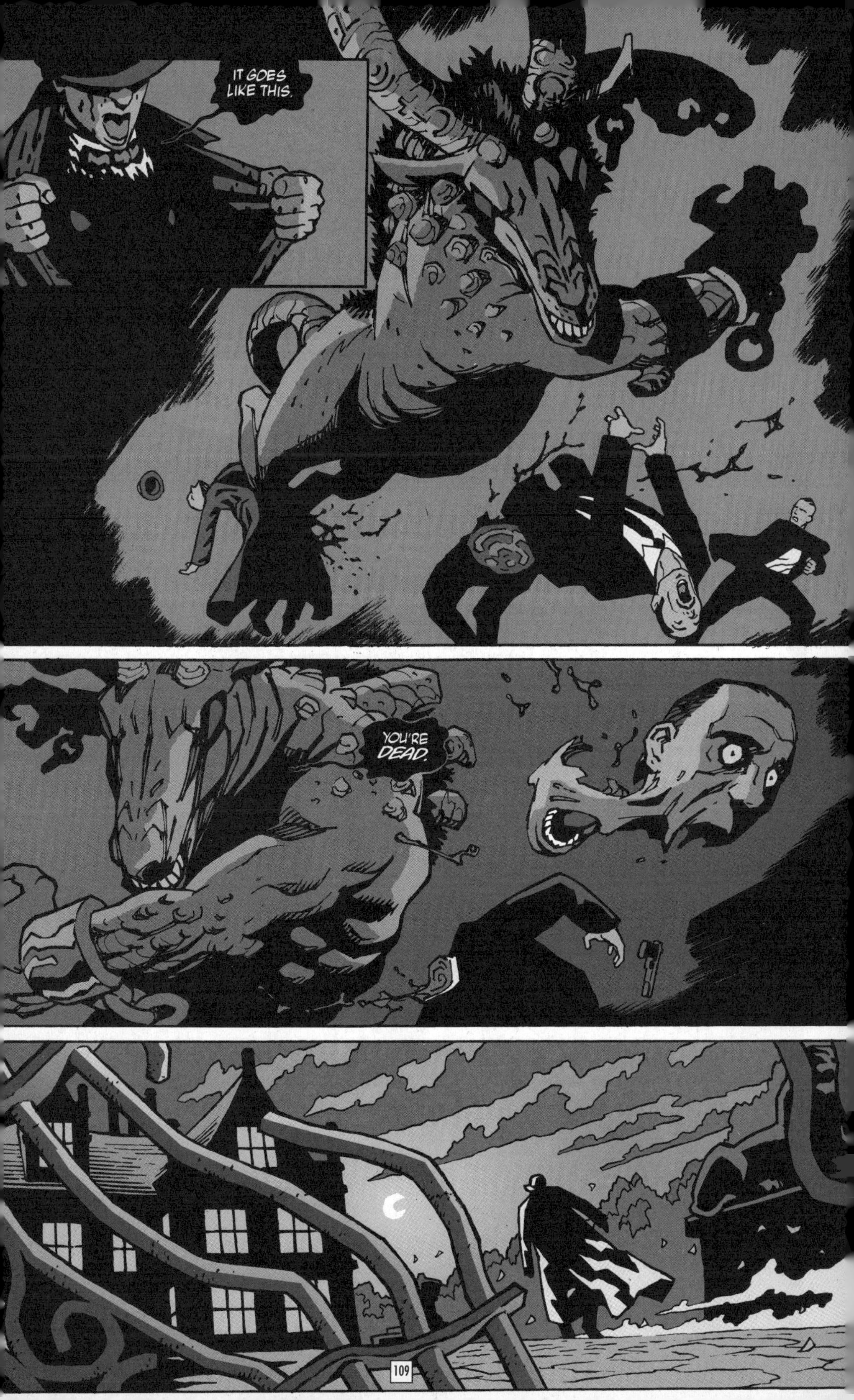
IT GOES LIKE THIS.
YOU'RE DEAD.

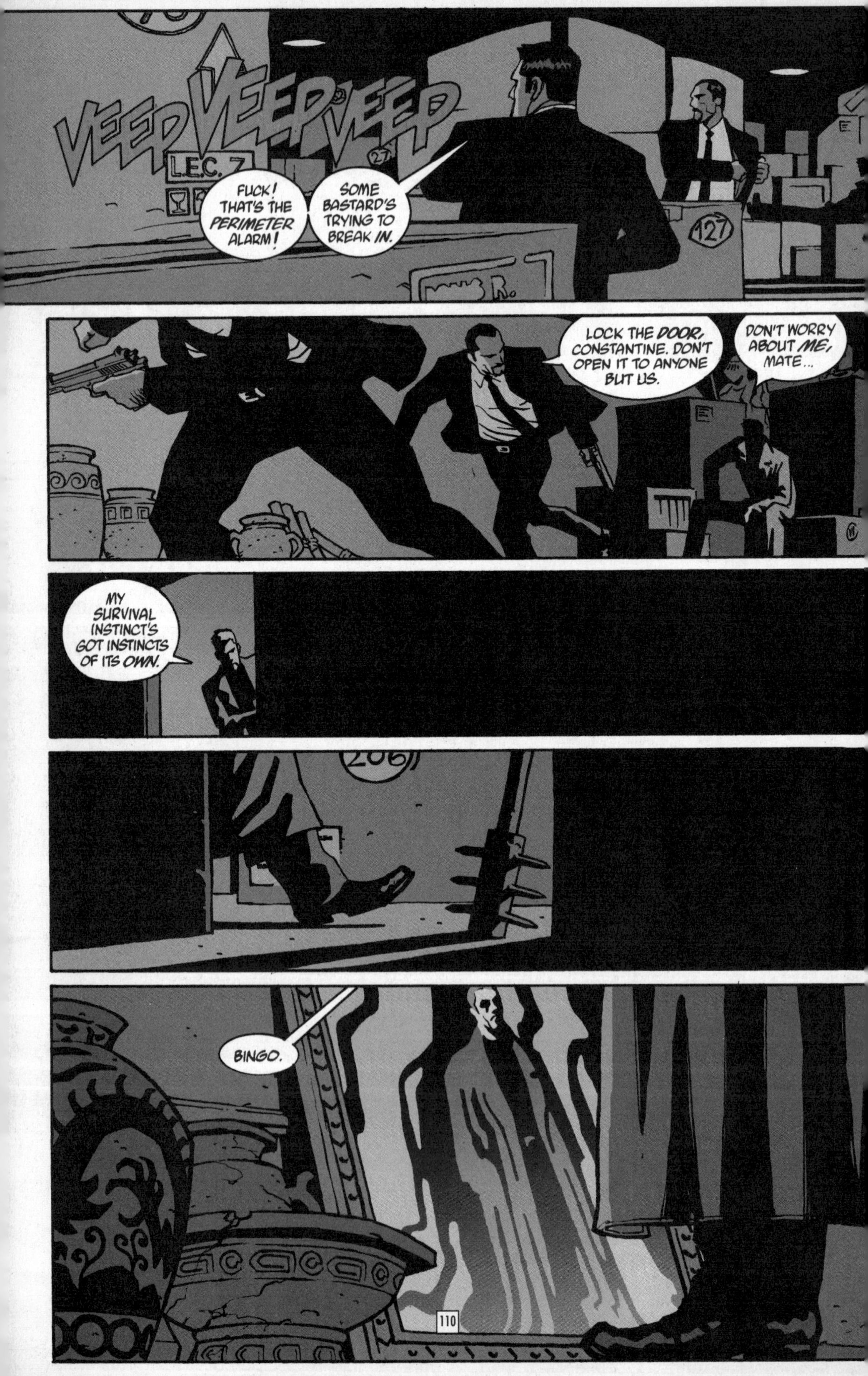
VEEP VEEP VEEP
L.E.C. 7
127
FUCK! THAT'S THE PERIMETER ALARM!
SOME BASTARD'S TRYING TO BREAK IN.
LOCK THE DOOR, CONSTANTINE. DON'T OPEN IT TO ANYONE BUT US.
DON'T WORRY ABOUT ME, MATE...
MY SURVIVAL INSTINCT'S GOT INSTINCTS OF ITS OWN.
206
BINGO.

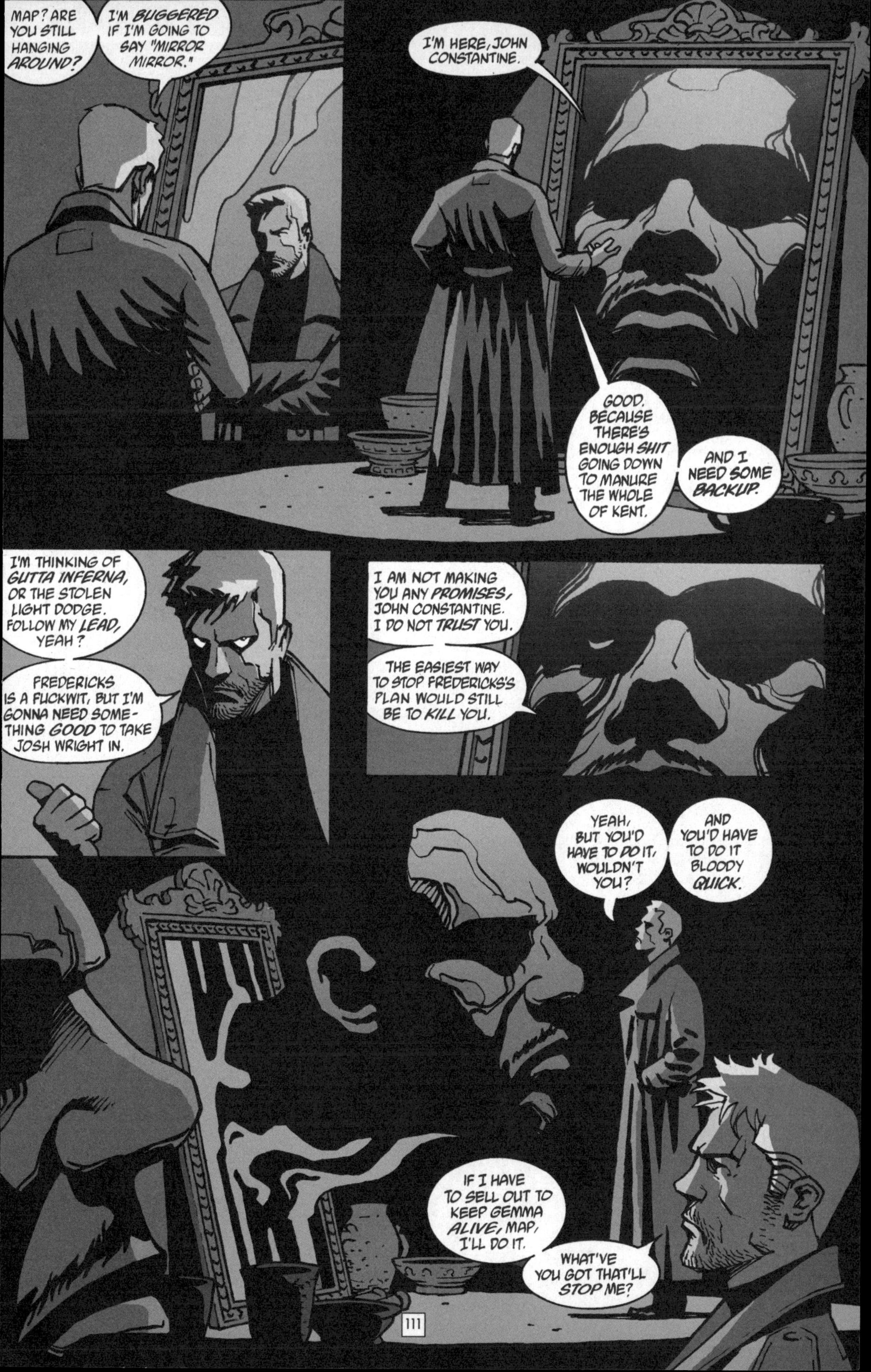
MAP? ARE YOU STILL HANGING AROUND?
I'M BUGGERED IF I'M GOING TO SAY "MIRROR MIRROR."
I'M HERE, JOHN CONSTANTINE.
GOOD. BECAUSE THERE'S ENOUGH SHIT GOING DOWN TO MANURE THE WHOLE OF KENT.
AND I NEED SOME BACKUP.
I'M THINKING OF GUTTA INFERNA, OR THE STOLEN LIGHT DODGE. FOLLOW MY LEAD, YEAH?
FREDERICKS IS A FUCKWIT, BUT I'M GONNA NEED SOME-THING GOOD TO TAKE JOSH WRIGHT IN.
I AM NOT MAKING YOU ANY PROMISES, JOHN CONSTANTINE. I DO NOT TRUST YOU.
THE EASIEST WAY TO STOP FREDERICKS'S PLAN WOULD STILL BE TO KILL YOU.
YEAH, BUT YOU'D HAVE TO DO IT, WOULDN'T YOU?
AND YOU'D HAVE TO DO IT BLOODY QUICK.
IF I HAVE TO SELL OUT TO KEEP GEMMA ALIVE, MAP, I'LL DO IT.
WHAT'VE YOU GOT THAT'LL STOP ME?

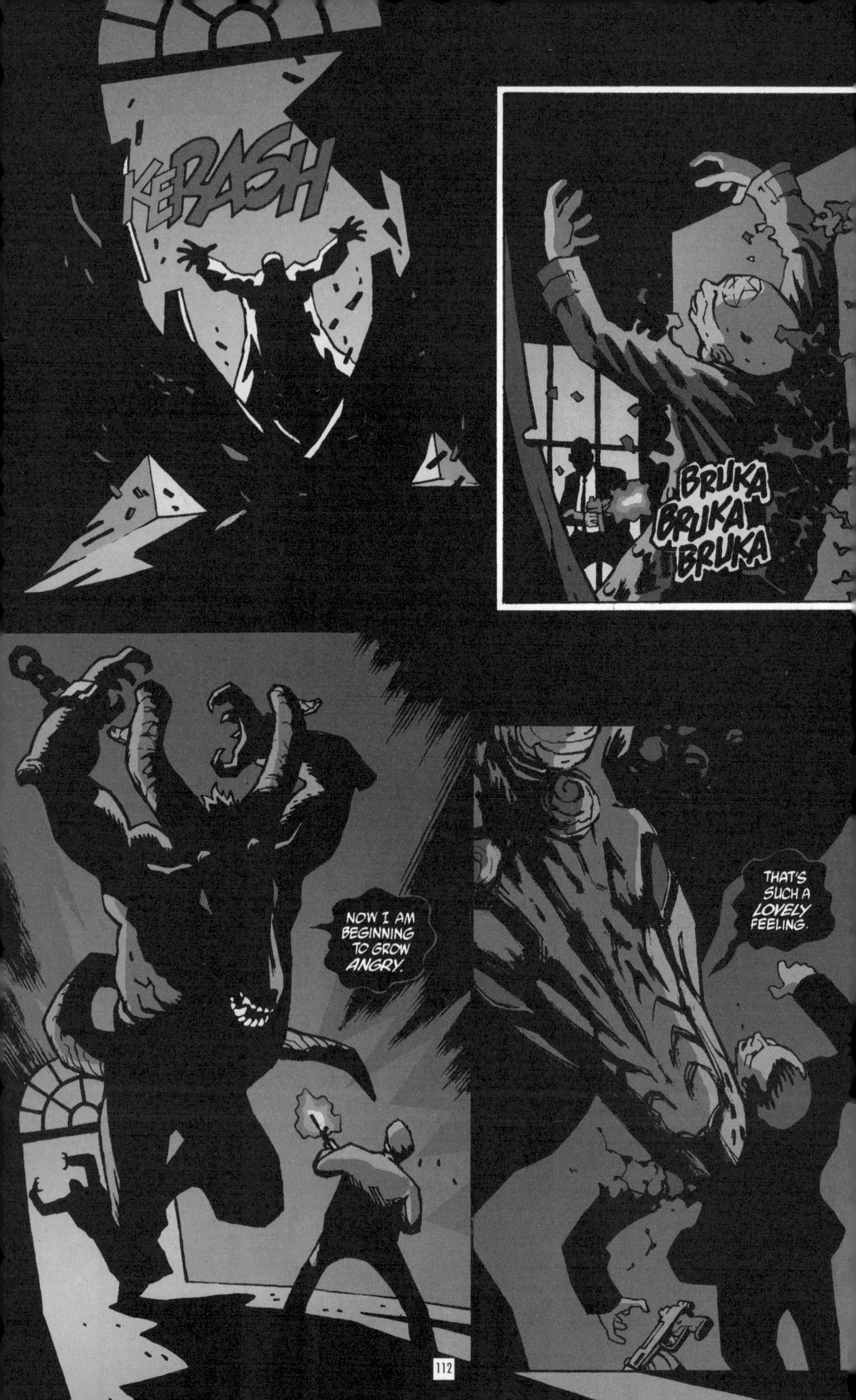
KERASH
BRUKA BRUKA BRUKA
NOW I AM BEGINNING TO GROW ANGRY.
THAT'S SUCH A LOVELY FEELING.

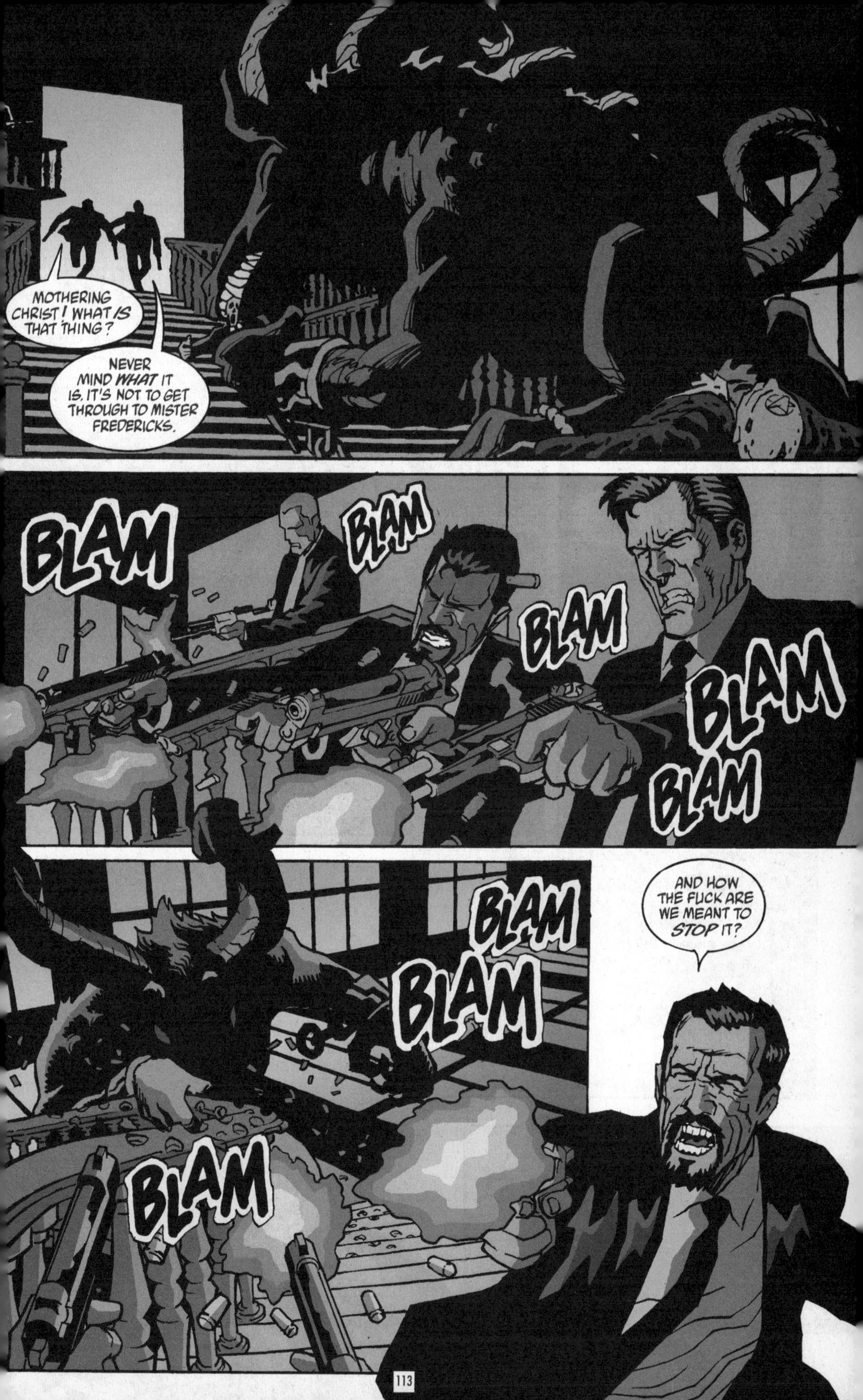
MOTHERING CHRIST! WHAT IS THAT THING?
NEVER MIND WHAT IT IS. IT'S NOT TO GET THROUGH TO MISTER FREDERICKS.
BLAM
BLAM
BLAM
BLAM
BLAM
BLAM
BLAM
AND HOW THE FUCK ARE WE MEANT TO STOP IT?
BLAM

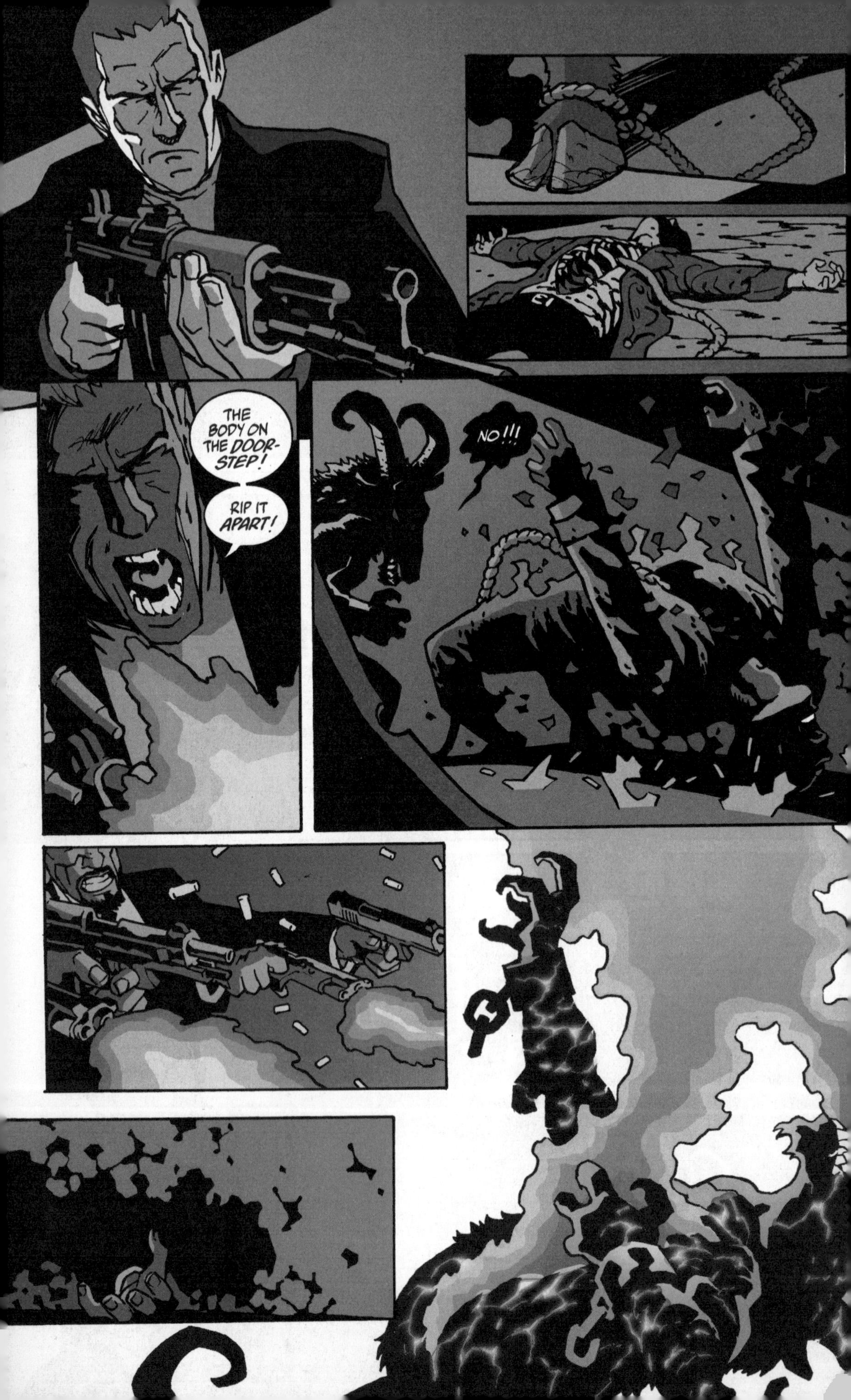
THE BODY ON THE DOOR-STEP!
RIP IT APART!
NO!!!

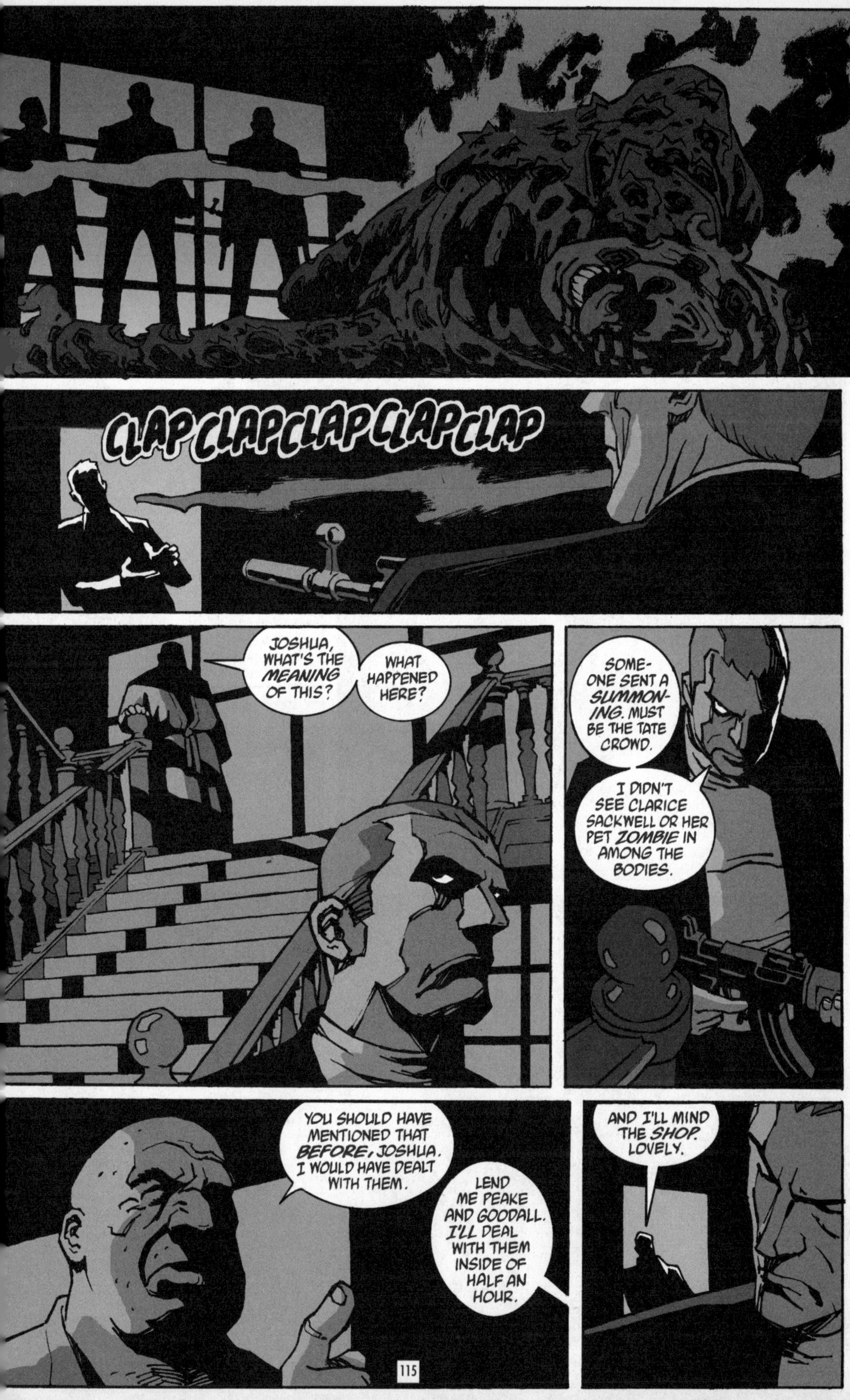
CLAP CLAP CLAP CLAP CLAP
JOSHUA, WHAT'S THE MEANING OF THIS?
WHAT HAPPENED HERE?
SOME-ONE SENT A SUMMON-ING. MUST BE THE TATE CROWD.
I DIDN'T SEE CLARICE SACKWELL OR HER PET ZOMBIE IN AMONG THE BODIES.
YOU SHOULD HAVE MENTIONED THAT BEFORE, JOSHUA. I WOULD HAVE DEALT WITH THEM.
LEND ME PEAKE AND GOODALL. I'LL DEAL WITH THEM INSIDE OF HALF AN HOUR.
AND I'LL MIND THE SHOP. LOVELY.

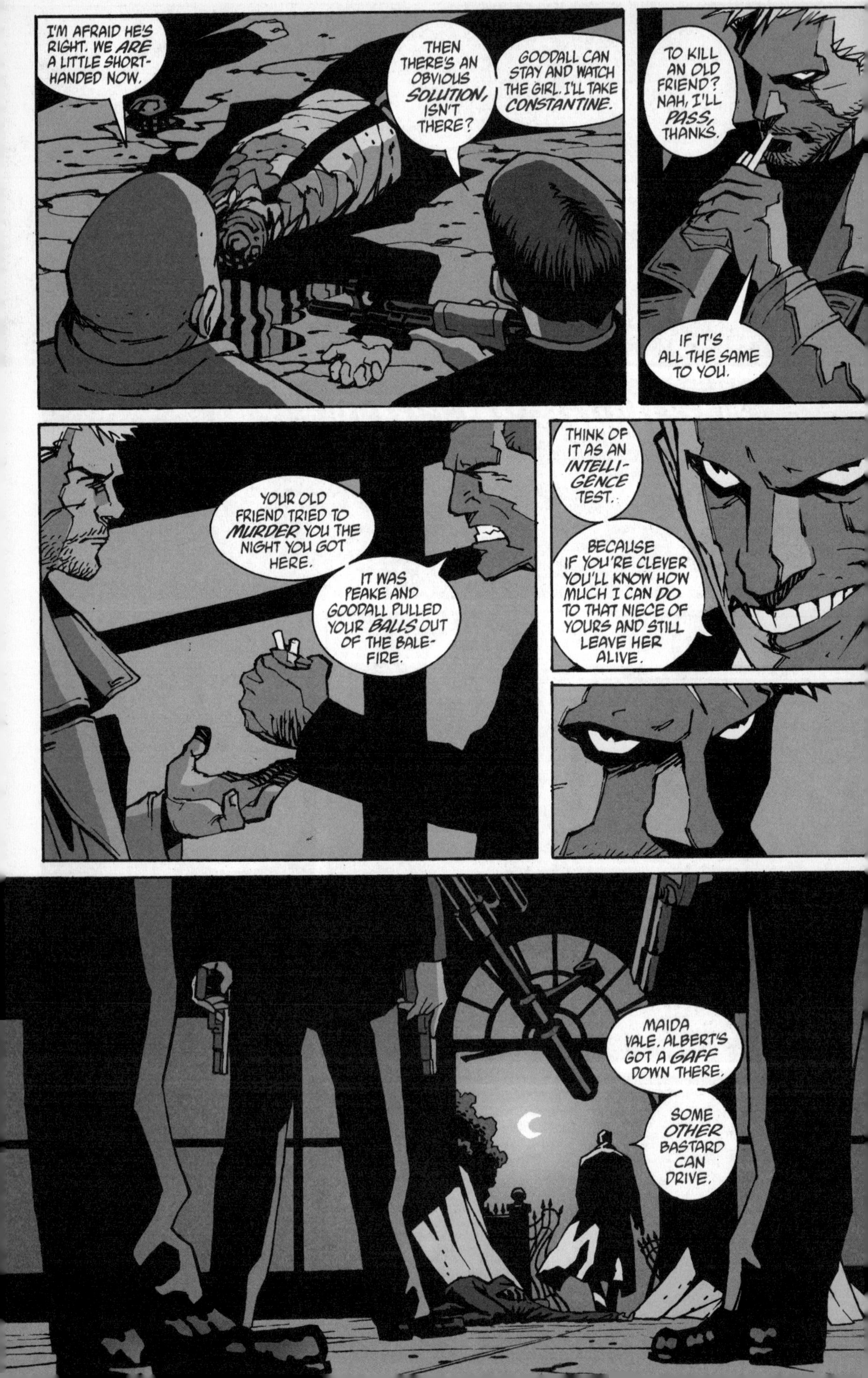
I'M AFRAID HE'S RIGHT. WE ARE A LITTLE SHORT-HANDED NOW.
THEN THERE'S AN OBVIOUS SOLUTION, ISN'T THERE?
GOODALL CAN STAY AND WATCH THE GIRL. I'LL TAKE CONSTANTINE.
TO KILL AN OLD FRIEND? NAH, I'LL PASS, THANKS.
IF IT'S ALL THE SAME TO YOU.
YOUR OLD FRIEND TRIED TO MURDER YOU THE NIGHT YOU GOT HERE.
IT WAS PEAKE AND GOODALL PULLED YOUR BALLS OUT OF THE BALE-FIRE.
THINK OF IT AS AN INTELLI-GENCE TEST.
BECAUSE IF YOU'RE CLEVER YOU'LL KNOW HOW MUCH I CAN DO TO THAT NIECE OF YOURS AND STILL LEAVE HER ALIVE.
MAIDA VALE. ALBERT'S GOT A GAFF DOWN THERE.
SOME OTHER BASTARD CAN DRIVE.

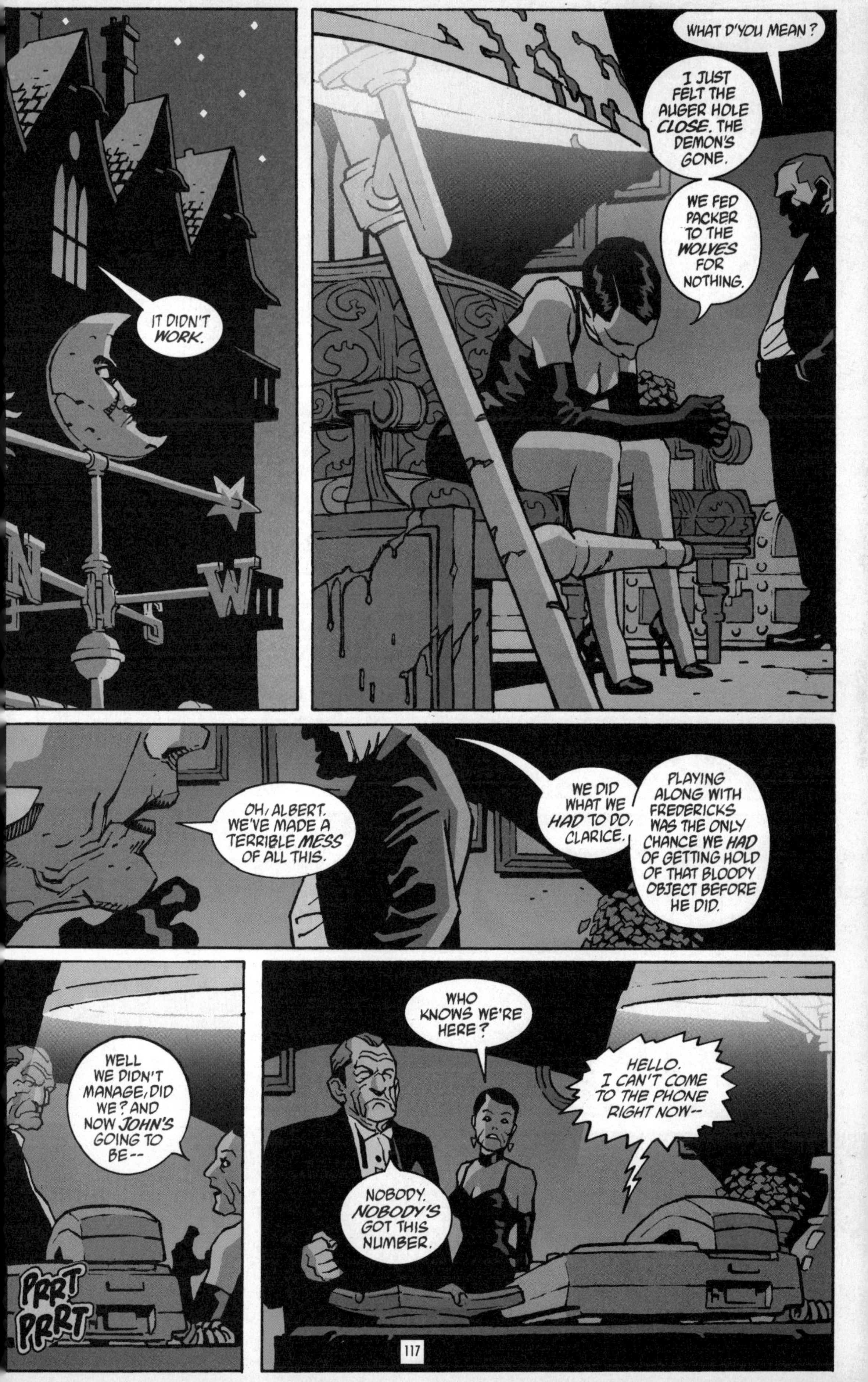
IT DIDN'T WORK.
WHAT D'YOU MEAN?
I JUST FELT THE AUGER HOLE CLOSE. THE DEMON'S GONE.
WE FED PACKER TO THE WOLVES FOR NOTHING.
OH, ALBERT. WE'VE MADE A TERRIBLE MESS OF ALL THIS.
WE DID WHAT WE HAD TO DO, CLARICE.
PLAYING ALONG WITH FREDERICKS WAS THE ONLY CHANCE WE HAD OF GETTING HOLD OF THAT BLOODY OBJECT BEFORE HE DID.
WELL WE DIDN'T MANAGE, DID WE? AND NOW JOHN'S GOING TO BE--
PRRT PRRT
WHO KNOWS WE'RE HERE?
NOBODY. NOBODY'S GOT THIS NUMBER.
HELLO. I CAN'T COME TO THE PHONE RIGHT NOW--

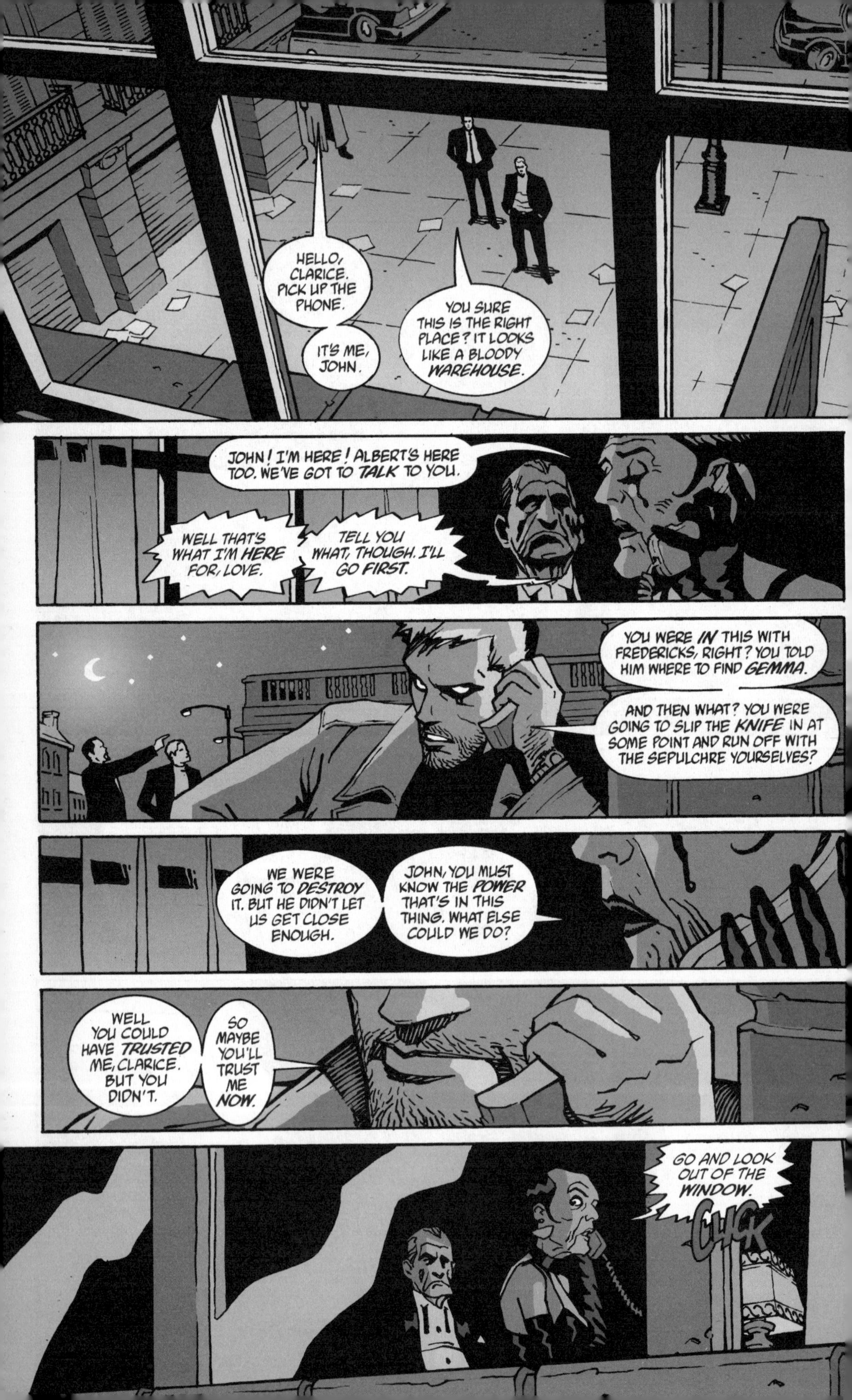
HELLO, CLARICE. PICK UP THE PHONE.
IT'S ME, JOHN.
YOU SURE THIS IS THE RIGHT PLACE? IT LOOKS LIKE A BLOODY WAREHOUSE.
JOHN! I'M HERE! ALBERT'S HERE TOO. WE'VE GOT TO TALK TO YOU.
WELL THAT'S WHAT I'M HERE FOR, LOVE.
TELL YOU WHAT, THOUGH. I'LL GO FIRST.
YOU WERE IN THIS WITH FREDERICKS, RIGHT? YOU TOLD HIM WHERE TO FIND GEMMA.
AND THEN WHAT? YOU WERE GOING TO SLIP THE KNIFE IN AT SOME POINT AND RUN OFF WITH THE SEPULCHRE YOURSELVES?
WE WERE GOING TO DESTROY IT. BUT HE DIDN'T LET US GET CLOSE ENOUGH.
JOHN, YOU MUST KNOW THE POWER THAT'S IN THIS THING. WHAT ELSE COULD WE DO?
WELL YOU COULD HAVE TRUSTED ME, CLARICE. BUT YOU DIDN'T.
SO MAYBE YOU'LL TRUST ME NOW.
GO AND LOOK OUT OF THE WINDOW.
CLICK

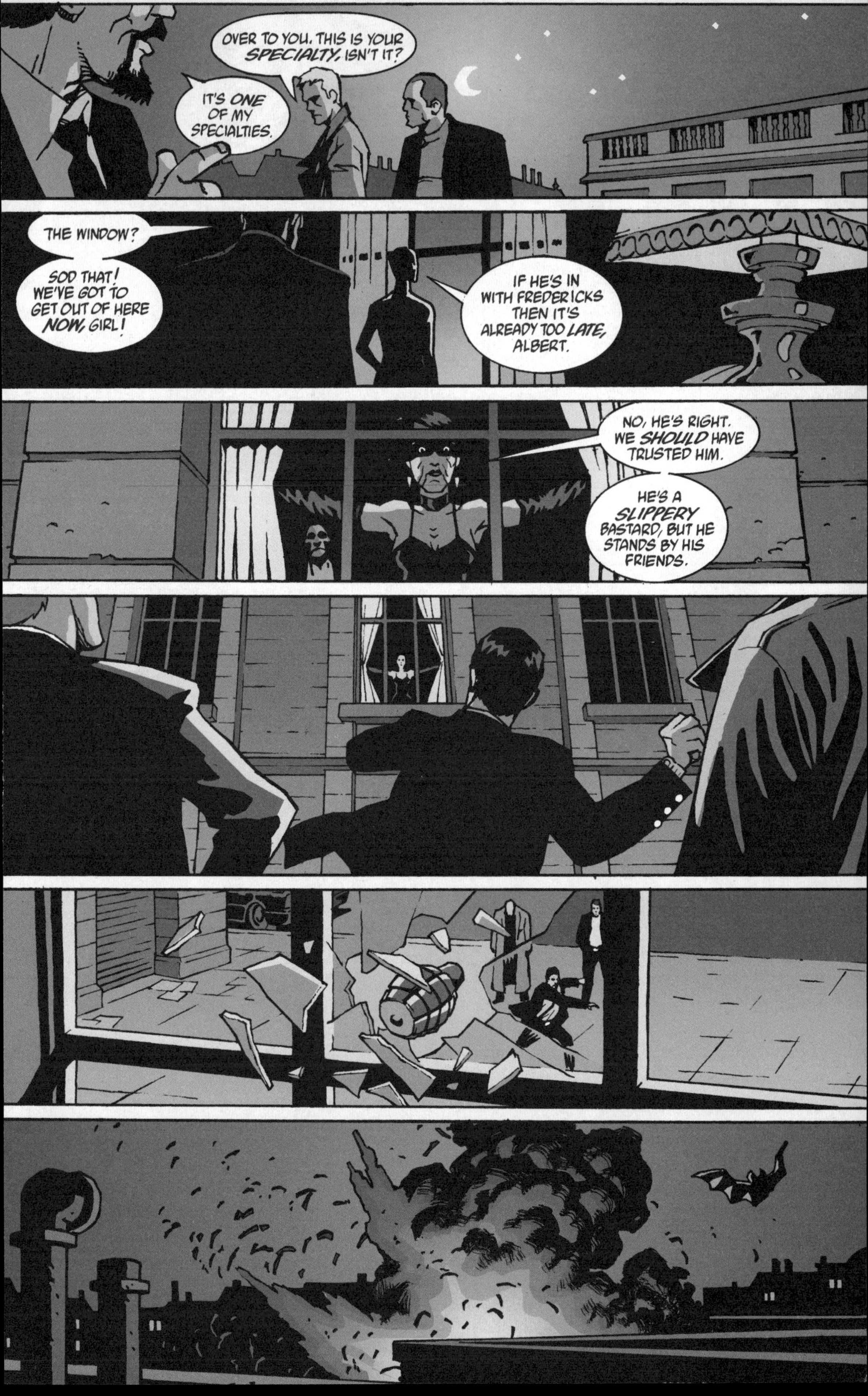
OVER TO YOU. THIS IS YOUR SPECIALTY, ISN'T IT?
IT'S ONE OF MY SPECIALTIES.
THE WINDOW?
SOD THAT! WE'VE GOT TO GET OUT OF HERE NOW, GIRL!
IF HE'S IN WITH FREDERICKS THEN IT'S ALREADY TOO LATE, ALBERT.
NO, HE'S RIGHT. WE SHOULD HAVE TRUSTED HIM.
HE'S A SLIPPERY BASTARD, BUT HE STANDS BY HIS FRIENDS.

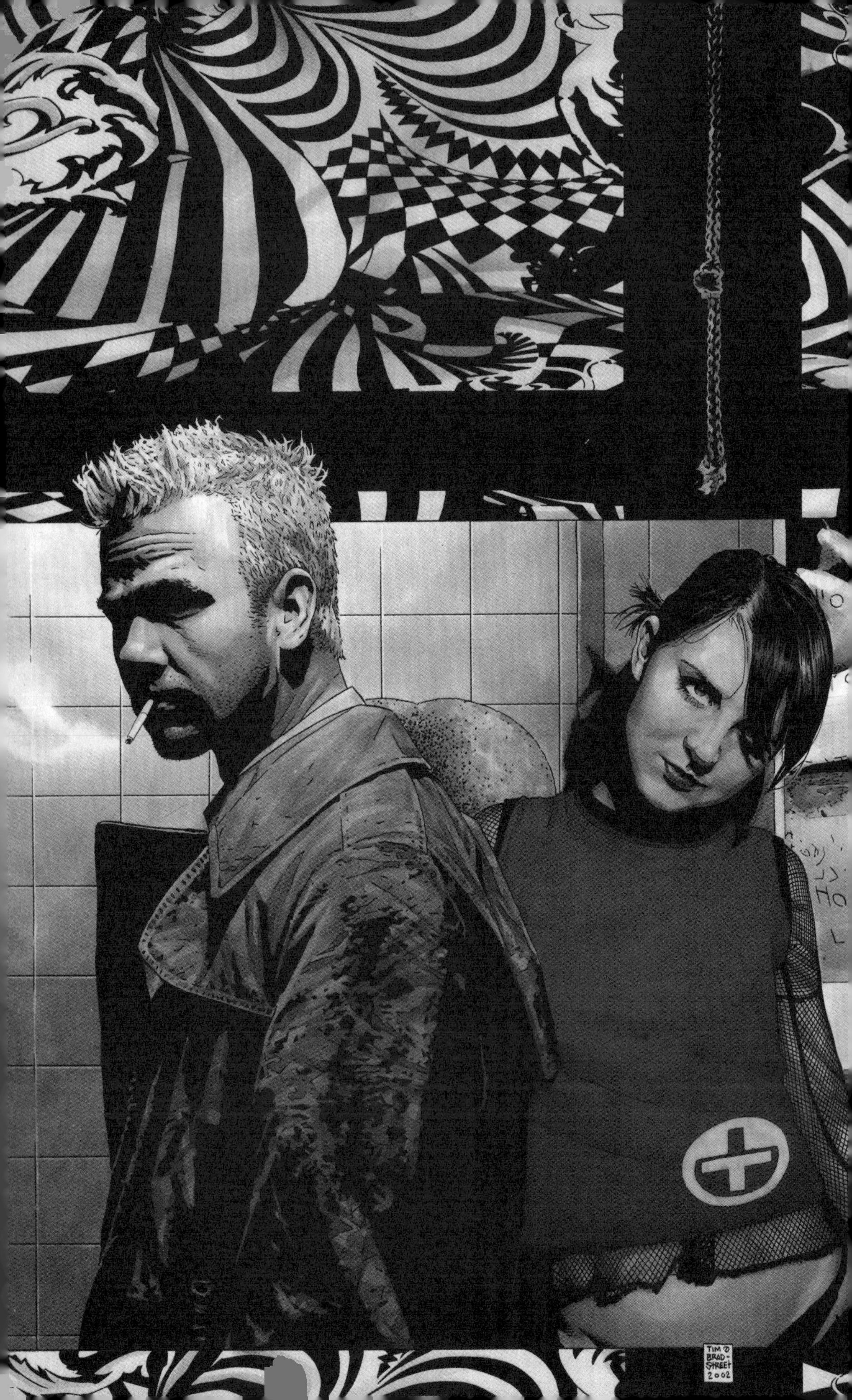
TIM
BRAD-
STREET
2002

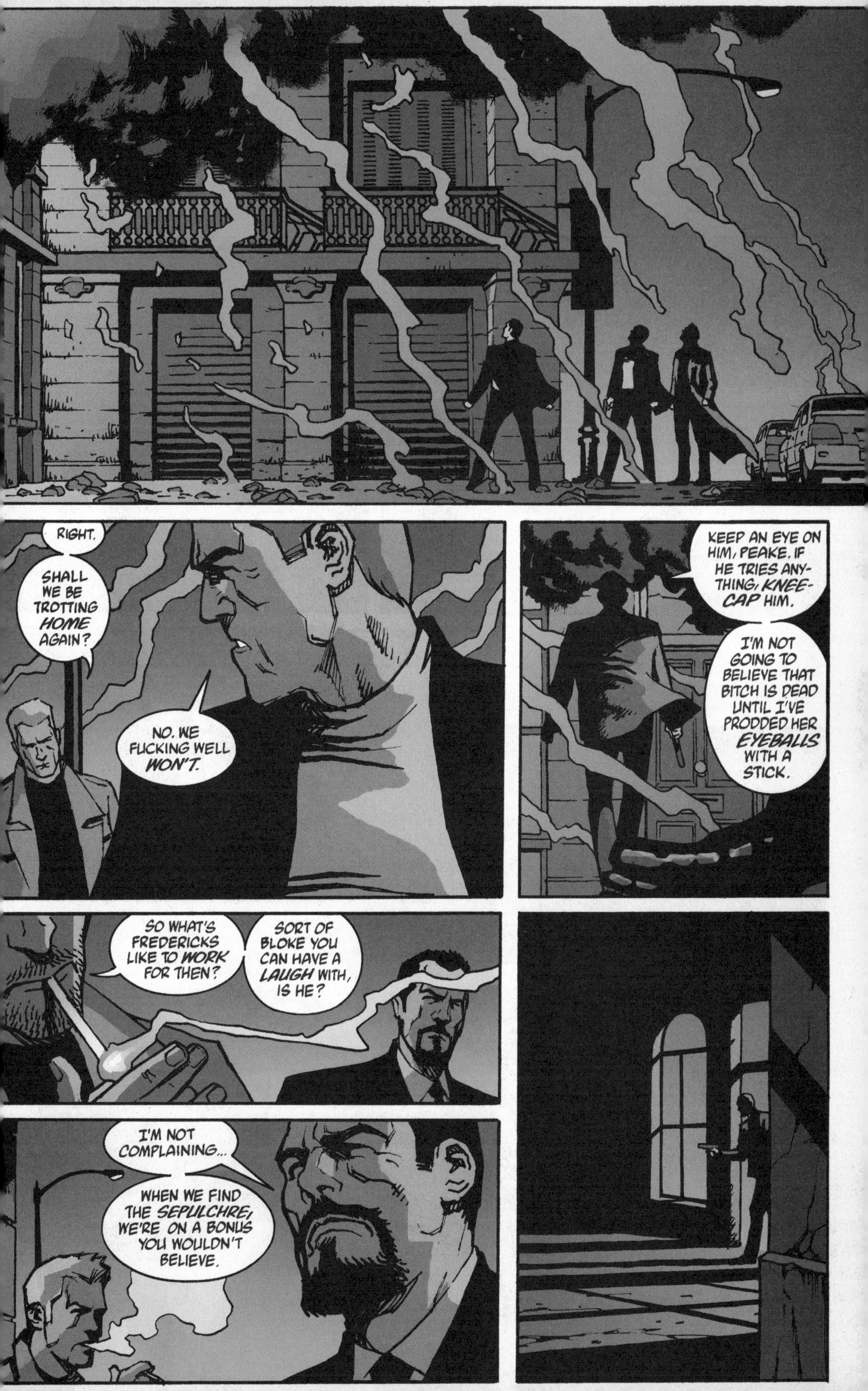
RIGHT.
SHALL WE BE TROTTING HOME AGAIN?
NO. WE FUCKING WELL WON'T.
KEEP AN EYE ON HIM, PEAKE. IF HE TRIES ANY-THING, KNEE-CAP HIM.
I'M NOT GOING TO BELIEVE THAT BITCH IS DEAD UNTIL I'VE PRODDED HER EYEBALLS WITH A STICK.
SO WHAT'S FREDERICKS LIKE TO WORK FOR THEN?
SORT OF BLOKE YOU CAN HAVE A LAUGH WITH, IS HE?
I'M NOT COMPLAINING...
WHEN WE FIND THE SEPULCHRE, WE'RE ON A BONUS YOU WOULDN'T BELIEVE.

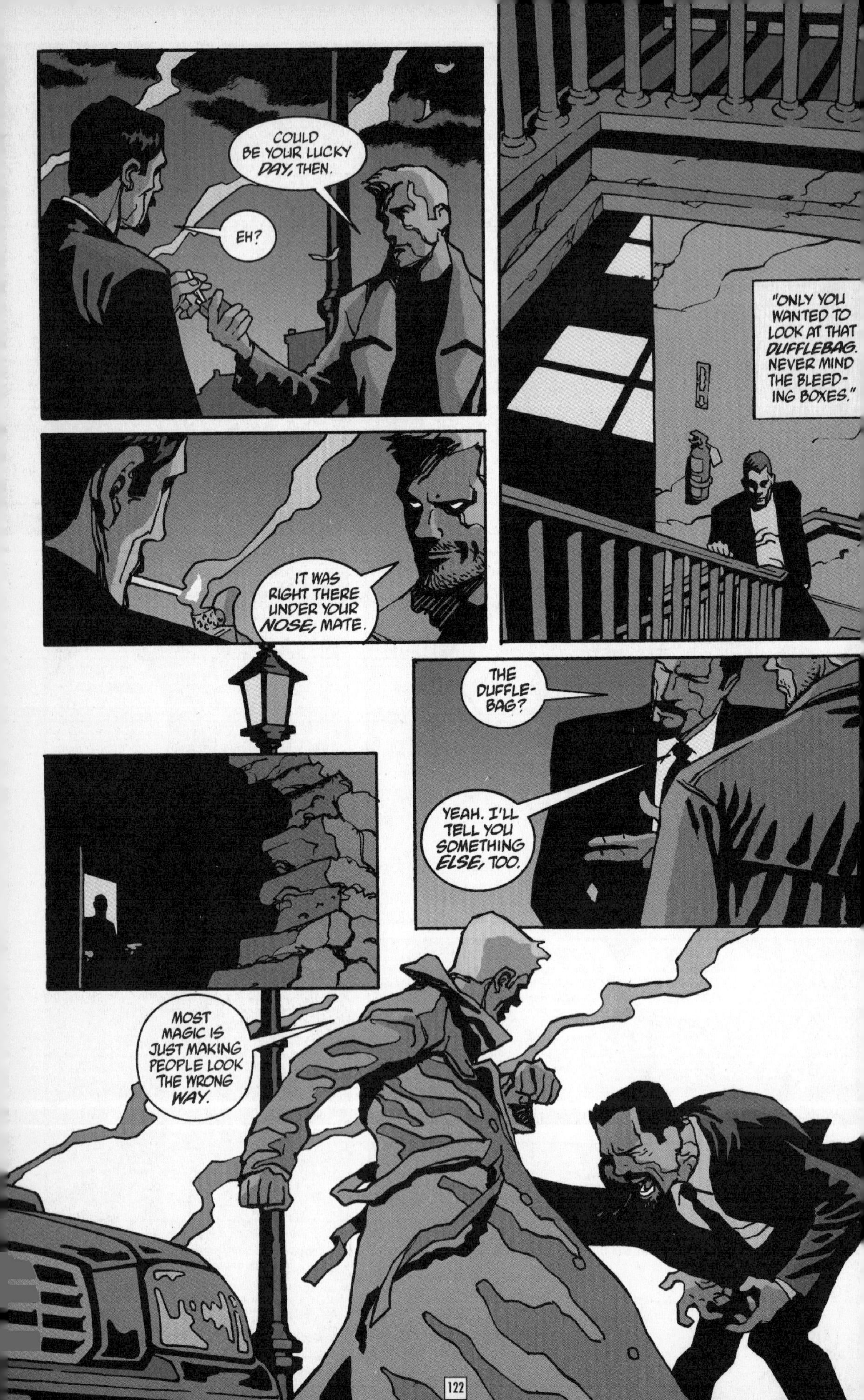
COULD BE YOUR LUCKY DAY, THEN.
EH?
"ONLY YOU WANTED TO LOOK AT THAT DUFFLEBAG. NEVER MIND THE BLEED-ING BOXES."
IT WAS RIGHT THERE UNDER YOUR NOSE, MATE.
THE DUFFLE-BAG?
YEAH. I'LL TELL YOU SOMETHING ELSE, TOO.
MOST MAGIC IS JUST MAKING PEOPLE LOOK THE WRONG WAY.

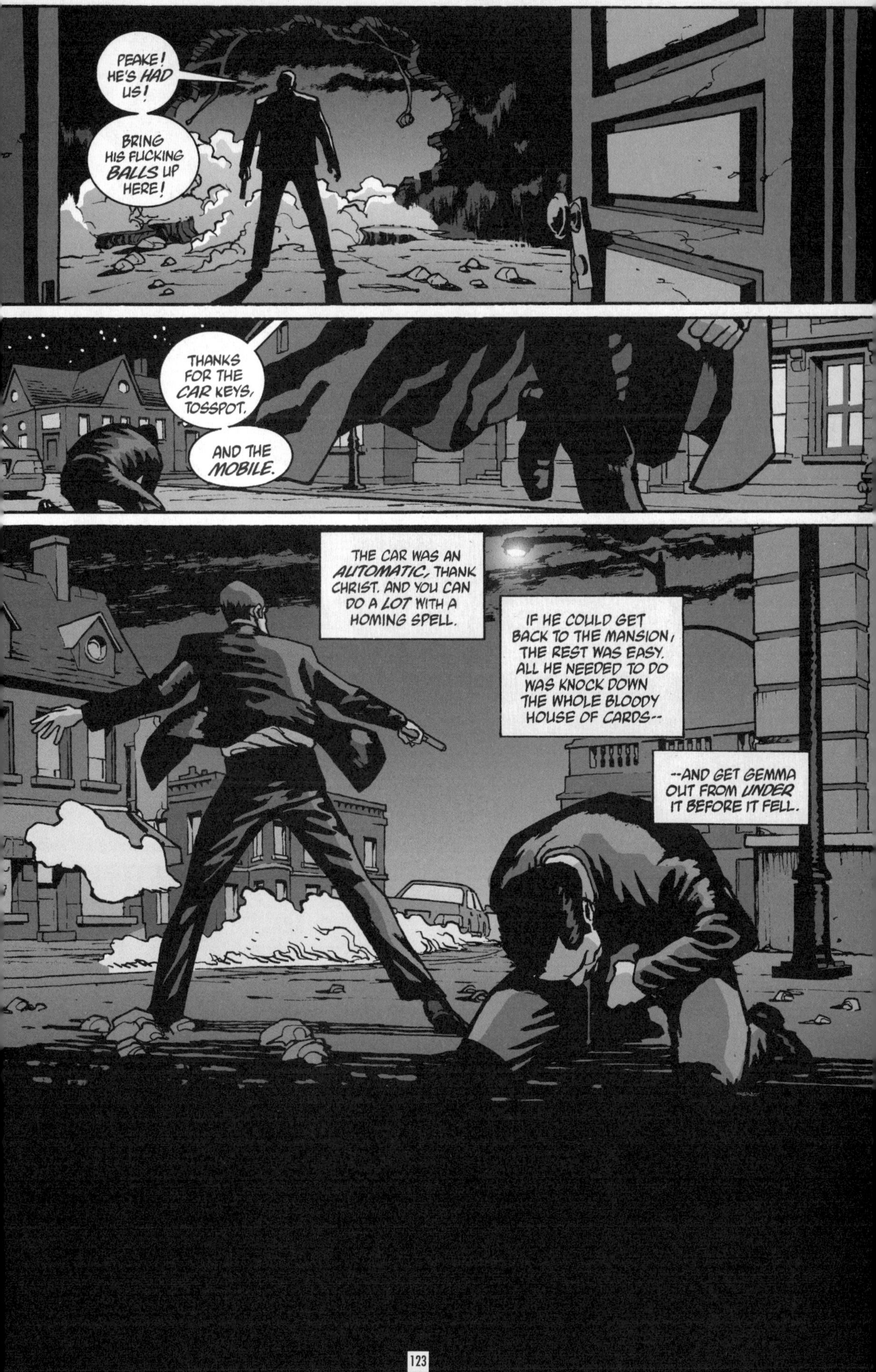
PEAKE! HE'S HAD US!
BRING HIS FUCKING BALLS UP HERE!
THANKS FOR THE CAR KEYS, TOSSPOT.
AND THE MOBILE.
THE CAR WAS AN AUTOMATIC, THANK CHRIST. AND YOU CAN DO A LOT WITH A HOMING SPELL.
IF HE COULD GET BACK TO THE MANSION, THE REST WAS EASY. ALL HE NEEDED TO DO WAS KNOCK DOWN THE WHOLE BLOODY HOUSE OF CARDS--
--AND GET GEMMA OUT FROM UNDER IT BEFORE IT FELL.

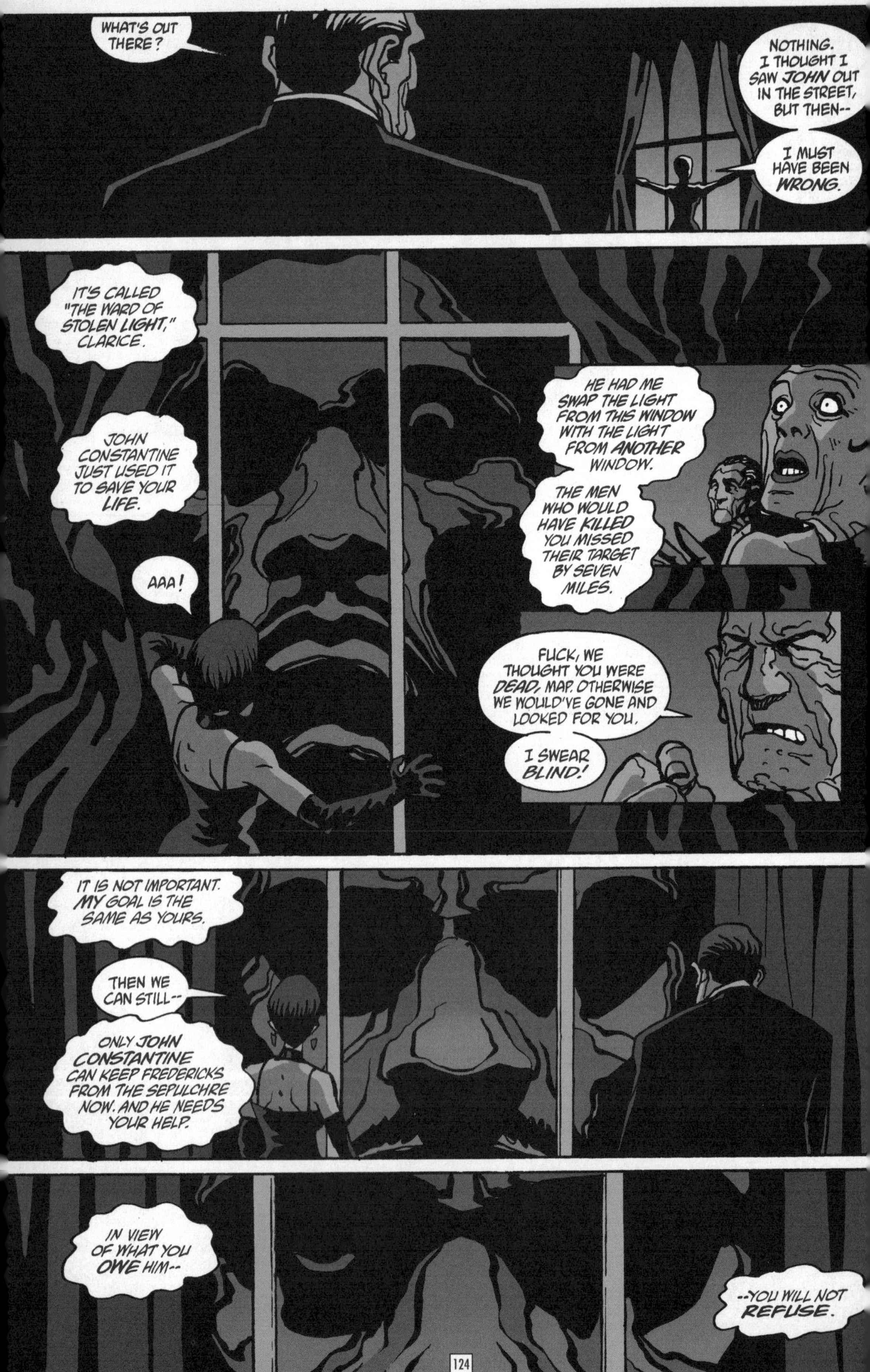
WHAT'S OUT THERE?
NOTHING. I THOUGHT I SAW JOHN OUT IN THE STREET, BUT THEN--
I MUST HAVE BEEN WRONG.
IT'S CALLED "THE WARD OF STOLEN LIGHT," CLARICE.
JOHN CONSTANTINE JUST USED IT TO SAVE YOUR LIFE.
AAA!
HE HAD ME SWAP THE LIGHT FROM THIS WINDOW WITH THE LIGHT FROM ANOTHER WINDOW.
THE MEN WHO WOULD HAVE KILLED YOU MISSED THEIR TARGET BY SEVEN MILES.
FUCK, WE THOUGHT YOU WERE DEAD, MAP. OTHERWISE WE WOULD'VE GONE AND LOOKED FOR YOU.
I SWEAR BLIND!
IT IS NOT IMPORTANT. MY GOAL IS THE SAME AS YOURS.
THEN WE CAN STILL--
ONLY JOHN CONSTANTINE CAN KEEP FREDERICKS FROM THE SEPULCHRE NOW. AND HE NEEDS YOUR HELP.
IN VIEW OF WHAT YOU OWE HIM--
--YOU WILL NOT REFUSE.

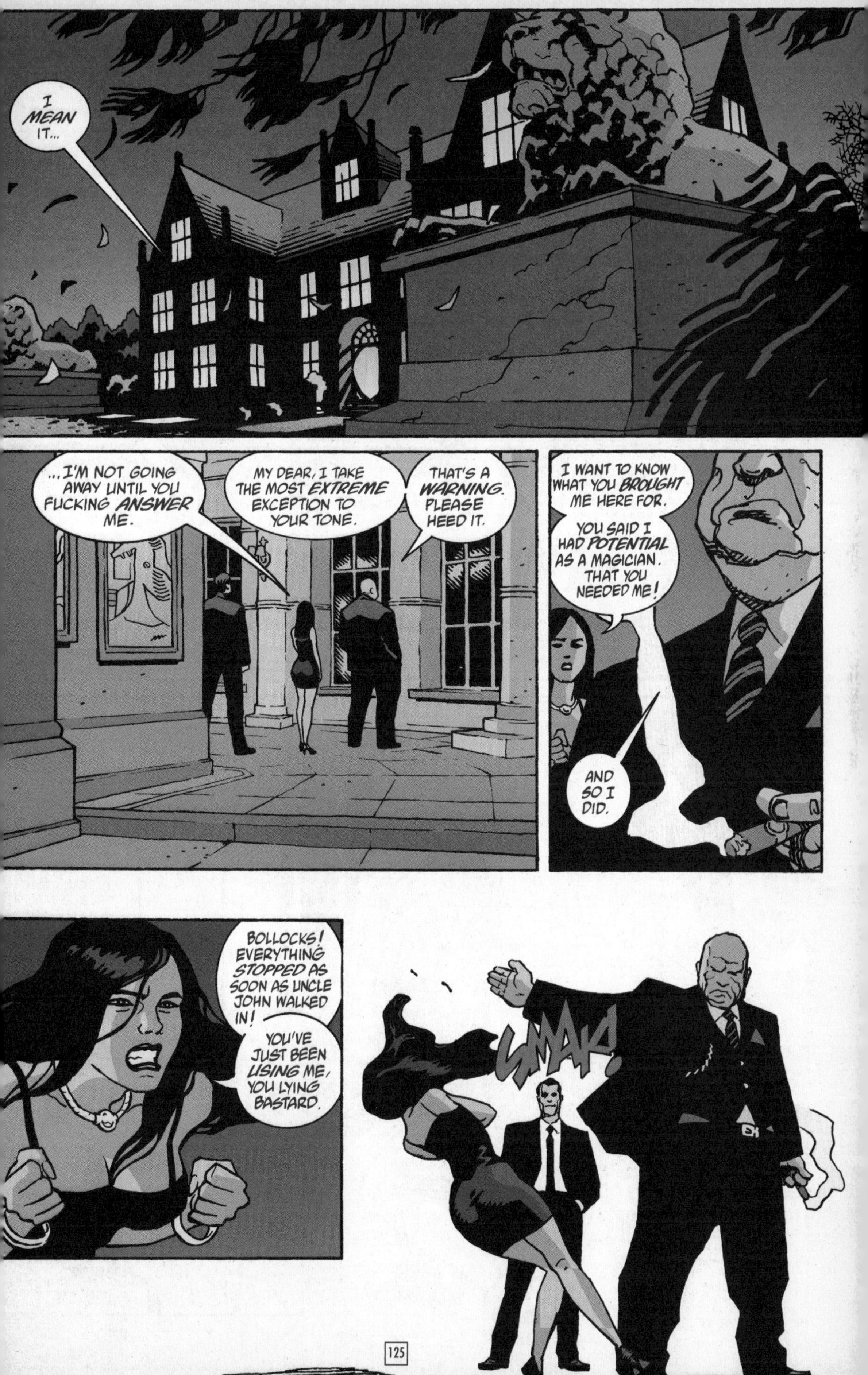

I MEAN IT...
...I'M NOT GOING AWAY UNTIL YOU FUCKING ANSWER ME.
MY DEAR, I TAKE THE MOST EXTREME EXCEPTION TO YOUR TONE.
THAT'S A WARNING. PLEASE HEED IT.
I WANT TO KNOW WHAT YOU BROUGHT ME HERE FOR.
YOU SAID I HAD POTENTIAL AS A MAGICIAN. THAT YOU NEEDED ME!
AND SO I DID.
BOLLOCKS! EVERYTHING STOPPED AS SOON AS UNCLE JOHN WALKED IN!
YOU'VE JUST BEEN USING ME, YOU LYING BASTARD.
SMAK!

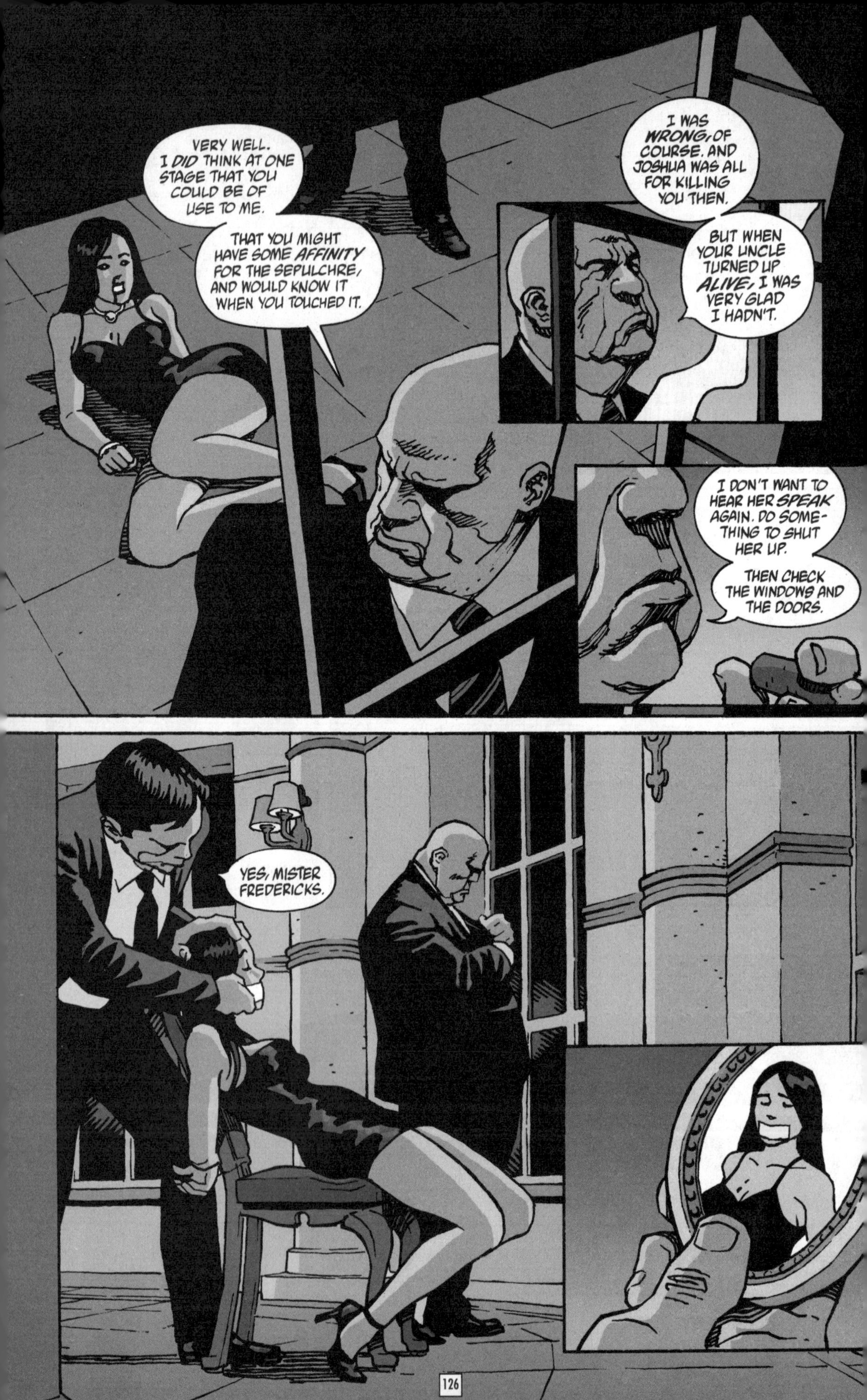
VERY WELL. I DID THINK AT ONE STAGE THAT YOU COULD BE OF USE TO ME.
THAT YOU MIGHT HAVE SOME AFFINITY FOR THE SEPULCHRE, AND WOULD KNOW IT WHEN YOU TOUCHED IT.
I WAS WRONG, OF COURSE. AND JOSHUA WAS ALL FOR KILLING YOU THEN.
BUT WHEN YOUR UNCLE TURNED UP ALIVE, I WAS VERY GLAD I HADN'T.
I DON'T WANT TO HEAR HER SPEAK AGAIN. DO SOMETHING TO SHUT HER UP.
THEN CHECK THE WINDOWS AND THE DOORS.
YES, MISTER FREDERICKS.

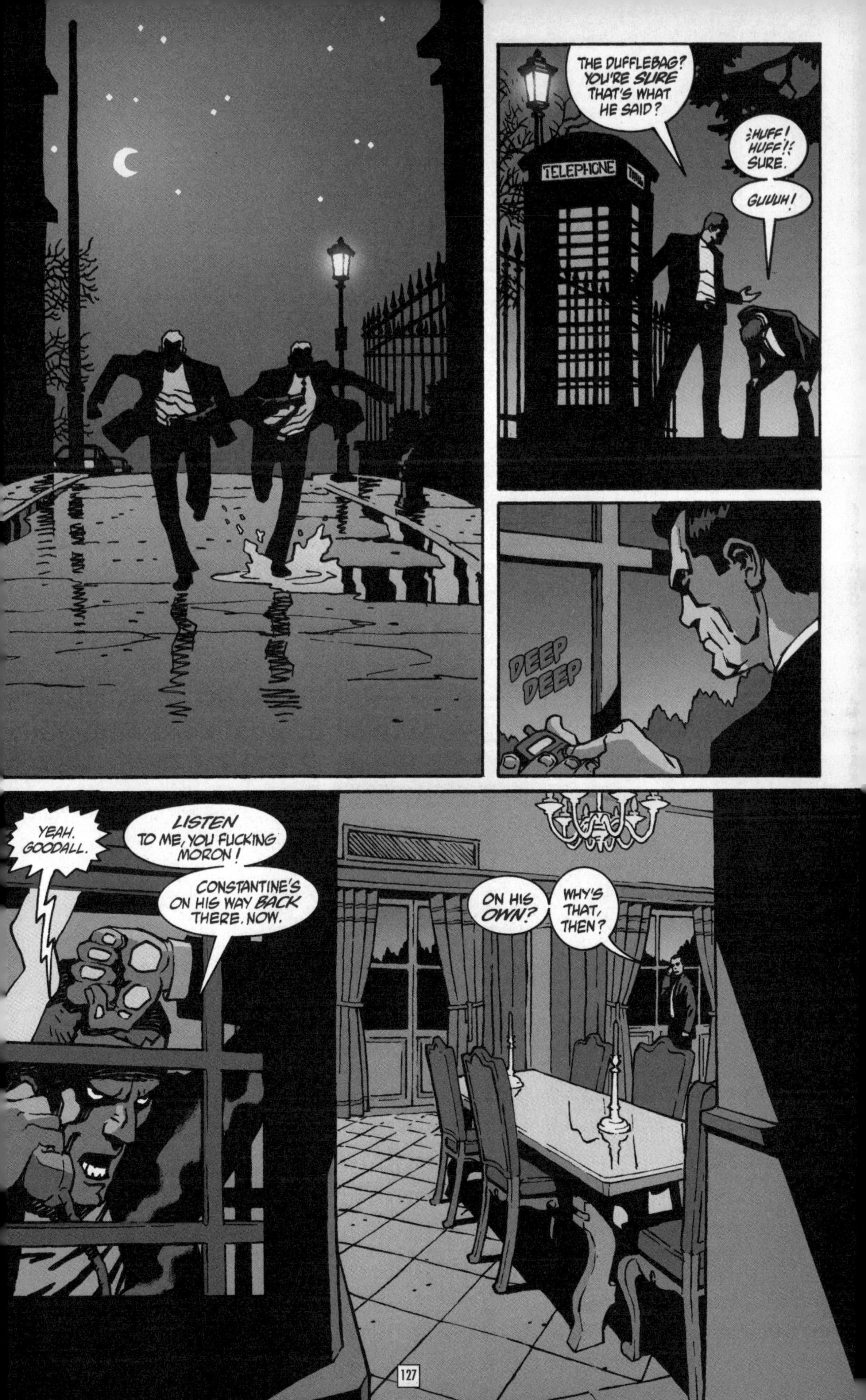
THE DUFFLEBAG? YOU'RE SURE THAT'S WHAT HE SAID?
HUFF! HUFF! SURE.
GUUUH!
TELEPHONE
DEEP DEEP
YEAH. GOODALL.
LISTEN TO ME, YOU FUCKING MORON!
CONSTANTINE'S ON HIS WAY BACK THERE. NOW.
ON HIS OWN?
WHY'S THAT, THEN?

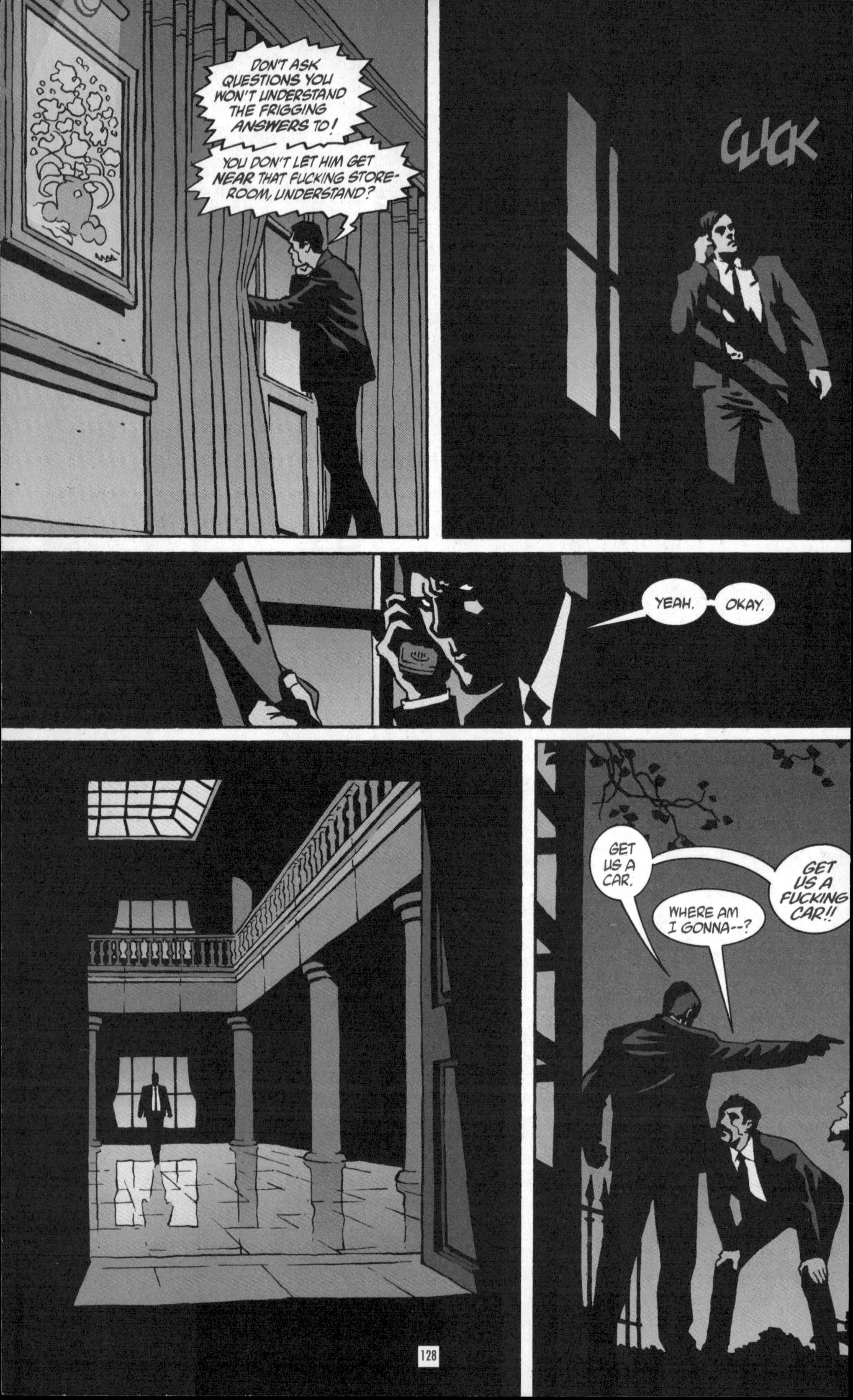
DON'T ASK QUESTIONS YOU WON'T UNDERSTAND THE FRIGGING ANSWERS TO!
YOU DON'T LET HIM GET NEAR THAT FUCKING STORE-ROOM, UNDERSTAND?
CLICK
YEAH.
OKAY.
GET US A CAR.
WHERE AM I GONNA--?
GET US A FUCKING CAR!!

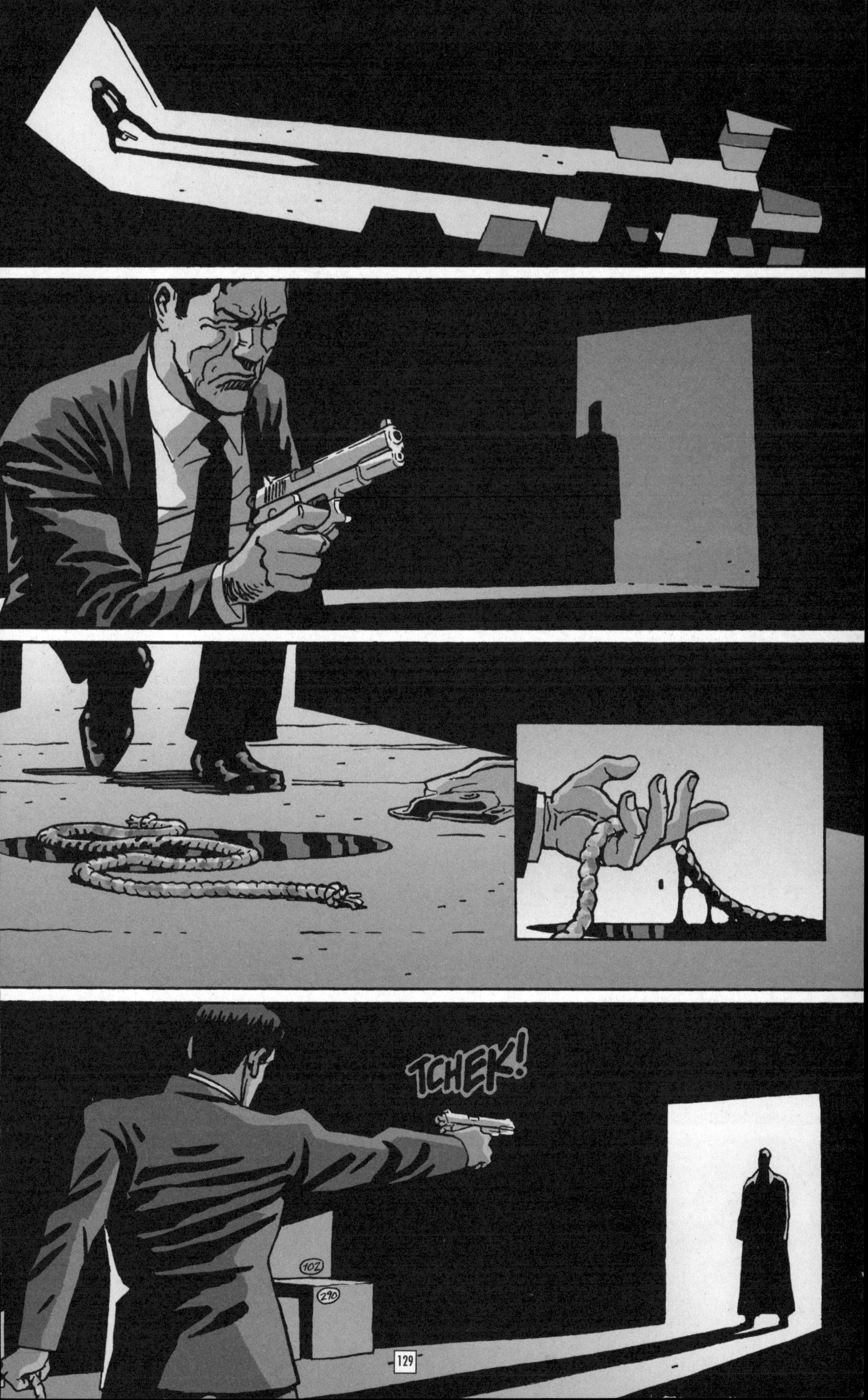
TCHEK!
102
290

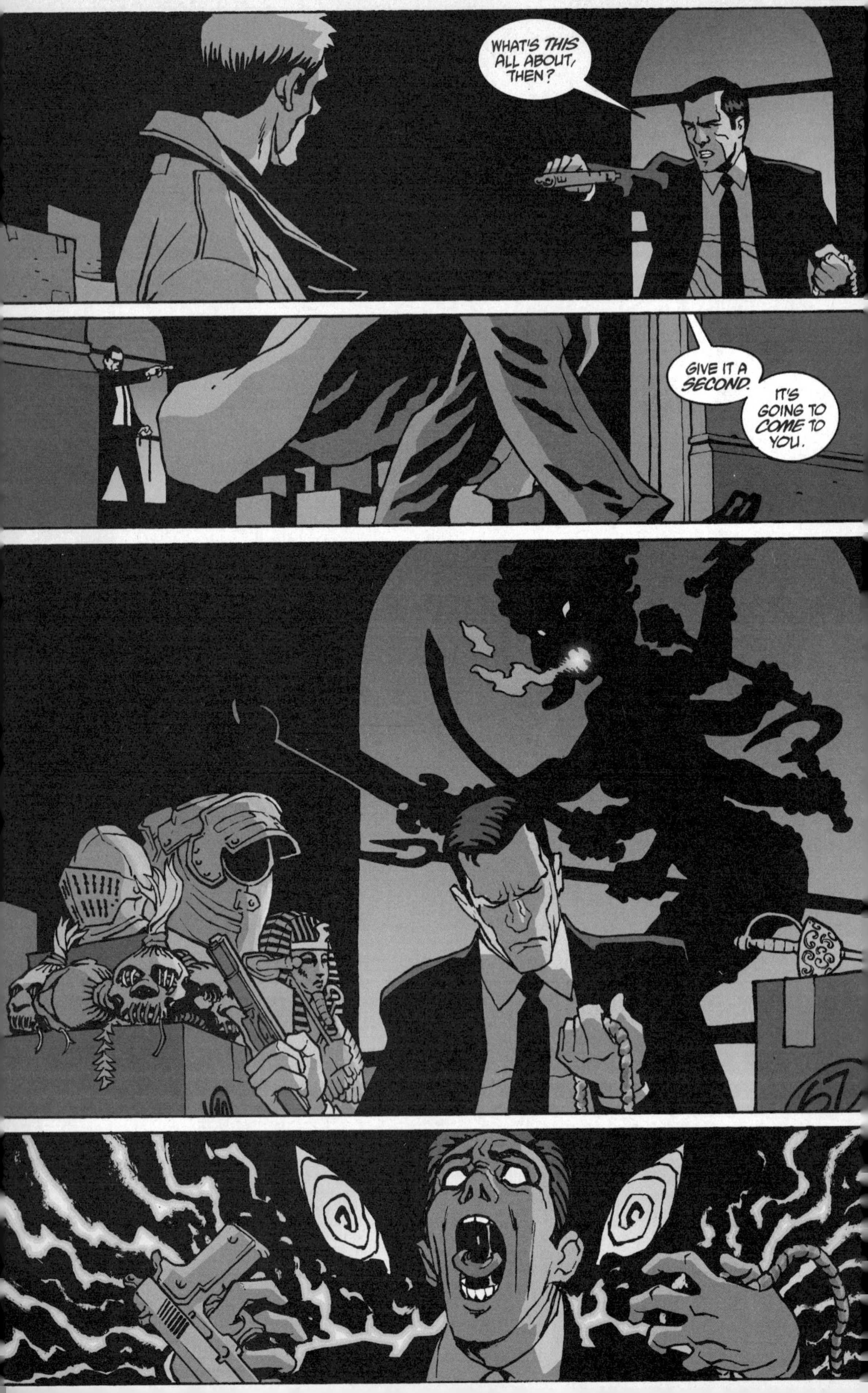
WHAT'S THIS ALL ABOUT, THEN?
GIVE IT A SECOND.
IT'S GOING TO COME TO YOU.

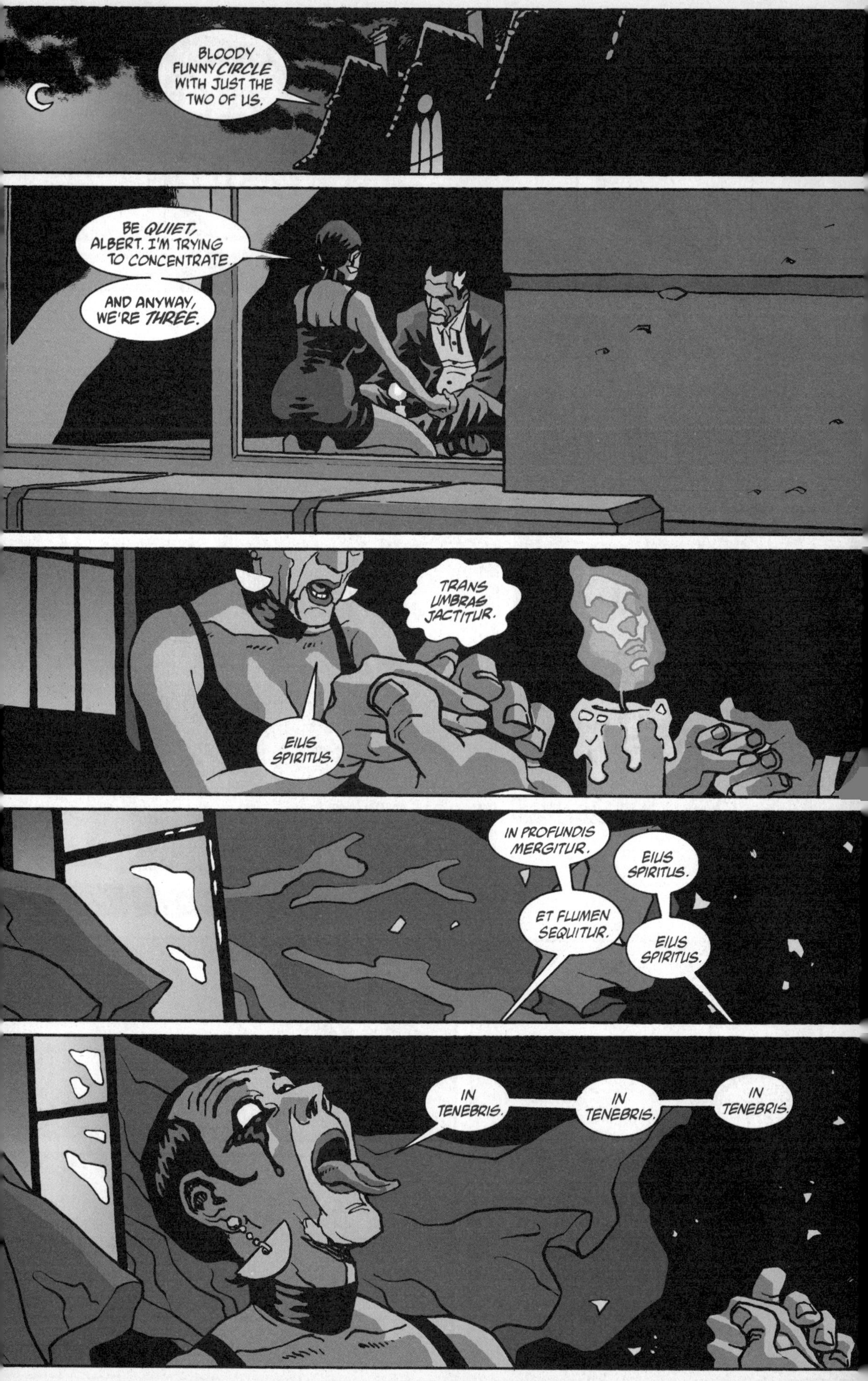

BLOODY FUNNY CIRCLE WITH JUST THE TWO OF US.
BE QUIET, ALBERT. I'M TRYING TO CONCENTRATE.
AND ANYWAY, WE'RE THREE.
TRANS UMBRAS JACTITUR.
EIUS SPIRITUS.
IN PROFUNDIS MERGITUR.
EIUS SPIRITUS.
ET FLUMEN SEQUITUR.
EIUS SPIRITUS.
IN TENEBRIS.
IN TENEBRIS.
IN TENEBRIS.

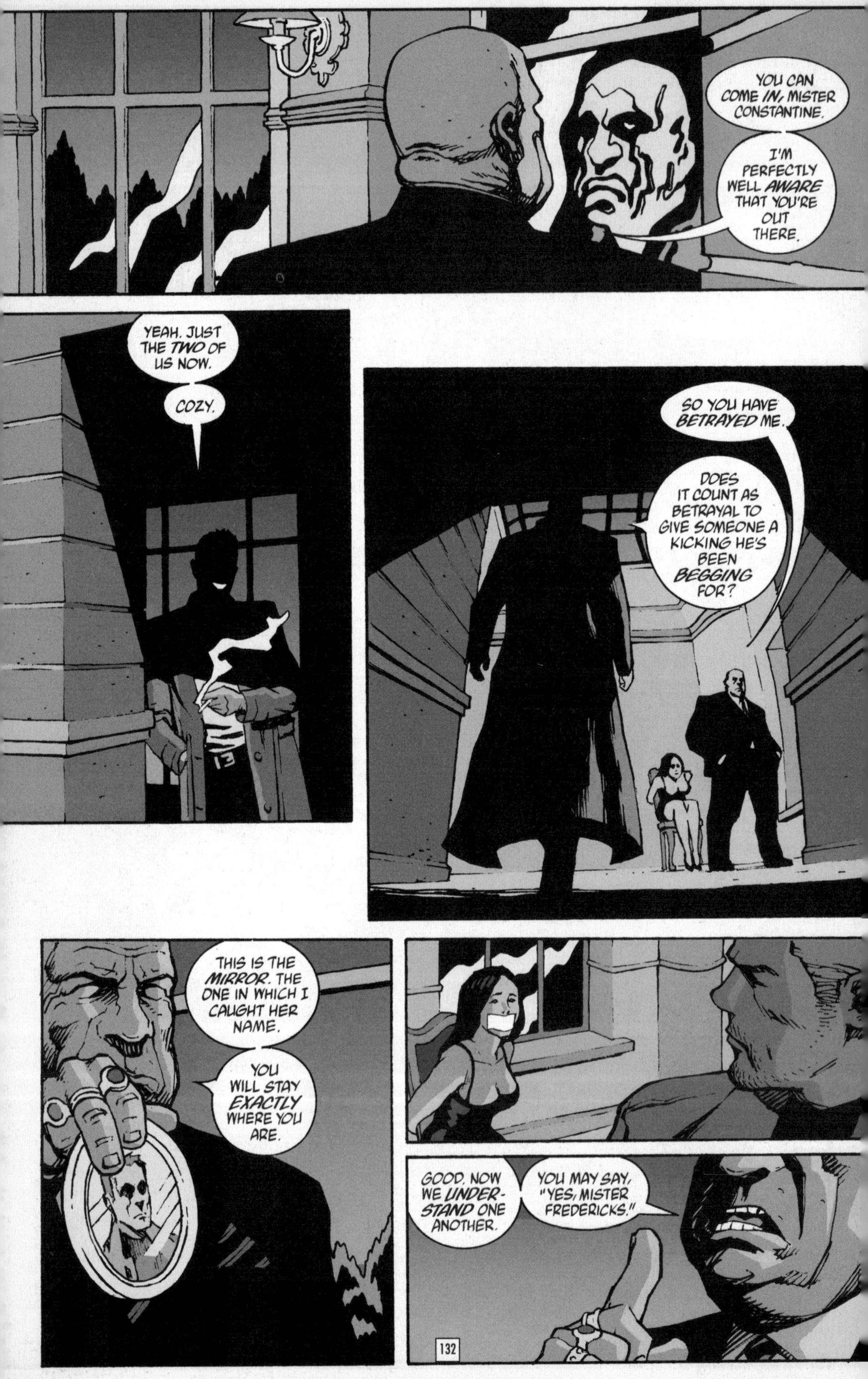
YOU CAN COME IN, MISTER CONSTANTINE.
I'M PERFECTLY WELL AWARE THAT YOU'RE OUT THERE.
YEAH. JUST THE TWO OF US NOW.
COZY.
SO YOU HAVE BETRAYED ME.
DOES IT COUNT AS BETRAYAL TO GIVE SOMEONE A KICKING HE'S BEEN BEGGING FOR?
THIS IS THE MIRROR. THE ONE IN WHICH I CAUGHT HER NAME.
YOU WILL STAY EXACTLY WHERE YOU ARE.
YOU MAY SAY, "YES, MISTER FREDERICKS."
GOOD. NOW WE UNDERSTAND ONE ANOTHER.

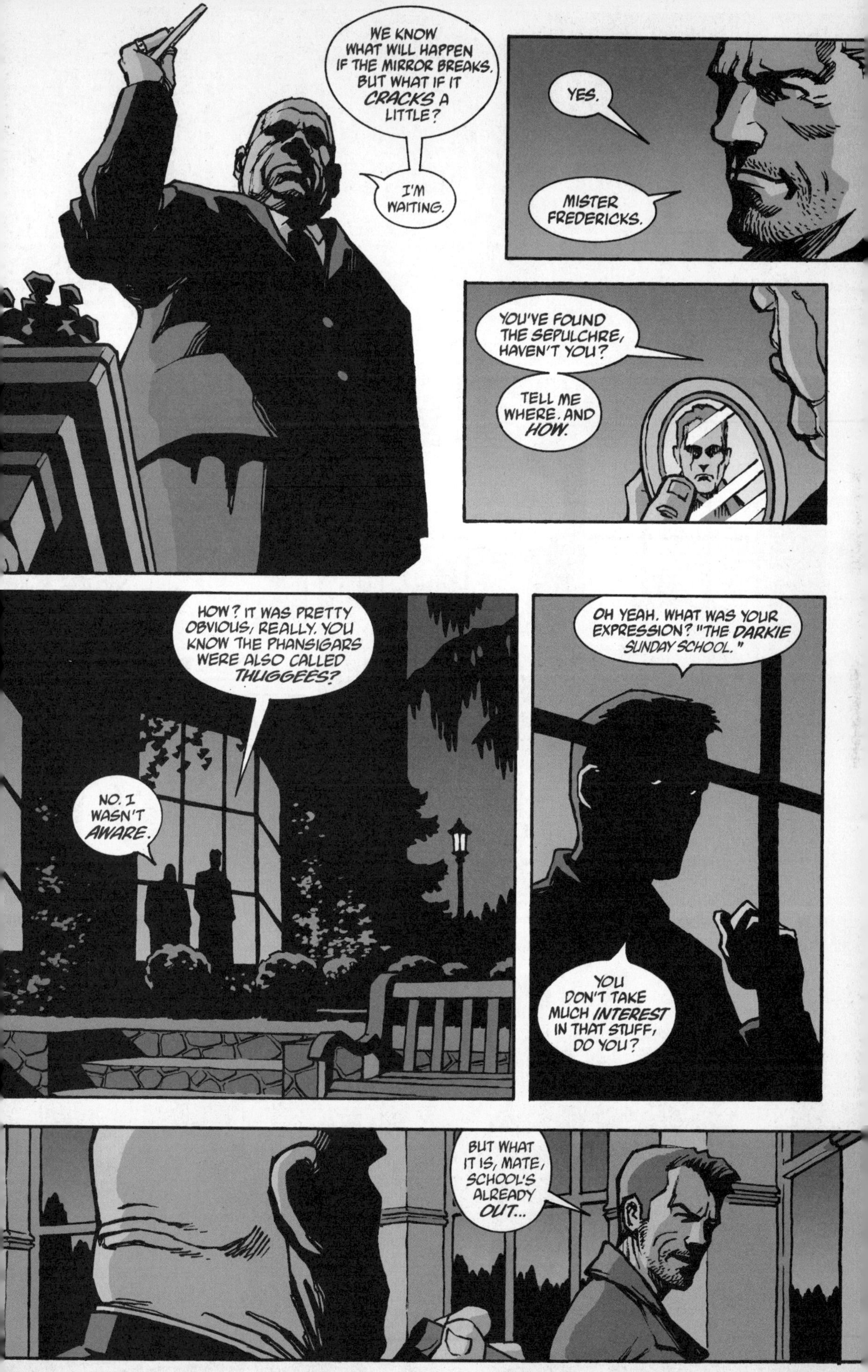
WE KNOW WHAT WILL HAPPEN IF THE MIRROR BREAKS. BUT WHAT IF IT CRACKS A LITTLE?
I'M WAITING.
YES.
MISTER FREDERICKS.
YOU'VE FOUND THE SEPULCHRE, HAVEN'T YOU?
TELL ME WHERE. AND HOW.
HOW? IT WAS PRETTY OBVIOUS, REALLY. YOU KNOW THE PHANSIGARS WERE ALSO CALLED THUGGEES?
NO. I WASN'T AWARE.
OH YEAH. WHAT WAS YOUR EXPRESSION? "THE DARKIE SUNDAY SCHOOL."
YOU DON'T TAKE MUCH INTEREST IN THAT STUFF, DO YOU?
BUT WHAT IT IS, MATE, SCHOOL'S ALREADY OUT...

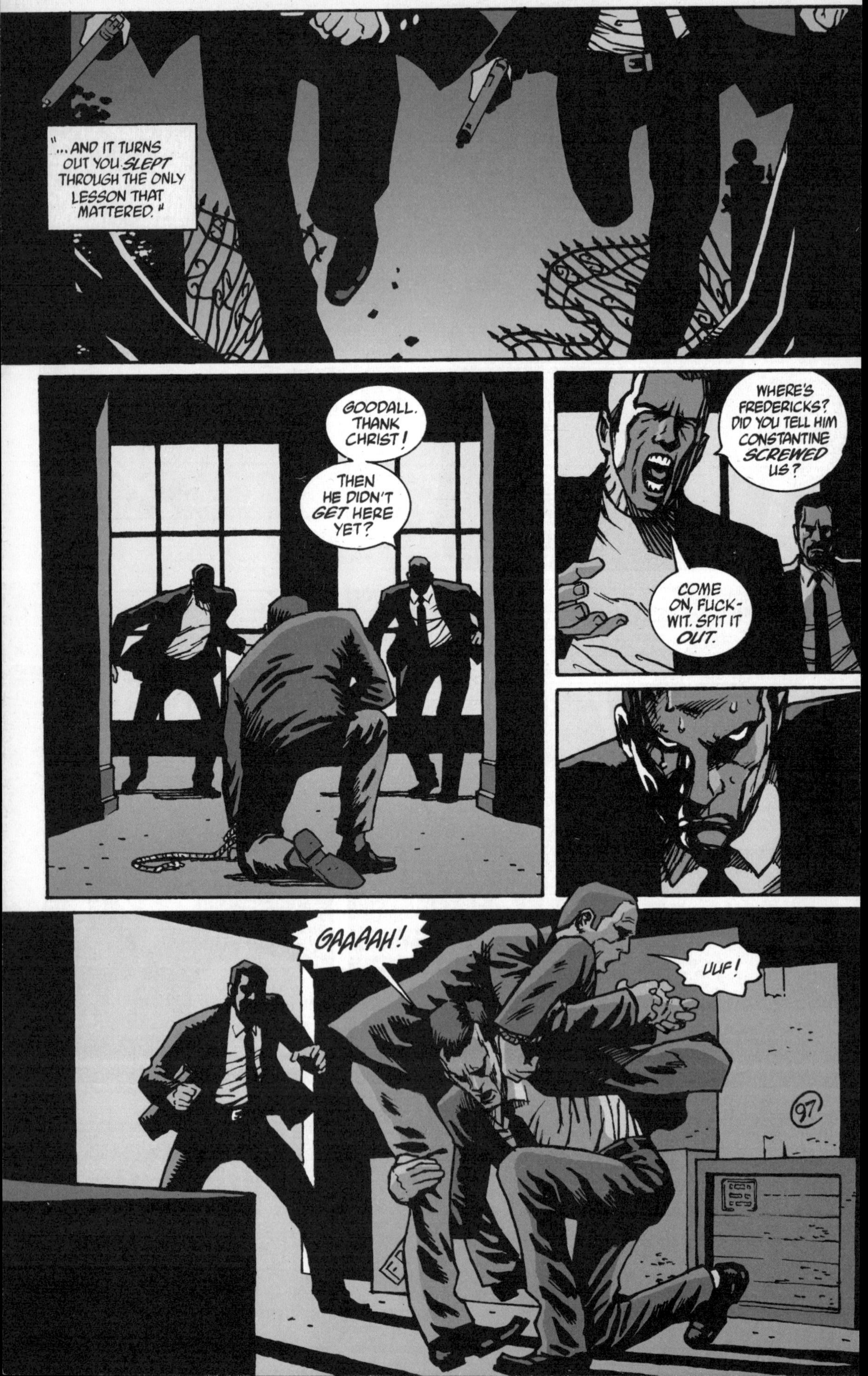
"...AND IT TURNS OUT YOU *SLEPT* THROUGH THE ONLY LESSON THAT MATTERED."
GOODALL. THANK CHRIST!
THEN HE DIDN'T *GET* HERE YET?
WHERE'S FREDERICKS? DID YOU TELL HIM CONSTANTINE *SCREWED* US?
COME ON, FUCK-WIT. SPIT IT *OUT*.
GAAAAH!
UUF!
97

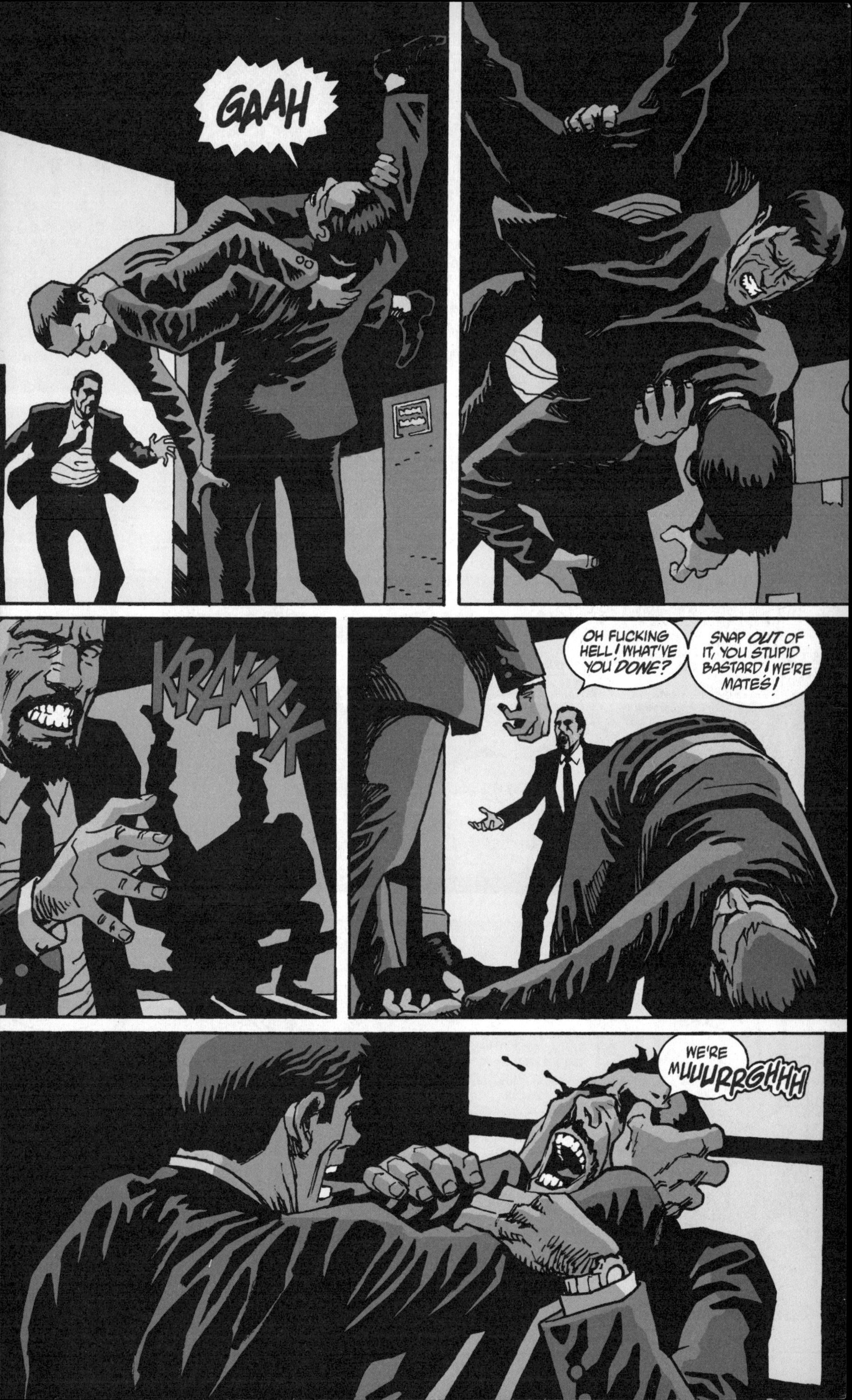
GAAH
KRAKKK
OH FUCKING HELL! WHAT'VE YOU DONE?
SNAP OUT OF IT, YOU STUPID BASTARD! WE'RE MATES!
WE'RE MUUURRGHHH

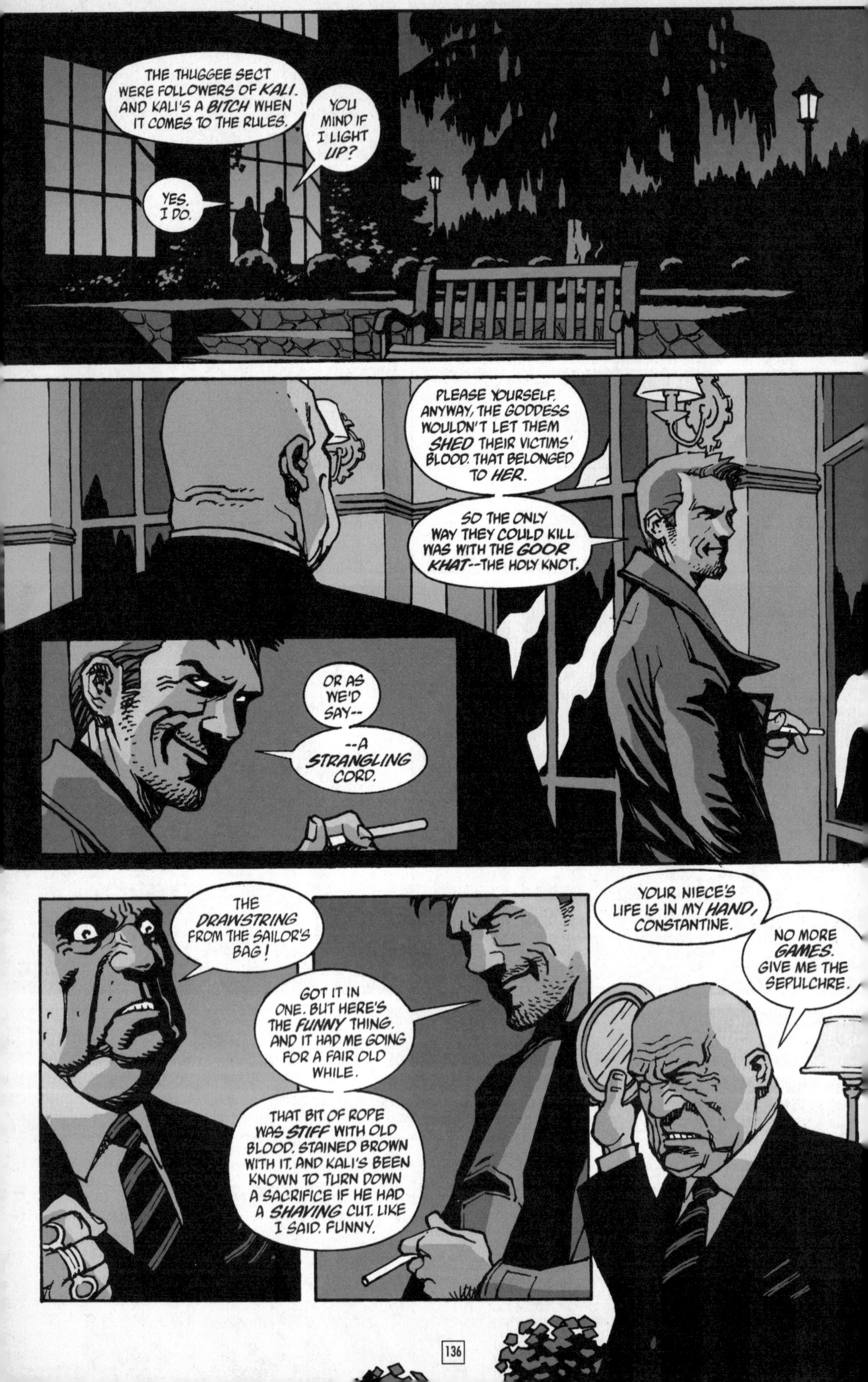
THE THUGGEE SECT WERE FOLLOWERS OF KALI. AND KALI'S A BITCH WHEN IT COMES TO THE RULES.
YOU MIND IF I LIGHT UP?
YES. I DO.
PLEASE YOURSELF. ANYWAY, THE GODDESS WOULDN'T LET THEM SHED THEIR VICTIMS' BLOOD. THAT BELONGED TO HER.
SO THE ONLY WAY THEY COULD KILL WAS WITH THE GOOR KHAT--THE HOLY KNOT.
OR AS WE'D SAY--
--A STRANGLING CORD.
THE DRAWSTRING FROM THE SAILOR'S BAG!
GOT IT IN ONE. BUT HERE'S THE FUNNY THING. AND IT HAD ME GOING FOR A FAIR OLD WHILE.
THAT BIT OF ROPE WAS STIFF WITH OLD BLOOD. STAINED BROWN WITH IT. AND KALI'S BEEN KNOWN TO TURN DOWN A SACRIFICE IF HE HAD A SHAVING CUT. LIKE I SAID. FUNNY.
YOUR NIECE'S LIFE IS IN MY HAND, CONSTANTINE.
NO MORE GAMES. GIVE ME THE SEPULCHRE.

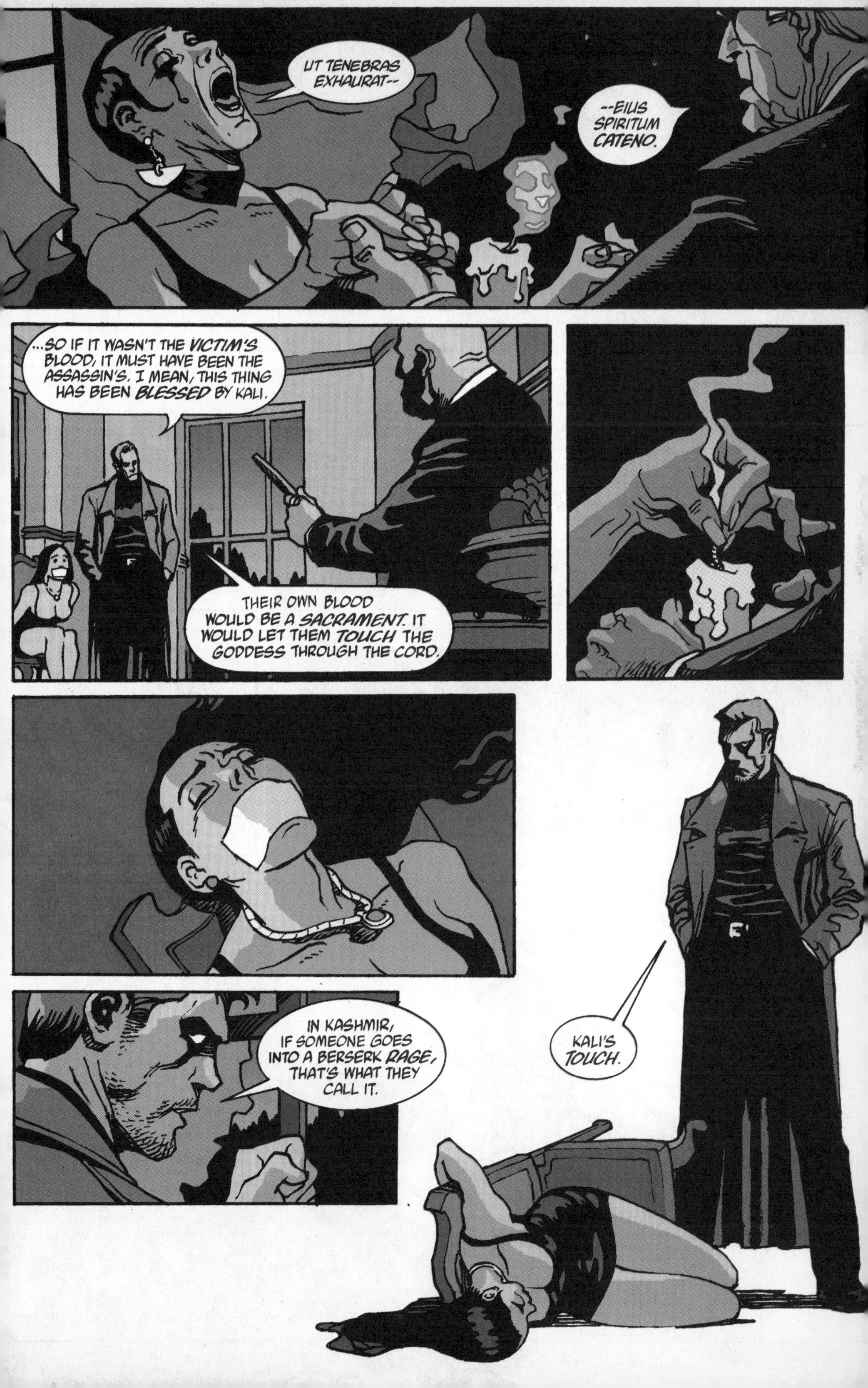
UT TENEBRAS EXHAURAT--
--EIUS SPIRITUM CATENO.
...SO IF IT WASN'T THE VICTIM'S BLOOD, IT MUST HAVE BEEN THE ASSASSIN'S. I MEAN, THIS THING HAS BEEN BLESSED BY KALI.
THEIR OWN BLOOD WOULD BE A SACRAMENT. IT WOULD LET THEM TOUCH THE GODDESS THROUGH THE CORD.
IN KASHMIR, IF SOMEONE GOES INTO A BERSERK RAGE, THAT'S WHAT THEY CALL IT.
KALI'S TOUCH.

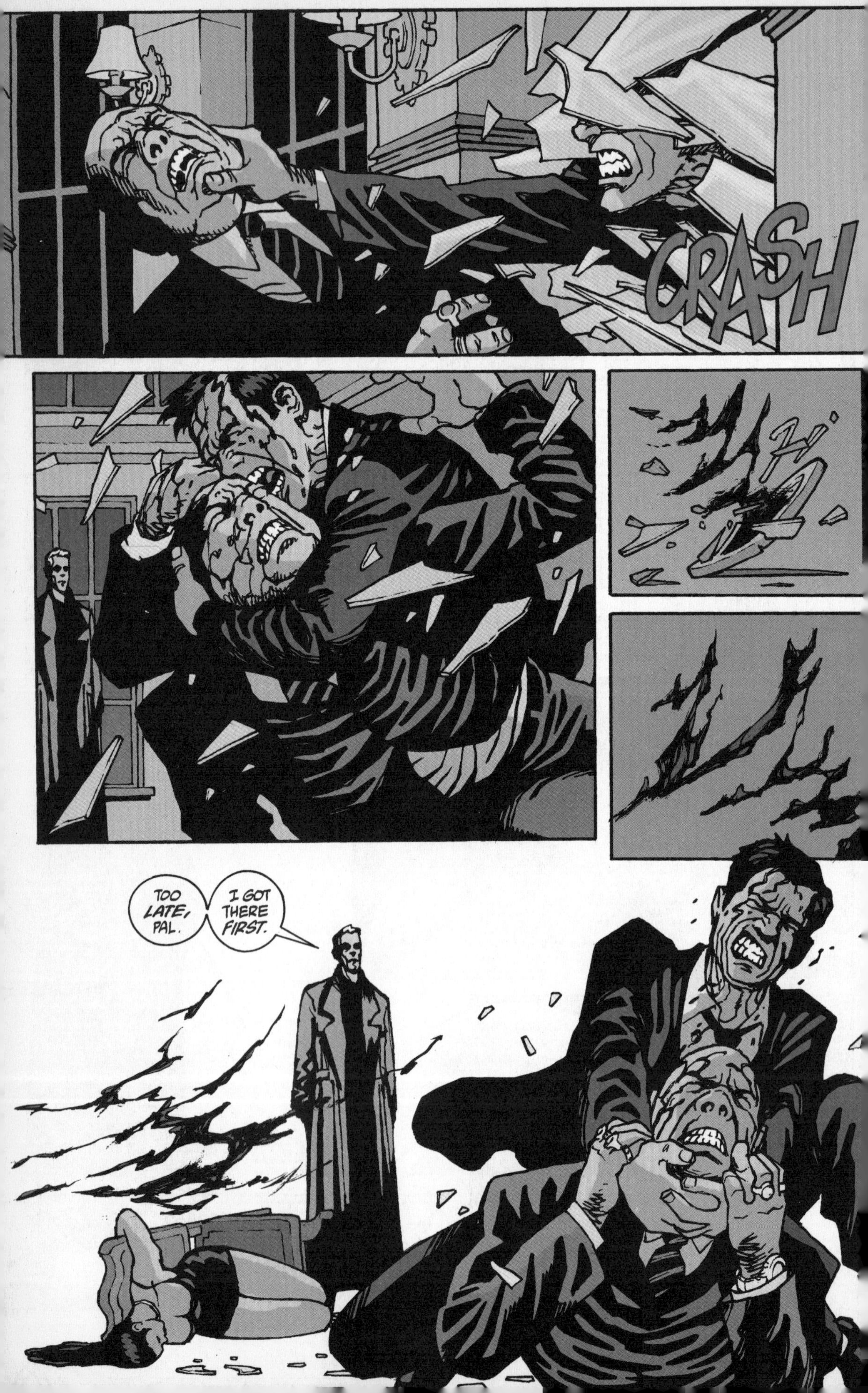
CRASH
TOO LATE, PAL.
I GOT THERE FIRST.

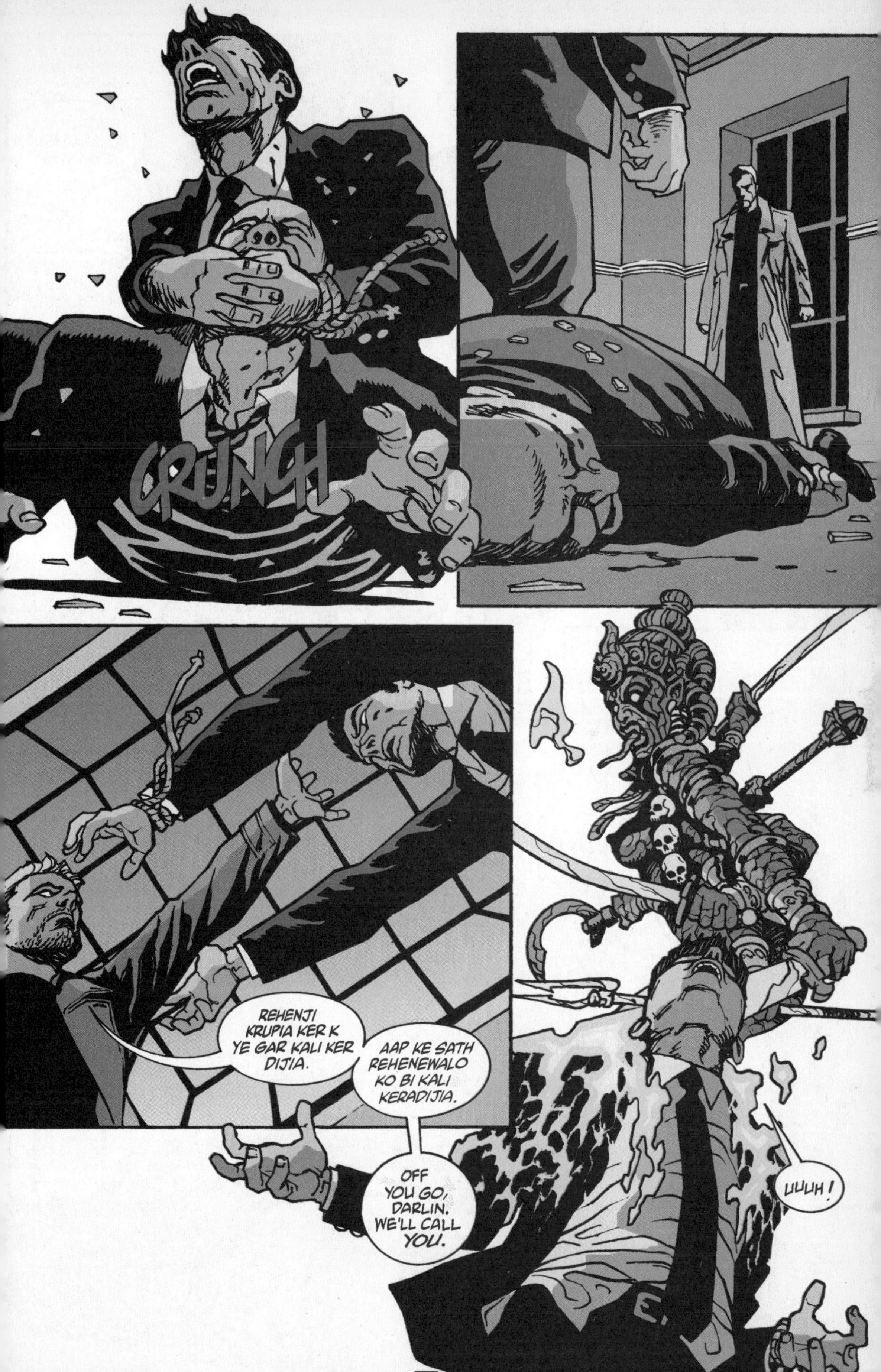
CRUNCH
REHENJI KRUPIA KER K YE GAR KALI KER DIJIA.
AAP KE SATH REHENEWALO KO BI KALI KERADIJIA.
OFF YOU GO, DARLIN. WE'LL CALL YOU.
UUUH!

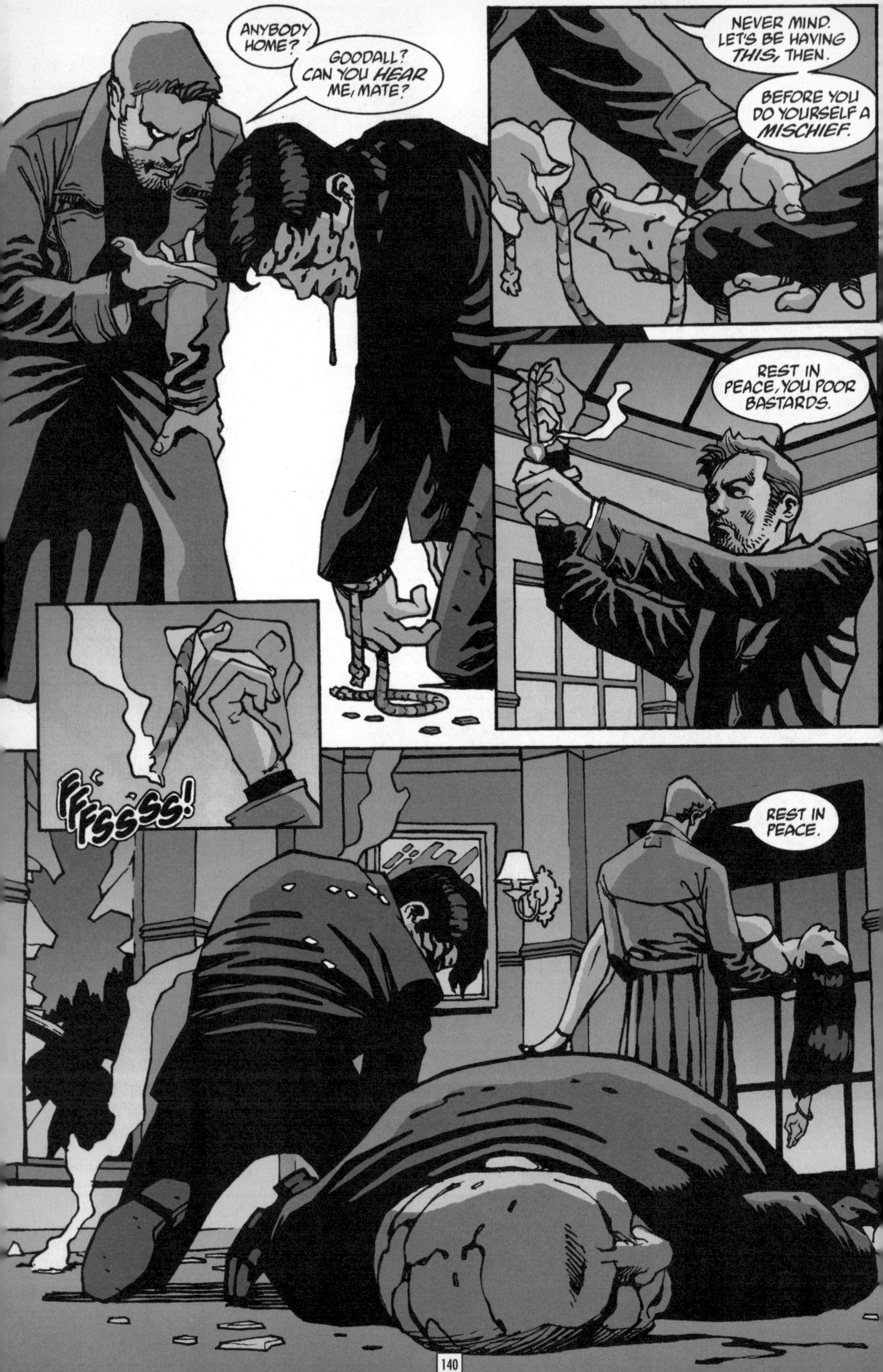
ANYBODY HOME?
GOODALL? CAN YOU HEAR ME, MATE?
NEVER MIND. LET'S BE HAVING THIS, THEN.
BEFORE YOU DO YOURSELF A MISCHIEF.
REST IN PEACE, YOU POOR BASTARDS.
FFFSSSSS!
REST IN PEACE.

"I'M SO SORRY ABOUT *GEMMA*, THOUGH."

"THAT WAS *MY* FAULT, JOHN. ALL MINE."

SHE'S FINE, CLARICE. SHE HATES MY *GUTS*, BUT SHE'S FINE.

THAT TRANCE YOU PUT HER INTO *WORKED*, THANK GOD. SHE WAS DOWN TOO DEEP FOR THE CURSE TO *FIND* HER.

MARTIN PACKE

1953-2002

NO, I'M MORE WORRIED ABOUT WHAT *FREDERICKS* WAS UP TO.

HE WENT TO A LOT OF TROUBLE TO *GET* THAT THING. CAN'T HELP WONDERING WHY.

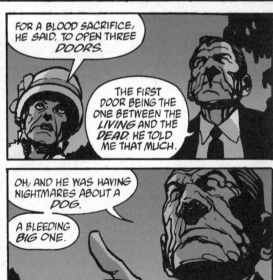

FOR A BLOOD SACRIFICE, HE SAID. TO OPEN THREE *DOORS*.

THE FIRST DOOR BEING THE ONE BETWEEN THE *LIVING* AND THE *DEAD*. HE TOLD ME THAT MUCH.

OH, AND HE WAS HAVING NIGHTMARES ABOUT A *DOG*.

A BLEEDING *BIG* ONE.

SOD IT. IT CAN COME AND BITE ME IN THE *ARSE* IN ITS OWN GOOD TIME.

CHIN CHIN.

TAKE *CARE* OF YOURSELF, JOHN.

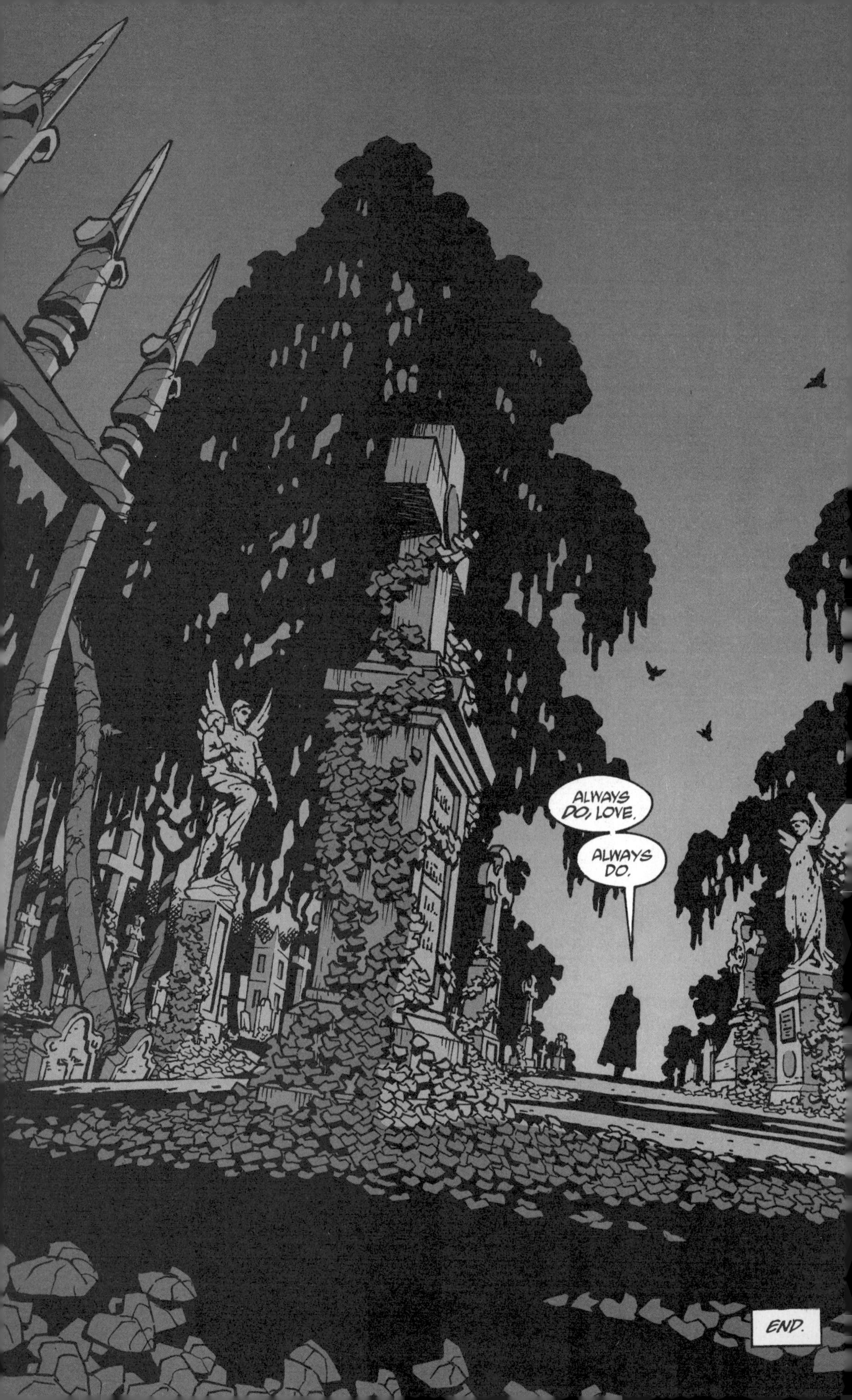
ALWAYS DO, LOVE.
ALWAYS DO.
END.

THE HELLBLAZER LIBRARY

14 definitive collections chronicling the legendary anti-hero and his journeys through Hell and back. Where horror, dark magic and bad luck meet, John Constantine is never far away.

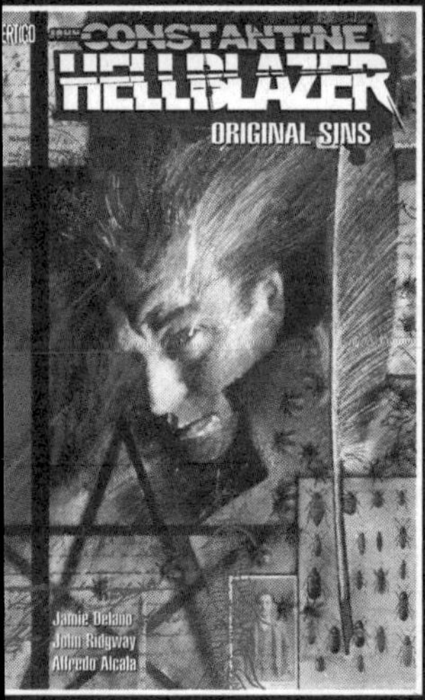

CONSTANTINE
HELLBLAZER
ORIGINAL SINS
Jamie Delano
John Ridgway
Alfredo Alcala

ORIGINAL SINS
JAMIE DELANO/VARIOUS

he volume that introduces John Constantine, aster manipulator of black magic, and hronicles the inescapable nightmares that ireaten his closest friends and loved ones.

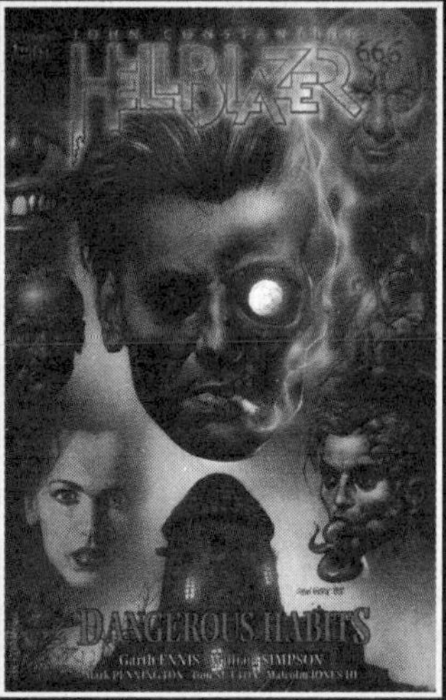

HELLBLAZER
DANGEROUS HABITS

DANGEROUS HABITS
GARTH ENNIS/VARIOUS

Constantine is diagnosed with terminal lung cancer and plays his most dangerous game ever in order to save his life while keeping his soul.

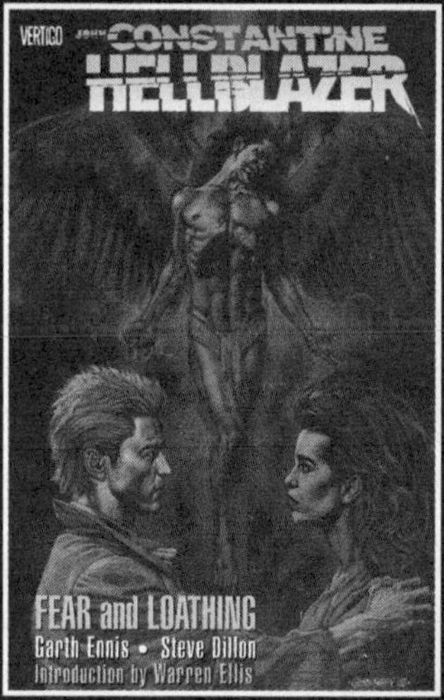

VERTIGO
CONSTANTINE
HELLBLAZER
FEAR and LOATHING
Garth Ennis • Steve Dillon
Introduction by Warren Ellis

FEAR AND LOATHING
GARTH ENNIS/STEVE DILLON

Constantine must dissuade his young niece Gemma from following in his troubled footsteps, as well as engineer a fall from heaven and cope with an upcoming birthday.

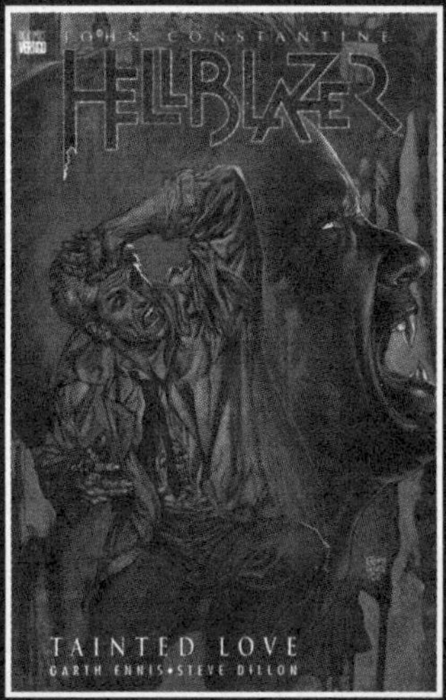

JOHN CONSTANTINE
HELLBLAZER
TAINTED LOVE
GARTH ENNIS•STEVE DILLON

TAINTED LOVE
GARTH ENNIS/STEVE DILLON

Constantine loses Kit, the love of his life, and spirals into homelessness and alcoholism. On the street he must deal with vicious vampires and revisit the scene of one of his earlier — and tragic — encounters with the black arts.

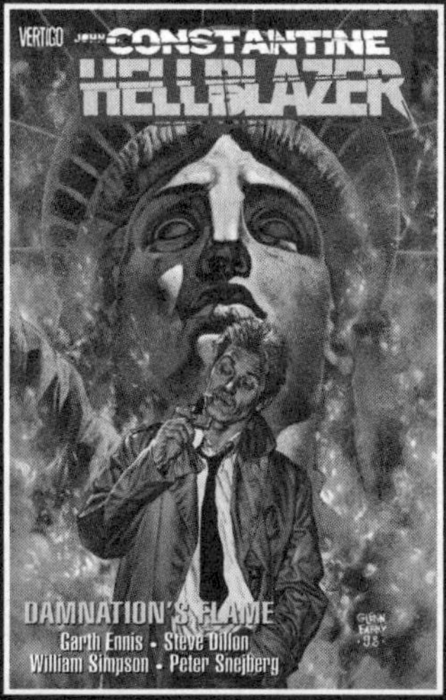

VERTIGO
CONSTANTINE
HELLBLAZER
DAMNATION'S FLAME
Garth Ennis • Steve Dillon
William Simpson • Peter Snejbjerg

DAMNATION'S FLAME
GARTH ENNIS/STEVE DILLON/ WILLIAM SIMPSON/PETER SNEJBJERG

Cleaned up but still distraught, Constantine heads to New York City, where his body takes abuse on the streets as his mind is hijacked into a voodoo hell.

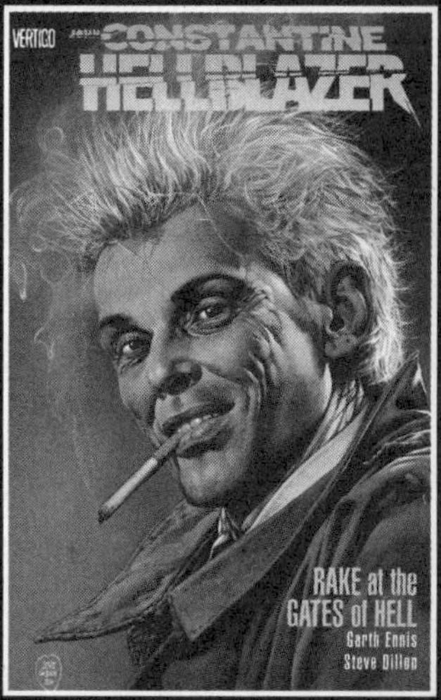

VERTIGO
CONSTANTINE
HELLBLAZER
RAKE at the GATES of HELL
Garth Ennis
Steve Dillon

RAKE AT THE GATES OF HELL
GARTH ENNIS/STEVE DILLON

Looking for revenge after twice being tricked by him, the Devil confronts Constantine one final time in hopes of destroying him once and for all. Meanwhile, Constantine meets with Kit and hears her bittersweet homecoming story.

ALL TITLES ARE SUGGESTED FOR MATURE READERS

SON OF MAN
GARTH ENNIS/JOHN HIGGINS
Constantine must put right an old mistake that has left his best mate Chas Chandler wrongly accused of killing a mob boss and an undead child about to unleash unimaginable evil on the world.

HAUNTED
WARREN ELLIS/JOHN HIGGINS
Constantine looks into the death of an old love and earns a savage beating for his trouble. But when the killer makes the mistake of exposing his identity, the Hellblazer teaches him the real meaning of revenge.

SETTING SUN
WARREN ELLIS/VARIOUS
Five short stories follow Constantine as he deals with a room-bound psychotic, the "crib" of a miscarried Antichrist, the guilty conscience of a World War II torturer, a desperate conspiracy theorist and the ghosts of old loves.

HARD TIME
BRIAN AZZARELLO/RICHARD CORBEN
Convicted for a murder he didn't commit, Constantine is sentenced to 35 years in an American maximum security prison. However, using his wits and mastery of black magic, he soon climbs the ranks to become top dog of his new, horrible environment.

GOOD INTENTIONS
BRIAN AZZARELLO/MARCELO FRUSIN
In the small town of Doglick, West Virginia, Constantine must confront the brothers of the man he went to prison for killing. While there, he rediscovers the fact that not all horrors are supernatural.

FREEZES OVER
BRIAN AZZARELLO/MARCELO FRUSIN
GUY DAVIS/STEVE DILLON
Held hostage by a blizzard, an urban legend know as the "Iceman" and three desperate gunmen, Constantine must gamble with his life in order t save a group of innocent hostages.

HIGHWATER
BRIAN AZZARELLO/VARIOUS
From a white supremacist stronghold in Idaho to an underground sex club in California, Constantine's trek across America comes to an end in the stately manor of a nemesis he barely even knew he had.

ALL HIS ENGINES
MIKE CAREY/LEONARDO MANCO
A mysterious plague puts millions into deadly comas, including Chas's granddaughter, Tricia. In looking for a cure, Constantine discovers a mad demon in a body woven out of cancer cells, and a diabolical plot to build franchised Hells throughout the cities of men.